The En[illegible]

Roy[illegible]ch

The Preliminary Declaration

By the solemn Act of Union between the two Grand Lodges of Free-Masons of England in December 1813, it was 'declared and pronounced that Pure Antient Masonry consists of three degrees and no more, viz., those of the Entered Apprentice, the Fellow Craft and the Master Mason, including the Supreme Order of the Royal Arch.'

David West

Hamilton House Publishing Ltd

hamiltonhousepublishing.com

Cover designed by Lawrie Morrisson.

ISBN: 978-1-8380715-0-9

First published 2020 by Hamilton House Publishing Ltd,
Rochester upon Medway, Kent, UK, ME2 3EA.

For information on Hamilton House Publishing Ltd and its list, visit hamiltonhousepublishing.com.

In association with

Lewis Masonic

This work is dedicated to

Matthew William Ralph West

With thanks to
Peter Currie, Glyn Jarrett,
and to Jenny as ever.

Other Masonic books by David West

Comments by readers

The Goat, the Devil, and the Freemason

A wonderful, infuriating, stimulating, and provocative book that is a joy to read. It provides a perfect counterpoint to all the pretentious rubbish about Freemasonry that we have suffered so long. I could not have been more entertained and enlightened. A very well written book that takes you from France to the Wild West to Ancient Egypt with quite a bit of the Holy Land thrown in! A great read, well presented and easy to understand for such a complicated subject. Thoroughly recommended.

A shorter history of Goats, Devils, and Freemasons

The faster reading edition of the 'Goat, the Devil and the Freemason'

Never be short of candidates again (Things to do when you have nothing to do)

Without doubt, David West and Lawrie Morrisson are two of the most far sighted and innovative Freemasons in England. Their successful lodge embraces a constant stream of new ideas and uses all the tools of modern technology. Its website is the envy of the many who seek to follow in its footsteps and replicate its success. This book shows how they did it.

Deism at the time of the founders of the Premier Grand Lodge

'To contemplate the intellectual faculties and to trace them through the paths of heavenly science even to the throne of God Himself.' Ever wondered what this means? This book makes it clear. Expertly written, making a subject that could be so difficult, very easy to follow. Enlightening and entertaining!

Managing the Future of Freemasonry

A candle in the dark. There's a surplus of Masonic writings today, but precious few delve as thoughtfully and thoroughly as Dr. West into the future of Freemasonry. He lays out his arguments in a logical, accurate, and sometimes humorous manner. His optimism is contagious.

Masonic Legends (with Matthew West)

Lively and immensely entertaining, you can dine off the facts in this book for years. A fascinating look at history and how it is often time warped to create myth and legend. A stunner of a book! I am on my second read, far too much information to take in on one pass. The research must have been immense. Its attention to detail is amazing – and it's often very amusing as well!

Contents

Nomenclature of the two Grand Lodges

It is usual to refer to the 1717/1721 Premier Grand Lodge as the *Moderns* and to the 1751 Grand Lodge as the *Antients*. In this book I refer to them as the *Premier* and the *Atholl* Grand Lodges (many of the latter's Grand Masters were Dukes of Atholl) to avoid confusion while analysing the phrase *Pure Antient Masonry*.

Preface

The Royal Arch raises passions. There are those who find chapter the most enjoyable of Masonic meetings, and those who find it dull and bewildering. It has always had a special status in Freemasonry, but we have to admit it is a continuing source of confusion.

We struggle with its place in *Pure Antient Freemasonry*. Is it the completion of the third degree, a continuation of the Craft or is there simply no ritual connection between the Craft and the Royal Arch? At our initiation each of us promised – without evasion, equivocation or mental reservation – to conceal our secrets, never to indite, carve or mark the least trace of them. How then, on being exalted, can we be expected to believe that they were engraved on a plate of gold by the three Grand Masters?

The Royal Arch and the third degree are fictional tales teaching a moral lesson, stories of inspiring if invented events. Symbolism, allegory, and metaphor are proper and useful literary devices, but there is a logic to their use. Consistency and coherence are vital if the story is not to disappoint but, sad to say, both fail in this.

The relationship between the Craft and the Royal Arch has long been an enigma. To resolve it we must go back into the eighteenth century. As the story unfolds we will see how the problems stem from a wrong turn taken towards the century's end, and how reversing it provides new meaning for the Royal Arch.

The Royal Arch as it is worked by the United Grand Lodge of England is the central focus of this book, but the different narrative and structure in Scottish, Irish, and York Rite working offer new perspectives from which to view the enigma.

First essay: the numbers in brief

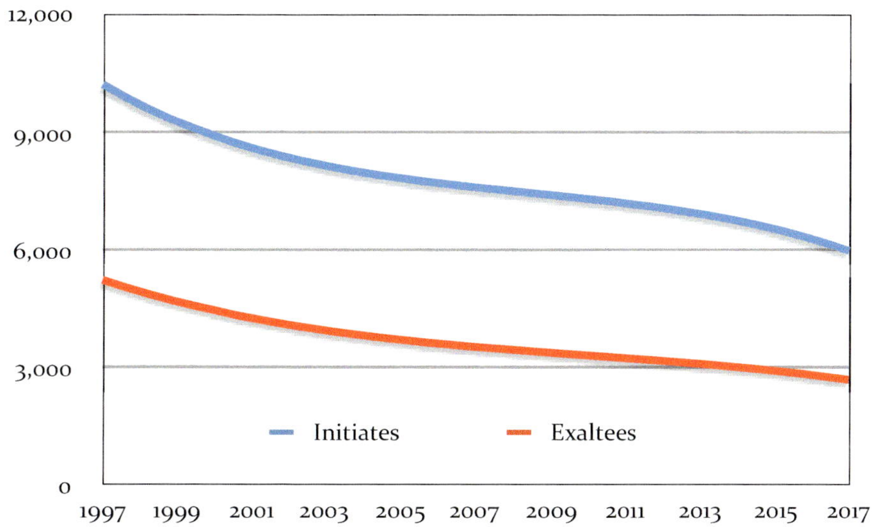

The graph above exhibits the trend[1] of exaltations in red and of initiations in blue. The gap between the two lines narrows towards 2017, indicating a decline in the ratio of exaltees to initiates.

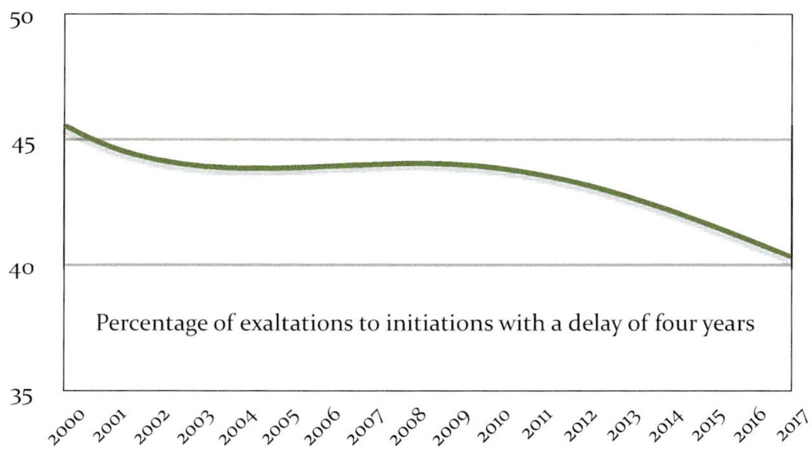

Since it is rare for initiates to join the Royal Arch immediately after initiation, it may be useful to build in a delay. The equation in the

[1] Polynomial order 3.

second graph is *exaltations as a percentage* (Y-axis) *per year* (X-axis) *of initiations four years earlier*. This trend also indicates a decline in the ratio of exaltees to initiates.

Resignation and exclusion

In recent years, an average of 37% of Craft masons have been members of the Royal Arch, with a high of 55% in Lincolnshire and a low of 32% in London.[1] Nevertheless, even those provinces with high Royal Arch penetration can find membership declining. Buckinghamshire has been above the national norm with 39% of Craft masons in the Royal Arch. In 2011, it gained sixty-one exaltees and joiners but lost eighty companions through resignation and exclusion (an impolite form of resignation). With twenty dying, its net loss was thirty-nine.

Inactivity

In England, resignation and exclusion from the Royal Arch averages just over three per cent a year, not an unhealthy figure, but inactivity also matters: companions who remain members but rarely attend. Inactivity often follows immediately on exaltation – many a grand officer has arrived to present a certificate to an exaltee who hasn't – and it is nothing new in Freemasonry. The 1876 *Freemason's Chronicle* complains that inactive Masons, hearing:

> *... that men of standing in society are daily entering our ranks ... he seeks and obtains admission, and then his ambition is satisfied.*

This explains inactivity by an external reason, little to do with Masonry itself. A similarly external cause results from attempts to increase exaltations by limiting Craft honours to Royal Arch members. The nineteenth century snob and the modern pyramid climber may have no real interest in the Royal Arch.

---

[1] 41% Cambridge (2018), East Lancs 40% (2018), Devon 37% (2017), Herts 37% (2017).

The Rusty Nail Program

Scottish Rite's House of the Temple, Washington, photo APK.

Many American lodges have been huge, sometimes with more than a thousand members, as illustrated by the scale of this Scottish Rite Temple in Washington. The average membership of the 450 lodges in Ohio is 166, five or six times the average in England, and impersonality must play a part in inactivity.

One US lodge found that 88% of its companions were inactive; only twelve of its hundred members attended lodge. Another analysed its inactive members:

> *Most had not been in Lodge for at least ten years. One man had not attended lodge since he had been raised in 1929. Four were past Masters, all of whom were afraid that they would embarrass themselves during a strict examination, because they were so "rusty". One past Master had not attended a Lodge since his year as Master, 1957.*

The *Rusty Nail Program* aims to overcome the embarrassment of forgotten signs and words, so that hitherto inactive members feel welcome and able to attend lodge, or indeed chapter, again.

Cohort

Losses to the *Grand Chapter Above* account for an annual average of three per cent of English membership, but resignation, exclusion and inactivity are the only factors over which we have some control. A 'wet finger' study of some London and Essex chapters indicated that in the ten years between 2006 and 2016, something over forty per cent of exaltees became inactive.

It is not easy to put statistics for resignation, exclusion and inactivity into one picture, but a sort of cohort analysis may serve.

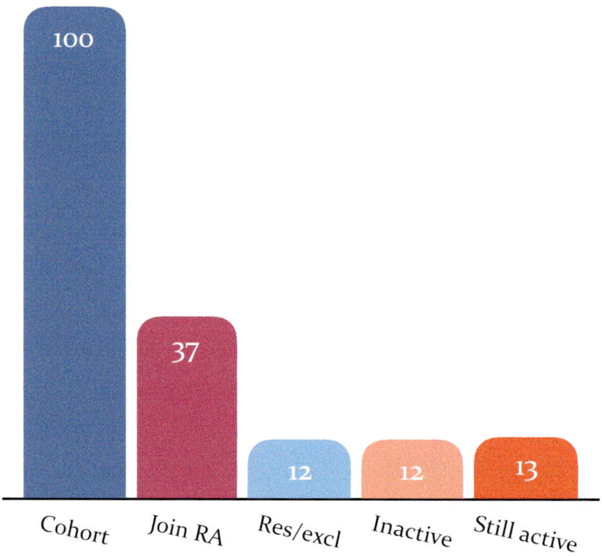

Of one hundred Craft masons, thirty-seven will be exalted into the Royal Arch. Over ten years, twelve of the thirty-seven will resign or be excluded and a further twelve will become inactive. After ten years, we are left with thirteen per cent of our cohort, thirteen active companions. This leads to the unfortunate conclusion that 87% of masons are not vitally interested in the Royal Arch. They are not convinced that it is the *keystone of the Masonic structure.*

Second essay: elsewhere

The constant smile of the Master of St Laurence Lodge No. 5511 in a real vault, a feature of many Scottish and Irish chapter rooms.

Scotland

Compare the declaration of the United Grand Lodge of England:

> *Pure Antient Masonry consists of three degrees and no more, viz., those of the Entered Apprentice, the Fellow Craft and the Master Mason, including the Supreme Order of the Royal Arch.*

with the Scottish Craft version:

> *The Grand Lodge of Scotland practises and recognises no degrees of masonry but those of Entered Apprentice, Fellow-Craft (including the Mark), and Master Mason.*

While the Mark is included, there is no mention of the Royal Arch in the Scottish Craft statement.[1] The Scottish Supreme Grand Royal Arch Chapter works independently of the Grand Lodge; the two bodies rarely have members of their executives in common, and Scottish chapters are not attached to lodges. The Grand Chapter states that it:

> *... practises and recognises no degrees of masonry but those of Mark Master,[2] Excellent Master, Royal Arch, Royal Ark Mariner, and the Babylonish Pass ...*

While the coverage of degrees is striking, the most important difference is that both Scottish bodies use the words *practises and recognises,* in place of the English phrase *consists of.* The significance of this is huge. The English declaration claims that the Craft and the Royal Arch alone are pure and ancient/antient, a claim demanding justification and in effect implying that all other orders are impure and modern. Neither Scottish body makes a claim to antiquity, purity, or exclusivity. In simply listing the orders they practise and recognise, the declarations require no justification.

There is no special precedence in Scottish practice for the Royal Arch. It is not seen as a necessary continuation of the Craft nor as specially related to it. A companion of the St. Andrew Royal Arch Chapter No. 146 writes:

> *I remember reading somewhere [that] the Royal Arch Degree was originally considered to be the second half or completion of the Master Mason Degree, and I will admit to be somewhat surprised ...*

The work

The legend of the Royal Arch in Scotland is much the same as that in English & Wales (whence it stems) with three differences. The

---

[1] The word *declaration* as such is not used in Scotland or in Ireland.

[2] In practice most Scottish masons are advanced to the Mark in a Craft lodge.

Jabulon word is retained as is the ceremony of the veils, known in Scotland as the degree of Excellent Master, a challenge and pass at each of four veils.[1] The three Craft degrees, the Excellent Master and the Mark are prerequisites for entry to the Royal Arch and as Grahame J. Smith, at the time Grand Scribe Ezra of the Supreme Grand Chapter of Scotland, said:

> *A candidate for the Royal Arch degree who has not received his Mark degree within a Craft lodge has to be advanced in the Mark lodge held within the chapter ... Normal Scottish practice is to open the chapter, read the minutes and conduct any business, then, if a candidate be present, adjourn ... English Constitution visitors who are not Mark Master Masons or Excellent Masters must retire for a time. It is not necessary for Irish Constitution visitors to retire as they work an equivalent system of degrees. A Mark lodge is now opened, the business of advancement ... is completed* [and the] *Mark lodge is closed. A lodge of Excellent Masters is then opened ... the candidate is obligated and instructed, then passes the blue, purple, and scarlet veils, receiving at each the appropriate sign, token and word which will be required of him later in the Royal Arch degree. He is then received as an Excellent Master.* [That] *lodge is closed ... the Chapter resumed, and English Constitution visitors are readmitted.*[2]

Chapters may confer the cryptic degrees as well as the Royal Ark

---

[1] An explanation of the veils is similar to the explanation of the robes and sceptres in the English Royal Arch. Duncan's Masonic Ritual and Monitor (1866) reads: *The blue veil is the peculiar colour of the three ancient, or symbolical degrees. It is an emblem of universal friendship and benevolence, and instructs us that in the mind of a mason those virtues should be as expansive as the blue arch of heaven. The purple veil, being produced by a due mixture of blue and scarlet ... teaches us to cultivate and improve that spirit of harmony between the brethren of the symbolic degrees and the companions of the sublime degrees. The scarlet veil is emblematical of fervency and zeal, the appropriate colour of the Royal Arch Degree. It admonishes us to be fervent in the exercise of our devotions to God, and zealous in our endeavours to promote the happiness of men. The white veil is emblematical of that purity of heart and rectitude of conduct which are essential to obtain admission into the divine sanctum sanctorum above.*

[2] Speaking at a regular convocation of the Supreme Grand Chapter of England, November 12th, 1997.

Mariner, which is not 'moored' to Mark Lodges as it is in England. They may also work the degrees of the Babylonish Pass, which form the Order of Knight Masons in Ireland.

Ireland

The lovely little temple in Skibbereen, Co. Cork
with some of its veils.

Irish masonry records three momentous events in Judaic history:

1. The building of Solomon's temple, depicted in Craft Freemasonry.
2. The rebuilding of the temple by Josiah, portrayed in Royal Arch Masonry.
3. Zerubbabel's quest to build a second temple, illustrated in Knight Masonry.

Three orders, although the Irish (Craft) declaration reads:

> *Pure Ancient Masonry consists of the following Degrees and no others, viz. – The Entered Apprentice, the Fellow Craft, the Master Mason and the Installed Master, but the Degrees of Royal Arch and Mark Master Mason shall also be recognized so long as the Supreme Grand Royal Arch Chapter of Ireland shall work only those two Degrees in the form in which they are worked at the passing of this Law.*

There is no mention in either list of Prince Masonry which gives many Irish lodge rooms their elegance and style.

Prince Masons: stalls, swords and armorial banners of members of the Chapter of Prince Rose Croix Masons No. 1, Cork. The oak stalls are more than 300 years old.

Irish masonry's recognition of the Royal Arch as *complementary* and *essential* but *separate* is not dissimilar to English usage. Both declarations use a little sleight of hand to include the Royal Arch: the Irish using an undefined process of recognition, the English using some unusual mathematics. Mathematically 3+1=4, but *mathematically* is not the same as *masonically.*

Like the Atholl Grand Lodge declaration, the English version should read:

> *Pure Antient Masonry consists of four degrees and no more, viz. the Entered Apprentice, the Fellow Craft, the Master Mason and the Royal Arch,*

but it doesn't.

Josiah

There is no obvious reason to connect Craft and Royal Arch in Ireland since there is no narrative link between the two. The principals in Ireland are the Excellent King, the High Priest and the Chief Scribe, and the story is taken from 2 Kings 22 and 23. This tells the story of the renovation of the first temple by King Josiah, perhaps forty years before the exile of the Israelites and perhaps ninety years before Cyrus granted their return.[1] There is no historical or archeological evidence for the life of Josiah, biblically assumed to be from 648 to 609 BCE, but there may be some evidence for his death. 2 Kings 23:29 reads:

> *Pharaoh Necho king of Egypt went up against the king of Assyria to the River Euphrates: and king Josiah went against him; and he slew him at Megiddo.* RED STAR

[1] Recorded on the Cyrus Cylinder, 539-538 BCE, and now in the British Museum.

The *Babylonian Chronicles* record an Egyptian army movement:

> *The seventeenth year: in the month Du'ûzu Aššur-uballit, king of Assyria, with a large army from Egypt, crossed the River Euphrates and marched against Haran* [YELLOW STAR] *to conquer it.*[1]

Haran was north-east of Judah and the Babylonians had taken it from the Assyrians in 610 BCE. In seeking to regain it in June/July the following year, Assyria was overthrown by the Medes and Babylonians, with some smaller states chancing their arm. Egypt had sought to support Assyria, and Josiah may have decided to assist Babylon by stationing his army across the Egyptian route.

Devout

The Old Testament presents Josiah as a devout rather than a military figure, ordering Hilkiah, the high priest, to divert the entrance fees charged by the doorkeepers to pay for workmen to

Visiting a chapter in Skibbereen, Co. Cork, Ireland.
Visitors are wearing blue and red sashes from left shoulder to right hip.
The Excellent King stands between the pillars.

[1] British Museum, B.M. 219.01. The 17th year is roughly 609 to 608 BCE.

repair the breaches of the house. During this restoration of the temple, the book of the law is found. The recognition that the people had not been obeying the law causes Josiah to rend his clothes (a biblical sign of contrition), to destroy the high places (associated with Ba'al, the most popular god in the Levant), and cut down the poles and groves (associated with the goddess Asherah), all as a biblical sign of kingly piety. The Josiah story has nothing to do with lost secrets but the discovery of the book of the law reveals a code enabling the reading of a lost name.

The York Rite

In North America, some Latin American countries and the Philippines, the Royal Arch is one of four CAPITULAR[1] degrees in the York Rite. It includes the Mark Master, Past Master, and Most Excellent Master as well as the Royal Arch.[2] The Capitular sequence is followed by the CRYPTIC degrees, the Select, Royal, and Super Excellent Master degrees, and by the COMMANDERY of Knights Templar, including the Order of the Red Cross, the passing Order of St Paul, the Order of Malta and the Order of the Temple.

A 1952 Indiana Royal Arch ritual features the usual discovery of the vault and block of white marble but then adds a *curiously wrought* box, with *inscriptions, in characters unknown*. Once it is opened, Joshua tells the brethren that:

> *The Grand Council is of the opinion that this most valuable discovery is an imitation of the Ark of the Covenant,*[3] *containing a true copy of the Book of Law, an imitation of a pot of manna and of Aaron's rod.*

---

[1] The *Oxford* gives *pertaining to the ecclesiastical.*

[2] The Mark Master degree is the same as the English version. The Past Master degree provides the esoteric knowledge of the chair of King Solomon. The Most Excellent Master degree is a grander version of the English Royal & Select.

[3] See *Masonic Legends,* David West & Matthew West, Hamilton House, 2018.

The box also contains a parchment with *a key*[1] *by means of which we may be able to read the characters.* Using this they discover:

> *… engraved on a triangular plate of gold … the long lost Master's Word which was lost upon the death of our Grand Master Hiram Abif and which the faithful of the Craft were to receive when future generations should discover it.*

1952 Indiana summary lecture

This lecture takes the exaltee through all the degrees encountered on the way to the Royal Arch, and thus describes the Capitular degrees of the York Rite.

> *And now … you have received all the instruction that pertains to our noble Craft. You have ascended by regular gradations to the summit of our sublime and Royal art. You have been conducted around the outer courts of the Temple, viewed its beautiful proportions, its massive pillars, its star decked canopy, its mosaic pavements, its lights, jewels and furniture. You have been introduced into the Middle Chamber, and you learned, by the example of our ancient brethren, to reverence the sacred name of Deity. You have entered the unfinished Sanctum Sanctorum and there, in the integrity and inflexible fidelity of the illustrious Tyrian, witnessed an example of firmness and fortitude never surpassed in the history of man* [IN THE THREE CRAFT DEGREES].
>
> *You have wrought in the quarries and exhibited specimens of your skill, and have been taught how to receive, in a proper manner your Masonic wages* [IN THE MARK AND MARK MASTER]. *You have regularly passed the chair and learned its important duties, a knowledge of which can alone qualify you to preside over the sons of light* [IN THE PAST MASTER DEGREE]. *You have been present and assisted at the completion and dedication of our mystic temple and for your zeal and fidelity to the Craft have received the congratulatory title of* MOST EXCELLENT MASTER.

[1] Similar to the Masonic alphabet at the end of the English Mark ritual book.

You have now witnessed the mournful desolation of Zion, the sack and destruction of the city and Temple of God and the utter loss, as the world supposed, of all those articles contained in the Holy of Holies. You have seen the chosen people of God forced by a foreign despot from the pleasant groves and peaceful vineyards of their native Israel and dragged into captivity on the banks of the far off Euphrates. [SUPER-EXCELLENT MASTER in the English Royal & Select] *But you have seen those afflicted sons of Zion visited, in the darkest night of their adversity, by a peaceful light from heaven which guided them over rough and rugged roads to the scene of their former glory.* [THE SOJOURNERS' JOURNEY IS DRAMATIC AND PICTURESQUE.]

You have seen them enabled by the Signet of Eternal Truth to pass the veils [EXCELLENT MASTER IN SCOTLAND BUT ROYAL ARCH IN CAPITULAR SEQUENCE] *that interposed between them and their fondest hopes. You have seen them successfully engaged in the great and glorious work of rebuilding the House of the Lord. And finally, you have seen the sacred treasures of the first Temple brought to light, and the blessed book restored to the longing eyes of the devout Israelites, to be the rule and guide, the comfort and support of the people of God throughout all future time* [ROYAL ARCH].

The workings of the Craft and Royal Arch in Scotland, Ireland[1] and North America, show a variety of ritual and management which should show us that our own way is not the only way, and thereby open our minds to the possibility of change.

[1] The oldest continuously working Grand Lodge, being founded in 1725.

Sequences following the Craft degrees

Scottish	Irish	English	York Rite
Mark Master Mason *advanced in Craft lodge*	Mark Master Mason	Mark optional	Mark Master Mason
Excellent Master (veils)	Installed Master	No equivalent	Past Master
No degree	No degree	No veils [a] Royal & Select [b]	Most Excellent Master [c]
Royal Arch Mason	Royal Arch Mason (veils)	Royal Arch Mason	Royal Arch Mason (veils)
Leading figure			
Zerubbabel	Excellent King (Josiah)	Zerubbabel	Joshua
Discovery			
Word	Book of Law then word	Word	Book of Law then word
Common continuations			
Royal Ark Mariner	Knight Mason [e]	Many [b] for example:	Cryptic Masonry
Babylonish Pass [d]	Prince Mason	Knights Templar Rose Croix	Commandery of Knights Templar
Notes			
[d] Knight of the Sword, Knight of the East, Knight of the East and West.	[e] Same content as Scottish knightly orders.	[a] except Bristol working [b] Optional	[c] Similar to Royal & Select degree of same name

Third essay: fudges and fictions

> *There are many additional different degrees/orders supplementary to Craft Freemasonry but the Holy Royal Arch*[1] *is the only true progression, or culmination, of Craft Freemasonry. These different degrees/orders are all worth-while organisations, but Chapter, or the Holy Royal Arch, is universally and correctly known and accepted as the Supreme Degree.* A ROYAL ARCH CHAPTER

Most companions never question the statement that the secrets lost on Hiram's death are those discovered by the sojourners in the vault, even though it is incoherent. Remember, that our initiation, each of us solemnly promised to:

> *… hele, conceal and never reveal any part or parts, point or points, of the secrets or mysteries of or belonging to Free and Accepted Masons in Masonry, which may heretofore have been known by, shall now, or may at any future time be communicated to* [US].

and that we would not:

> *… write those secrets; indite, carve, mark, engrave, or otherwise them delineate, or cause or suffer it to be done by others if in* [OUR] *power to prevent it, on anything moveable or immoveable under the canopy of heaven, whereby or whereon any letter character or figure or the least trace of any letter character or figure may become legible or intelligible to* [OURSELVES] *or anyone in the world.*

Nevertheless, on our exaltation, we are expected to believe that on the orders of the original three Grand Masters[2] these same secrets were engraved on a plate of gold. The implication is that when Solomon declared the secrets of a Master Mason to be lost, he was

[1] The Royal Arch is 'holy' only in the English constitution.

[2] Why three? No other lodge, grand or private, has three masters.

telling a porky – certainly indulging in some *evasion* and *equivocation*, and probably some *mental reservation* as well. Our obligation and the discovery simply do not fit together.

Allegory and history

To recap, we know that the tales associated with the building and re-building of a temple at Jerusalem are allegories – fictional tales yielding lessons on morality and life, like Bunyan's *Pilgrim's Progress* or Swift's *Gulliver's Travels* – and so we do not expect them to correspond to historical fact. Nevertheless, we do expect them to make sense: to be coherent and internally consistent.

It matters little that there is no historical or archeological evidence for Hiram Abif; no evidence that he was a Master Mason; none that he built a temple; none that he suffered death in refusing to reveal the secrets of his exalted degree. Taken as an allegory, his story is dramatic, more or less coherent, and a lesson in courage, integrity, and fidelity.[1] It provides an example of how the Masonic life should be lived, and how we should die.

In the same vein, there is very little evidence, historical or archeological, for a pre-Herodian second temple, certainly none to support the Royal Arch narrative. Had there been any evidence, it was destroyed in the building of Herod's (third) temple, commenced in 19 BCE and destroyed by the Romans in 70 CE. The sojourners' discovery, as exciting as it is, has no evidence to sustain it. It too is an allegory, a dramatic fiction, providing a moral lesson in humility, courage and loyalty.

The third degree and Royal Arch tales are satisfying on their own, but together they are incoherent; a secret never to be revealed is incompatible with a secret engraved; one tale belies the other.

---

[1] An excellent discourse is found in 'The Legend of Hiram Abif', Jerry Marsengill, *Transactions of A. Douglas Smith, Jr. Lodge of Research*, No. 1949, Vol. 2, Oct 1988.

Spells and charms

An incantation is a spell or charm used to produce a magical effect, magic being the fictitious art of contriving events. The quote which opens this essay is really no more than an incantation, seeking to create a binding connection between the Craft and the Royal Arch without rationale, evidence or justification. No reason is offered for its claims that the Royal Arch is the only **true** progression and that it is **universally** and **correctly** known as the Supreme degree, and this is true of all such attempts to establish an abiding link.

A provincial strategic plan calls for the Royal Arch to be:

> *The Holy Royal Arch … provides the vehicle by which the last part of the **journey** through Pure Ancient Masonry is **completed**. It is **not an optional extra** but the means by which a Master Mason **completes** his basic Masonic knowledge and experience.*

No justification is offered for there being a Masonic journey, none that the Royal Arch is its completion, and none that exaltation is required, not optional.

Another province calls, again without justification, for the Royal Arch to be *recognised, accepted and acted upon as the essential order,* and in 2003, Grand Lodge declared that the Royal Arch is *indissolubly* linked to the Craft. Such affirmations are more commonly declarations of intent, like *I will always love you*. The only way that the Royal Arch's link to the Craft could be an indissoluble statement, is if it were a tautology, a matter of definition or meaning.[1] The statement *murder is wrong* is a tautology, true by definition, because *murder* means *wrongful killing*. The equation 2+2=4 is another tautology because in the system of mathematics 2+2 means 4. Without justification, the 2003 statement was little more than conjuration.

---

[1] See *Deism at the time of the founders*, David West, Hamilton House, 2nd edition 2018.

Lovelocks on a bridge in Slovenia. Photo Petar Milošević.

It was soon agreed to be unhelpful, and an attempt made to clarify it, but that brought little more than a change in tone, as if patience was wearing thin.

> *... there still seems to be some doubt in the minds of some Companions about the continuing link between the Craft and the Royal Arch, and some feeling that the enhancement in the status of this Order has broken the link. Such, Companions, is not the case ... There is no compromise here, Companions: that bond is to remain as strong and as close as ever, and the Royal Arch should be regarded by all as the important final step in pure Antient Freemasonry.*

The final clause *(should be regarded ...)* can only be interpreted as an edict, as indeed can:

- *you must not doubt*
- *you must ignore such feelings*
- *there is no compromise*
- *the bond is to remain*

... but a command is not evidence.

Fudge and faith

The *Preliminary Declaration* that:

> ... *Pure Antient Masonry consists of three degrees and no more, viz., those of the Entered Apprentice, the Fellow Craft and the Master Mason, including the Supreme Order of the Royal Arch.*

is commonly agreed to be a fudge, a form of words to enable the two grand lodges to slide around a disagreement over the Royal Arch, which might have delayed or even prevented the union. As Knoop & Jones write:

> ... [it] *was treated by most Masonic historians of the nineteenth century ... not as a statement of historical fact but as a mythical claim, not to be taken seriously.*[1]

Nevertheless, forms of words continue to be sought. In 2018 Grand Lodge tried again:

> *The Craft and the Royal Arch should get on together not because the Book of Constitutions tells us that they must, but rather because there is an obvious synergy between the two.*

Recall that only 13% of all Freemasons become active companions of the Royal Arch and that 87% of Masons remain unconvinced that a brother's Masonic experience is complete only when he has been exalted – little evidence for any *obvious synergy*.

The relationship between Craft and Royal Arch has become an article of faith, but that faith has been fatally compromised. If you have been brought up in English Royal Arch ritual, you will recall the words of the Most Excellent Zerubbabel:

> *We congratulate you on being exalted into Royal Arch Masonry, at once the foundation and keystone of the whole Masonic structure. You may perhaps imagine that you have this day taken a fourth degree in Freemasonry. Such, however, is not the case. It is the Master Mason's*

---

[1] *The Genesis of Freemasonry*, Douglas Knoop & G.P. Jones, Manchester Univ. Press, 1947.

completed, for when you were raised to the third degree you were informed that by the untimely death of our Master Hiram Abif the secrets of a Master Mason were lost, and that certain substituted secrets were adopted to distinguish all master masons until time or circumstances should restore the genuine.

Although many companions have not noticed, the Royal Arch is no longer officially connected with the third degree. Keith Tallon reminds us that the words in red were removed in 2004.[1] The Supreme Grand Chapter insists that the Royal Arch should no longer be described as the completion of the third degree, but since that has long been its unique selling point, how is the Royal Arch now to be sold? We are told:

> *... we must adopt a different approach, and stress that a man only becomes a complete Mason when he takes this very important additional step into this Order.*

Complete Mason

But who are complete Masons? Resist, please, the temptation to answer that a complete Mason is one who is exalted into the Royal Arch. This traps us into a circular argument, such that the sentence:

> *When he is exalted into the Royal Arch, a man becomes a complete Mason*

is tantamount to:

> *When a man is exalted into the Royal Arch, he is exalted into the Royal Arch.*

The absence of any USP should tell us something – that there is no connection – but decrees and incantations continue to be made. Signboards in Masonic centres tell us that Core Freemasonry consists of four steps, rather like the Atholls' declaration that *Antient Freemasonry consists of four Degrees.* This particular attempt to provide a 'forever link' combines incantation with edict. What does *core* mean? By what criteria do we decide what is and what is

---

[1] 'Evolution of the Royal Arch Ritual', Keith Tallon, *The Masonic Study Society*, 2016.

not core? Defining the core as the three Craft degrees and the Royal Arch, produces more circularity:

Core Freemasonry consists of the three Craft degrees and the Royal Arch

becomes:

The three Craft degrees and the Royal Arch consist of the three Craft degrees and the Royal Arch.

Why the word *interdependent*? The *Oxford* gives *mutually dependent, dependent upon each other*. What provides this mutual dependence? What supports the exhortation, *You really should, you know?*

The fudge that caused the problem holds Masonry in its thrall. It is taken for granted that the Royal Arch has an intimate connection with the Craft and that all we have to do is to find words to express it – but by now we should recognise that there are no words. Edicts and commands, even when supported by the carrot of promotion in Craft, are admissions of failure.

Fourth essay: ancient and antient

The *Preliminary Declaration* is part of the *General Laws and Regulations for the Government of the Craft* and its spelling of *antient* has a (t) in the middle. The website of the Supreme Grand Chapter of England has the sentence, *Royal Arch is considered to be the completion of 'pure ancient Masonry'*, with a (c) in the middle.

Ancient?

For ancient (c), the *Oxford* gives *of early origin, going far back*. By this criterion, the Royal Arch is not ancient. Going far back, our early brethren worked a ritual of one or two degrees and might have declared (but didn't) that *pure and ancient Freemasonry consisted of two degrees and no more, viz., the Entered Apprentice, and the Fellow Craft.* The third degree was an innovation, adopted by most lodges perhaps by 1750/60, and the Royal Arch another, adopted somewhat later.[1] Few Masons were aware of it before turn the century. As Yasha Beresiner writes:[2]

> *... the available evidence indicates that the degree was not taken seriously even by the* [ATHOLL GRAND LODGE] *until 1766 and probably only from December 1771. In the intervening period, Laurence Dermott kept the Royal Arch active almost single handedly. Early documents of the* [ATHOLL GRAND LODGE] *make minor, if any, reference to the Royal Arch. Laurence Dermott found in the Royal Arch an*

[1] The second half of the 18th century was a great time for creating new degrees. The Mark, the KT, the Rose Croix, the Red Cross of Constantine, the Royal Order of Scotland stem from this period. Jean-Marie Ragon listed more than 1,400 degrees, few of which have survived. *Tuileur général de la francmaçonnerie*, Collignon, 1861.

[2] *Royal Arch: The Fourth Degree of the Grand Lodge of the Antients,* Batham Royal Arch Lecture for 2000.

excellent tool to use against the [PREMIER GRAND LODGE]. *He did not, however, implement the Order until the establishment of the Supreme Grand Chapter … which took the Royal Arch initiative away from him.*[1]

The exposures from *Three Distinct Knocks* (1760), through *Jachin & Boaz* (1762), and *Shibboleth* (1765), like William Preston, writing from 1773 to 1818, make no mention of the Royal Arch, although *Hiram: or the grand master key* of 1766, claims to have been written by *Member of Royal Arch.*[2]

The first Grand Chapter

The Premier Grand Lodge steadfastly refused to recognise the Royal Arch, despite the first Grand Chapter being founded by its members, one of whom was the Grand Secretary, James Heseltine, who said the Royal Arch:

… is a private and distinct society. It is part of Masonry but has no connection with Grand Lodge.[3]

Heseltine has often been accused of hypocrisy but may have been speaking the exact truth. (We will come back to this later.) The Atholl Grand

[1] No Grand Chapter was associated with the Atholl Grand Lodge.

[2] There is no other mention in the book, although a toast is listed *to the memory of P. H. Z. L and I. A.* Perhaps Z refers to *Zerubbabel.*

[3] 1774 letter, quoted in *Freemasons' Book of the Royal Arch*, Bernard E. Jones, Harrap, 1957.

Lodge, of course, treated Royal Arch as a fourth degree,[1] and it is in these opposing views, that we find the provenance of the unhappy compromise that is the *Preliminary Declaration.* It enabled the union, but its unhappiness comes back to haunt us.[2]

But antient?

While the Royal Arch cannot be considered *ancient,* it might still be *antient.* We are accustomed to referring to members of the Atholl Grand Lodge as the *Antients* (t), although a warrant for a lodge at Mottram in Longdendale in the Peak District, signed by Laurence Dermott himself begins: *We, the Grand Lodge of the Most Ancient* (c) *& Honourable Fraternity of Free & Accepted Masons.*[3]

In the eighteenth century, the spelling varied but the spelling *antient* (t) fell out of use in the early nineteenth century, and so we are free to adopt it – not as a **des**cription but as a **pres**cription. We can **pres**cribe that antient (t) Freemasonry consists of the Craft and Royal Arch and, as in Scottish practice, simply list the orders for which UGLE takes responsibility. Some wording might be:

> *The United Grand Lodge of England recognises and practises only the three degrees of the Craft and the Royal Arch, which it refers to as 'Pure Antient Freemasonry.'*

This effectively reverses the 2018 UGLE statement that *the Craft and the Royal Arch should get on together not because the Book of Constitutions tells us that they must, but rather because there is an obvious synergy between the two.* There is no synergy between the two orders today. All we can be sure of now is that UGLE

---

1 Installation was also treated as a degree by the Atholl Grand Lodge. One of several accusations that they laid against Premier Grand Lodge was that the latter had *allowed the esoteric ceremony at the installation of a master to fall into disuse.* Such accusations explain their description of themselves as *Ancients/Antients* and of the Premier Grand Lodge as *Moderns*, a calculated insult.

2 There was no public statement of the *Preliminary Declaration* until 1853.

3 T.M. Carter, 'Provincial Warrants', part II, *AQC*, Vol. 42, 1930.

recognises the two and only the two of them. In adopting this or similar wording, we derive the benefit that there is no need for justification.

To use an analogy, the *Fédération Internationale de Basketball* is the sole competent authority for the sport of basketball throughout the world, recognised as such by the International Olympic Committee. Why doesn't it include netball? Because it doesn't. No justification is needed. Basketball is what it does. Netball isn't. By the same token, the Craft and the Royal Arch are what UGLE does. KT and Rose Croix aren't.

What, then, about the word *pure*? Adding no apparent semantic value, it may have been inserted into the *Preliminary Declaration* as part of an attempt to stop the proliferation of orders: declaring them *impure*, not part of real Masonry. While the Duke of Sussex wanted nothing to do with the Mark, KT and Rose Croix, today these orders are universally accepted as properly Masonic,[1] so the word *pure* does no work at all, and the declaration might read:

> *The United Grand Lodge of England recognises and practises only the three degrees of the Craft and the Royal Arch, which it refers to as 'Antient Freemasonry.'*

This different approach, something which UGLE has said it seeks, absolves us from attempts to defend the indefensible, instead simply legislating for the use of a word.

---

[1] The right to the title *Masonic* seems to need clarification. The recent proliferation of orders, some quite silly, may even justify a form of control – something to delight the ghost of the Duke of Sussex!

Fifth essay: eighteenth century

The prologue to a 1952 Indiana Royal Arch ritual declaims:

> *Without the Royal Arch, the Master's degree is like a song half sung, a tale partly told or a promise unfulfilled.*

Such a sentiment implies that the role of the Royal Arch is to complete the third degree, by re-discovering the 'genuine' secrets of the Master Mason, but eighteenth century third degrees are unanimous that the substitution following the death of Hiram Abif, was permanent. William Preston makes this clear:

> *Solomon ... expressed his sorrow at the loss which the Craft had sustained by the death of his friend ... and said by his death the secrets of a Master Mason must now be lost to future generations ... the first sign or other form used at raising the body should supply the loss, and be equally honoured with his approbation.*[1]

Note the phrases:

- *must now be **lost** to future generations*
- *the first sign ... should **supply** [REPLACE] the loss*
- *be **equally honoured** with his approbation*

With the approval of King Solomon, the original secrets (words) of a Master Mason were replaced; lost to future generations because the replaced secrets (words) would be used no more, and thus eventually forgotten. All eighteenth century exposures say much the same thing, that the new replaced the old. Since *Preston does not seem to have derived much of his material from previous authors of catechisms,*[2] their similarity to Preston may act to validate them on this point.

---

[1] *William Preston and his work*, Colin Dyer, Lewis Masonic, 1987.

[2] 'The Lectures of English Craft Freemasonry', P.R. James, *AQC*, Vol.79, 1966.

English exposures

In what is taken to be the first mention of the third degree, Prichard's *Masonry Dissected* of 1730, the text is fairly familiar:

You're a heroik fellow; from when came you?
From the East
Where are you a-going?
To the West
What are you going to do there?
To seek for that which was lost and is now found.
What was that which was lost and is now found?
The Master-Mason's word.
How was it lost?
By three great knocks of the death of our master Hiram.

and also:

... they agreed that if they do not find the word in him or about him, the first word should be the master's word.[1]

Note that Prichard uses *word,* not *secret,* and says nothing about the original being restored. What was 'lost' was the word in use previously. It was lost because three were needed to communicate it but there were only two left; found because a new word replaced it. *Three Distinct Knocks,* which appears in 1760, is also clear that the *key-word,* as TDK calls it, will never be restored:

And Solomon told them that if they could not find a key-word in him, or about him, it was lost; for there were but three in the world that knew it, and it can never be deliver'd without we three are together; but now one is dead, therefore it is lost.

The same is true of *Jachin & Boaz* (J&B) and *Hiram.* There is some variation in wording due to less than skilful plagiarism, nonetheless it is plain that in no English exposure is there any hint

---

[1] *The Early Masonic Catechisms,* Douglas Knoop, G.P. Jones, Douglas Hamer, *Quatuor Coronati* Lodge, 1975.

of the original master's word being recovered. Since it was replaced, not lost, mention of recovery would be perverse.

French exposures

French exposures[1] of a similar date have much in common with the English, although with two major differences.

Firstly, almost all use the name *Adoniram* instead of *Hiram*. Joannes Snoek writes that many *of the French versions of the Hiramic Legend are either preceded by or start with a discussion of who the hero of the story was and what was his real name.* Hiram is discounted because he was a worker in metals, so they conclude that the builder must have been *the architect of the temple,* biblically named Adoniram.[2]

Secondly there is no reference to the rule of three. The master's word is replaced for fear that Adoniram had been forced to reveal the original, a much more sensible reason. This is displayed in *Le Sceau Rompu*, the broken (waxen) seal, of 1745.

> *The Masters agreed together, out of fear that the Master's word had been revealed, that the first sign to make its appearance in the grip that would be used to raise him, & the first word that would be uttered, should serve in future for Masters.*

Note the phrase *should serve in future for Masters,* used *tout court*. The word used is a version of the familiar M-word. *La Désolation des Entrepreneurs Modernes* (1747) and *Le Maçon Démasqué* (1751) translate it as *the flesh falls from the bones.*

No re-discovery

To re-emphasise the point: in no English nor French third degree

---

[1] *The Early French Exposures,* ed. Harry Carr, *Quatuor Coronati* Lodge, 1971.

[2] 'The Evolution of the Hiramic Legend in England and France', *Heredom* 11, 2003. The only biblical mention of Adoniram relevant to the building of the temple is in 1 Kings 5:14 where he is placed in charge of the forced labour cutting wood from forests of Lebanon.

exposure, nor in Preston, is there any suggestion that the original Master Masons' word would or could be re-discovered. The word was never lost, but simply replaced – in English rituals because of the rule of three, and in French rituals for fear that the original had been compromised. The original word was *not* found in the vault, because it was never hidden there – or anywhere else. As an analogy, consider changing the password for an app on your computer. You may remember the old password as well as the new, but only the new one will work.

The *Francken MS.*

Now let us turn to the other side of the story, the Royal Arch. The *Francken MS.* represents the earliest version of the Ancient and Accepted Scottish Rite or Rose Croix but it also contains a Royal Arch ritual.

Henry Andrew Francken (*c.* 1729-1795) was born in what is now the Netherlands but spent most of his life in Jamaica, with a couple of years in Albany, NY, USA. He was employed in Jamaica by the Admiralty in legal roles, as the official Dutch interpreter, and later as a customs inspector. The manuscript was translated from the French of Étienne Morin (1717-1771), a collector of *haut grades* of Masonry, whom Francken met in 1763. It was not unusual in the late eighteenth century (and subsequently) for Masonic adventurers to augment their income by initiating and conferring honours for new and often bizarre rites, many of which they invented themselves. Morin conferred his rite on Francken and appointed him Deputy Inspector-General, in which role Francken took the order to America.[1]

[1] Morin *created dozens of other Inspectors … often itinerant degree pedlars* Arturo de Hoyos and S. Brent Morris, *Committed to the Flames*, Lewis Masonic, 2008. They instance Antoine Bideaud who conferred Scottish Rite degrees for $46 each.

The most complete version is the 1783,[1] 281 pages long. It is highly unlikely that the degrees were ever performed as written. The staging and costumes are fantasy; complex and expensive.

Enoch and after

And Enoch walked with God: and he was not; for God took him. Gerard Hoet (1648–1733) Bizzell Bible Collection, University of Oklahoma.

Francken's thirteenth and fourteenth degrees are the most relevant to the Royal Arch, with complex tales of Enoch[2], the flood (dated 1656 BCE) and Moses. God appears to Enoch in a dream, showing him a plate of gold under the ninth of nine arches underground, with the sacred name *enlightened* upon it.

Enoch builds a temple underground as in his dream and, instructed by God, tops it off with a stone trap door and iron ring. He engraves the sacred name on a golden plate and lays it under the ninth arch.

Only he knows the name, which he is forbidden to pronounce, but then Noah builds the ark, the deluge ensues, and the temple, and the name, is lost.

[1] *Francken Manuscript 1783*, Henry Andrew Francken, Kessinger Reprints.

[2] The *Book of Enoch* appears in neither the Hebrew or Christian Bible. Traditionally written by the great-grandfather of Noah, it is now dated between 300-100 BCE.

Much later, Moses meets God on Mount Sinai and he also learns the name, which Francken translates as *I am a strong & jealous God, most mighty puissant*. Moses is likewise told never to pronounce it and so this pronunciation is also lost, even though God promises that in the fullness of time Moses' posterity will find it engraved on a golden plate.

Later still, Solomon commences the building of his temple. During the digging for the foundations, a quantity of *riches such as vases, gold and silver urns, marble, porphyry,*[1] *jaspers and agate columns, with a number of precious stones* are found. Guessing a temple was previously built in this spot, Solomon chooses another location. A secret vault, at the end of another nine arches, is constructed for the use of the three grand masters, *the number of two was insufficient to enter in there, three absolutely necessary.*

Other masons who know of the vault, *ask that some of them might be introduced in to that secret place*. Solomon refuses but, like Moses, says that *God will permit one day that you will come to the knowledge of what you now desire*. He then sends Joabert, Stolkin and Guibelum to excavate more of the ruins of Enoch's temple. They discover the golden plate and Solomon tells them:

> *... the promise of God* [IS] *accomplished ... he had promised to Noah, Moses and David that one day the true name of him, by which he was to be invoked, should be discovered on a golden plate.*

The name was written in ancient Samaritan characters to prevent strangers using it in their *necromances or magic experiments.*[2] The golden plate is hidden once more in Solomon's vault. Francken's

[1] An igneous rock, used in Royal Ark Mariners; purple the most desirable colour.

[2] Invoking the name of God to achieve magical effects. For example, Cornelius Agrippa (1486-1535) writes in his *Venomous Magic* of the 3 spheres of creation and the use of *sympathies* between them to draw power from the celestial sphere to the elemental, a model going back to the apocryphal Hermes Trismegistus. See *A Shorter History of Goats, Devils and Freemasons*, David West, Hamilton House, 2018.

account continues, with complexity building on complexity, but we stop him here with the sacred name ready to be discovered.

There is little written about the Francken MS. other than two technical articles. In one John Hamill analyses the watermark, handwriting and provenance,[1] and in the other Brent Morris additionally discusses Francken's life,[2] but in the case of what is probably the oldest English Royal Arch ritual, the *Sheffield MS.*, we are fortunate to have John Acaster's article.[3]

1819 view of Sheffield, rural life giving way to industrialisation.

The *Sheffield MS.*

The manuscript itself is a small handwritten book, dated to about 1785, now in the Sheffield Masonic library, with the text available

1 'The Third *Francken MS.* of the Rite of Perfection', *AQC* Vol. 97, 1984.

2 'Henry Andrew Francken & his Masonic Manuscripts,' *World Conference on Freemasonry, Fraternalism and History*, May 2015. Available online from the Scottish Rite Research Society at scottishriteresearch.com.

3 *Peerings from within the Royal Arch*, John Acaster, Prov. Grand Lodge of East Lancashire.

online at SCRIBD. The first part seems a précis of the ritual and is followed by a catechism in four or five sections.[1] Much is familiar to modern ears, although with some unusual expressions. For example, in answer to a familiar challenge, itself missing in the text, the sojourner replies:

> *We are not of those runagates and parasites who, like the sons of Belial quitted their Brethren in distress, forsook the city and the Holy Temple and fled to the common enemy, neither are we of the inferior sort who were left to till the ground, dress the vines and cultivate the land.*[2]

In digging the foundations, the sojourners discover the usual pedestal bearing the names of the three Grand Masters, together with the sacred name on a plate of gold.

Two legends

We will return to the *Sheffield MS.* in the hands of John Acaster a little later but we should note that here, as in Francken, it is the sacred name, and only the sacred name, that is recovered, a name of course not subject to alteration. In the Royal Arch, represented by the *Sheffield MS.* and Francken, there is a re-discovery; in the third degrees, represented by the exposures and Preston, there is none. It becomes obvious that in the eighteenth century there were two legends: one in the Craft about the Master Mason's word, and another in the Royal Arch about the sacred name.

The Master Mason's word and the sacred name are different entities, stemming from different legends, and this is fundamental.

---

[1] Only 4 sections are numbered but *The Mystical Knowledge of the Temple* is perhaps a 5th.

[2] *Runagate* is an obsolete word meaning *renegade, vagabond, fugitive* or *apostate* (the last probably metaphorical), which occurs in Psalm 68:6 of the *Book of Common Prayer*, 1662: *He is the God that maketh men to be of one mind in an house, and bringeth the prisoners out of captivity: but letteth the runagates continue in scarceness.* The King James uses the word *rebellious*. The phrase *sons of Belial* usually means *worthless people*. On its own *Belial* may refer to a/the devil.

Sixth essay: two legends

The fact of the two legends seems never before to have been recognised, even though the resolution of the enigma of the Royal Arch fundamentally depends, upon it.

The *Master Mason's Word* legend says that the original word of a Master Mason[1] was substituted (not temporarily but permanently) on the death of Hiram Abif: in English rituals because of the rule of three, and in French rituals for fear that the original word had been compromised (a rather more sensible explanation).

The *Sacred Name* legend says that the name of God was hidden in a vault, lost when the temple was destroyed and re-discovered by the sojourners digging the foundations for the second temple.

Nothing sacred appears in eighteenth century third degrees, because the third is about the loss of the *Master Mason's Word,* and its immediate replacement, or substitution.

There is no substitution in early Royal Arch ritual because it is about the loss and re-discovery of *the sacred name,* for which there can be no substitute.

Certificate

The Master Mason's word was a certificate of competence. In the days of operative masonry, so the legend goes, most masons were illiterate and written certificates would have been of little use.

[1] The title *Master Mason* is used in the Royal & Select to refer to those whom today we might call architects/contractors. The introduction to the R&S ritual says, *whereas all overseers were in possession of the necessary trade secrets, a Master Word was essential to enable anyone to negotiate contracts, employ craftsmen and talk on equal terms with other Masters.* I am sorry that the excellent introduction cannot be attributed. Richard Bowyer writes: *The consensus is that it was a group of people involved with the re-writing of the ritual when Peter Glynn Williams was Grand Secretary (1986-1997).*

Nevertheless, the clerk of works still needed to be sure the man in front of him was what he claimed to be, and the possession of the Master Mason's word enabled a mason to *prove* his ability.

Possession of the word in early operative days was equivalent to a skilled trade certification today,[1] and it was this word that masons promised never to indite, carve, mark or otherwise delineate. The reason is obvious. Had an operative mason improperly revealed the word, it would have been seized upon by one of those dreaded cowans to steal work from good masons. The value of the word is demonstrated by the ruffians. Preston writes:

> *... the first ruffian ... stated that the temple being nearly finished, he should be obligated to travel into other countries for subsistence, and as the secrets of a Master Mason which he [Hiram] possessed, if revealed to him, would always entitle him to distinction; he therefore earnestly requested that those secrets should be immediately disclosed.*[2]

and by the lengths they were prepared to go to gain. They:

> *... demanded of our Master the secrets of his exalted degree, warning him that death would be the consequence of a refusal.*

Proving

So proving mattered a lot and, in theory at least, it still does today. If the word and sign of a Mason become known by *the uninitiated or popular world who are not Freemasons*, they might gain illegitimate access to a lodge. It is the job of the Inner Guard *to admit Freemasons on proof*. He reports to the Junior Warden whose duty it is to ensure that no *unqualified person gains admission to our assemblies.* When opening a lodge in the third degree the Master instructs Brother Junior Warden:

> *You, being acquainted with the proper method, will prove the brethren*

[1] For example, the UK National Vocational Qualifications (NVQs).

[2] This makes the first ruffian sound quite courteous!

master masons by signs and demonstrate that proof to me by copying their example.

When the Worshipful Master sanctions, confirms and declares that the secrets *shall designate you and all MMs throughout the Universe,* he is formally announcing the word to be used henceforth to prove a Master Mason qualified, in place of the previous word. Of course, there could be only one such 'certificate' word in use at any one time, a word that both masons and their potential employers could recognise. On the death of Hiram Abif, it is *not* the case that the Master Mason's word was lost *for a period of nearly five hundred years*. It was never lost at all; simply discarded in favour of another.

The Sacred Name legend

The *Master Mason's Word* legend has nothing to do with what the sojourners find. The legend of finding the *sacred name* belongs to the Royal Arch. In this legend, the name was hidden in the vault with other treasures, to prevent its capture by enemy forces and to preclude its use by magicians. The whereabouts of the vault were lost during the destruction of Jerusalem by the Babylonians in 597 BCE,[1] and was re-discovered by the sojourners, digging the foundations for the second temple.

Permission to rebuild sacred edifices had been granted (to all subject nations) by Cyrus the Great in 539/538 BCE, as recorded on the Cyrus Cylinder.[2] So in this legend, the sacred word was lost for nearer sixty than five hundred years. There was no (masonic) prohibition on inditing the sacred name, so Solomon's engraving in the vault was not improper.

---

[1] There is extra-biblical evidence for 597 in the *Babylonian Chronicles* but none for 587. Francken puts the destruction down to Solomon's frisky sex life, saying that he *soon forgot the goodness of God and gave himself up to all licentiousness* [SO] *God put it in the heart of Nebuchadnezzar, king of Babylon, to lay siege to Jerusalem.*

[2] *A shorter history of Goats, Devils and Freemasons,* David West, Hamilton House, 2018.

What was lost?

There is no Jewish legend to the effect that YHWH was ever lost, but its pronunciation has been. Before the use of *niqqud,* dotting or pointing marks to indicate vowels, the twenty-two letter Hebrew alphabet consisted only of consonants. Pronunciation of unknown words was impossible. In early times, the sacred name was pronounced quite normally, but gradually it became the custom to avoid it. By the third century BCE, it was used only inside the temple, and when that was destroyed by the Romans in 70 CE, it was not used at all and the pronunciation was lost:

Mesha stele, containing the earliest known reference (840 BCE) to Yahweh.

> *... the name of God (Yod Hé Vav Hé) may not be sounded. It is customarily pronounced 'Adonai' and when ... vocalised it is given the vowels of that word (Shev Ḥolam Kamatz).*[1]

When transferred from the Hebrew to the Latin alphabet, this became *Jehova,* and so as the *Encyclopedia* says,

> *... the word 'Jehova(h)' is an artificial composite. Modern scholarship believes the original pronunciation of the name was 'Yahveh'.*

[1] The *New Jewish Encyclopedia,* ed. David Bridger, Berman House, 1976.

In Royal & Select Masters the sacred name is hidden in the vault, written in three languages: Syrian (essentially Aramaic, incidentally the language of Jesus), Chaldean (the Akkadian language of Babylon) and Egyptian, so that:

> *... if the children of Israel should ever be carried into captivity and remain so long as to forget their mother tongue, yet on their return it might, if found, be restored by means of the other languages.*

Is the fear of forgetting their mother tongue rational? Spoken Hebrew did die out in the years following the third Jewish-Roman war 132-136 CE and Hebrew is said to be the only dead language that has been fully revived.

Why did they think the other languages would help? By the time of Cyrus the Great, Aramaic was the *lingua franca* of the Levant. In common with Hebrew, it had no vowels, but Chaldean and Egyptian both had five (as does English). No one could pronounce the Aramaic, but educated men like Ezra and Nehemiah could pronounce the Chaldean and Egyptian words, similar enough in sound and meaning to give clues to the Aramaic.

Again, we should remind ourselves that this is a matter of legend and not history. Neither Ezra nor Nehemiah were around at the supposed time of the rebuilding of the temple, and while the Royal & Select offers a neat way of discovering the pronunciation, it has no evidential value. Its ritual was written in the nineteenth century and re-written in the 1980s and 1990s.

Francken again

The *Master Mason's Word* legend and the *Sacred Name* legend both appear in Francken but in separate and distinct contexts. The *Sacred Name* legend occurs in his thirteenth and fourteenth degrees while the *Master Mason's Word* legend is mentioned only in his fifth degree. Here he talks, more briefly, of third degree matters and, indulging in a flight of fancy, tells how Hiram Abif's heart was:

> *... exposed to the public view in [AN] urn with a sword pierced through it ... At the end of the nine days, the heart was embalmed and deposited in [AN] obelisk, with triangular stone on which were engraved in Hebrew the letters IMB.*

The 'I' is said to be the initial of the previous master's word (Francken does not say what it was) and 'MB' the initials of the new word. So, in the eighteenth century, the sacred name belonged to the Royal Arch story and the Master Mason's word to the Hiramic story; again two distinct legends.

An aside

The meaning of the tetragrammaton is in dispute. Karen Armstrong gives a fascinating interpretation:

> *When Moses asks his name and credentials, ... he answers: 'I Am Who I Am.' What did he mean? He certainly did not mean, as later philosophers would assert, that he was self-subsistent Being. Hebrew did not have such a metaphysical dimension at this stage and it would be nearly 2000 years before it acquired one ... 'Ehyeh asher ehyeh' is a Hebrew idiom to express a deliberate vagueness ... So when Moses asks who he is, God replies in effect: 'Never you mind who I am!' or 'Mind your own business!'*[1]

Christine Hayes agrees that *Ehyeh Asher Ehyeh Asher,* means *I am that I am,* but when going back down the mountain, she suggests that Moses converts this to the third-person, *Yahweh Asher Yahweh,* – *He is who he is*, later abbreviated to *Yahweh.*[2] In the time of Moses Judaism was polytheistic, so a name was needed to indicate a god, as in Psalm 82. In monotheism, *God* suffices. There is only one.

---

[1] *A History of God*, Karen Armstrong, Random House, 1999.

[2] *Introduction to the Old Testament*, The Open Yale Courses Series, 2006.

Seventh essay: help from John Acaster

John Acaster

The *Sheffield MS.* is more straightforward than Francken, being restricted to the Royal Arch. As such, it uses only the *Sacred Name* legend. In answer to *What is the signification of the Temple?* it reads:

> *The terrestrial temple built by King Solomon was a figure* [SYMBOL] *of our saviour Christ and his church. For when the Son of God suffr'd the temple of his holy body to be destroy'd and risen again from the dead; then he raised up to us the Christian Church, which is the true spiritual house & temple where God liveth and dwelleth for ever.*

In Sheffield, the building of the temple is an allegory for the creation of the Christian Church: the temple a metaphorical representation of Jesus, the destruction of the first a representation of the crucifixion, the building of the second a representation of the resurrection. In the Craft, we see the physical construction of a physical temple, while in the Royal Arch we see the spiritual construction of a spiritual temple.

At a time when 99.9% of people in the UK believed in a Christian God and accepted the literal truth of the Bible,[1] it is easy to see how a Mason would be ready revisit the temple as a mystical entity in the Royal Arch, having studied it as a physical entity in the Craft. This may also help to explain the presence of the Mark degree in Scottish and Irish declarations. It serves to illustrate the derivation of the mystical from the physical.

The significant biblical references in Sheffield are *Haggai* 2, and *1 Peter* 2. To these John Ancaster[2] adds Isaiah 28:16:

> *Therefore thus saith the Lord God, Behold, I lay in Zion for a foundation a stone, a tried stone, a precious corner stone, a sure foundation.*

and Psalm 118:22, with clear kinship to the Mark: *The stone which the builders refused is become the head stone of the corner.* Haggai 2:4&7 reads:

> *… be strong, all ye people of the land, saith the Lord, and work: for I am with you, saith the Lord of hosts … And I will shake all nations, and the desire of all nations shall come: and I will fill this house with glory, saith the Lord of hosts.*

Taken together, these texts are taken to foreshadow 1 Peter 2:4-7:

> *To whom coming, as unto a living stone, disallowed indeed of men, but chosen of God, and precious, ye also as lively stones are built up a spiritual house, an holy priesthood, to offer up spiritual sacrifices acceptable to God by Jesus Christ. Wherefore also it is contained in the scripture: behold, I lay in Sion a chief corner stone, elect, precious, and he that believeth on him shall not be confounded … the stone which the*

---

[1] In 1760, 93.6% were Anglicans, 5.2% non-conformists, 1.1% Catholics, 0.1% Jews, 'Counting Religion in England and Wales: the Long Eighteenth Century, c. 1680-c. 1840', Clive D. Field, *Journal of Ecclesiastical History*, Vol. 63, No. 4, October 2012.

[2] *Peerings from within the Royal Arch*, E. John T. Acaster, Provincial Grand Lodge of East Lancashire.

builders disallowed, the same is made the head of the corner.[1]

In Christian thought, it is usual to associate Haggai's *desire of all nations* with Jesus, who is metaphorically taken to be Isaiah's foundation stone of the Church, with parallels in the Mark.[2]

Rejection

The stone is rejected by the builders in the Mark, because it is not what was expected; the overseers reject a keystone for which they have no plans. Jesus was rejected by the people because he was not the Messiah they expected. (*Christ* is Greek and *Messiah*, Hebrew. Both mean *the anointed*.) As Karen Armstrong points out,[3] Jesus was born into a society traumatised by violence. For example, the Roman general Publius Quintillius Varus (46 BCE - 6 CE) crucified 2,000. The people looked for a Messiah who would drive the Romans out and return Israel to the golden age of King David.

Importance

Psalm 118 says that the rejected stone was the most important. The rejected stone in the Mark, the keystone without which the arch cannot stand, had been thrown into the rubbish. Jesus, the rejected Messiah, the foundation stone without which God's church cannot be built, was laid in an unused tomb.[4] The mason

---

[1] Similar expressions are found in Matthew 21:42, Mark 12:10, Luke 20:17 and Acts 4:11. One asks whether the Old Testament foreshadows the New, or the New was written to be foreshadowed by the Old.

[2] Haggai 2:7 reads differently in other versions of the Bible. A detailed analysis is provided by Frank W. Hardy, who examines the phrase in its Hebrew, Greek, Syriac and Latin versions and writes: *On the one hand 'the desired of all nations' could be taken as a prophecy of Christ, and mean 'the [One] desired of all nations,' while on the other hand it could be taken as a preface to the remarks in the following verse about silver and gold, and mean 'the [things] desired of all nations.'* The strongest reason for adopting a non-messianic interpretation, he writes, is that the phrase *they will come* is plural. The text does not say *and he will come.* 'The Desired of all Nations in Haggai 2:7', *Historicism,* No. 12, October 1987.

[3] *Fields of Blood,* The Bodley Head, 2014.

[4] According to Luke 23:53. The gospels differ on the details.

who made the rejected stone finds it. Jesus rises from the dead.

The *Sheffield MS.* is replete with temple metaphors for Jesus, the Christian church and the afterlife. For example, the cherubim[1] at each end of the mercy seat, signify the Old and New Testaments.

Model of the Ark from the Wilderness Tabernacle, kibbutz Almog, near the Dead Sea.

Together they contain the doctrine of the Church, shown by their wings curving towards each other. The golden doors of the temple represent Christ, the way[2] by which his followers enter into eternal happiness. The golden candlestick, with its six branches and seven lights, represents the illumination of the path to eternal happiness by Jesus and the ministers of the Church. Acaster writes:

The Royal Arch provided remarkable revelations to its Companions in a period when schooling was scarce ... The Royal Arch in its earliest

---

[1] A *cherub* (plural *cherubim*) is not a baby boy with wings. Such figures are *putti* (singular *putto*) purely decorative. Cherubim are fearsome beings in *Ezekiel* 1:5-25.

[2] *Jesus answered, 'I am the way and the truth and the life. No one comes to the Father except through me.'* John 14:6.

period gave a satisfying and clear interpretation of the Bible message for Christians.

The prayer in Sheffield is:

Grant, we beseech thee Almighty God, that we may be always attentive to thy great and glorious attributes which are all infinitely perfect and that as far as in us lies imitate thy Divine Goodness …

This *old commencing prayer* (Acaster's term) tells us that we are *pledged to imitate Divine Goodness*. This, Acaster writes, is the central message of the Royal Arch *which has been blurred through the later adoption of an Anglican Collect*. The *great and glorious attributes* are symbolised by the triangle within a circle to which alone we bow.

Thus, in the Royal Arch, eighteenth century companions dedicated themselves to divine perfection, and it is no wonder that it came:

… to be known as the root, heart, and marrow of Masonry. Indeed, the Royal Arch degree appealed to the heart and soul of 18th century brethren: the three Craft degrees appealed to their heads.

Looked at this way, the Sheffield provides a clear connection between Royal Arch and Craft, a connection which is Christian but also Masonic, illustrated by symbols.[1]

---

[1] To fully comprehend it, one needs to be a Christian and probably a trinitarian. I am neither, hence my grateful use of Acaster's work.

Eighth essay: whence the compression

IN THE EIGHTEENTH CENTURY, THERE WERE TWO SEPARATE LEGENDS. IN ONE, THE SACRED NAME WAS LOST AND LATER FOUND. IN THE OTHER, THE WORD OF A MASTER MASON WAS REPLACED. THE COMPRESSION OF THE TWO LEGENDS INTO ONE IS THE ROOT CAUSE OF THE PROBLEMS OF THE ROYAL ARCH.

Speaking of the 1989 Royal Arch fuss, Richard Sandbach wrote:

> [THE] *mischief arises from mistaken and muddled work by revisers of the ritual and by those who later, in an excess of misplaced zeal allowed what is only a recognition word ... to be referred to as if it were a divine name.*[1]

De-Christianising

At the union in 1813, the Duke of Sussex sought to de-Christianise Freemasonry. In the Craft religious references were and are incidental to the narrative so the task of de-Christianisation was not too difficult, although some phrases remain such as *that bright morning star*.[2] The inclusion of biblical quotes was simply a normal style of writing in the Christian culture of the eighteenth century.[3]

On the other hand, the Royal Arch was conceived as a Christian allegory so its religious references were not incidental, and de-Christianisation thus undermined it. Acaster comments:

> *No wonder then that nowadays we cannot make out the vision and ideals which originally caused the Royal Arch to succeed.*

---

[1] 'Compatibility', *Understanding the Royal Arch*, Lewis Masonic, 1992.

[2] *I, Jesus have sent mine angel to testify unto you these things in the churches. I am the root and the offspring of David, and the bright and morning star.* Revelation 22:16.

[3] In the *Freemasons Magazine and Masonic Mirror* in January 1868, Bro. H.B. White quotes an old ritual: Q: *Why was you deprived of metals when raised a M.M?* A: *As Judas betrayed Christ for thirty pieces of silver, so I was deprived of metals that I might not have the price of blood about me.*

The changes made in the compression

The compression forced a reversal of meaning in the third degree by the addition of the words in red below:

> *… and that certain substituted secrets were adopted to distinguish all master masons until time or circumstances should restore the genuine,*

to facilitate a false addition to the Royal Arch:

> *When you were raised to the third degree you were informed that by the untimely death of our Master Hiram Abif the secrets of a Master Mason were lost, and that certain substituted secrets were adopted to distinguish all master masons until time or circumstances should restore the genuine.*[1]

The compression also caused an improper use of the word *genuine.*

> In the *Sacred Name* legend, the name of God was lost and later recovered. There was no substitution and, since there was only ever one name, there was no question of it being anything other than *genuine.*
>
> In the *Master Mason's Word* legend, one trade qualification word was replaced by another. Neither word was more genuine than the other, although only one could be in use at any time.

Another error is the phrase *five hundred years,* an irrelevant period from the switch of the trade qualification word in the *Master Mason's Word* legend, to the re-discovery of the name of God in the *Sacred Name* legend.

> The time between lost and found in the *Sacred Name* legend is no more than sixty years; that is from Nebuchadnezzar's razing of Jerusalem to the groundworks for Zerubbabel's temple.
>
> There is no time between lost and found in the *Master Mason's Word* legend because one word was simply switched for another.

---

[1] Modern Domatic ritual

These errors are the origin of the Royal Arch troubles.

The Sussex ritual

My first thought was that de-Christianisation compressed the two legends into one. As John Hamill says:

> *In 1817, the Duke of Sussex summoned the original Grand Chapter and the members of the Antients' former Royal Arch and 'united' them into the United Grand Chapter, a name that lasted a very few years until the present title of Supreme Grand Chapter was adopted. The administrative links between the Craft and Royal Arch were put into place but little else was done.*
>
> *In 1834, there being some doubt as to what the proper ceremonies were, the Duke of Sussex set up a special committee to investigate and recommend to the Grand Chapter what they should be. This they did and their deliberations were approved by both the Duke and the Grand Chapter. It was ordered that they should be adopted by all of the chapters then in existence and those that might come into being in the future.*[1]

The '*Sussex ritual*' was never published and by several accounts has languished in the Grand Secretary's safe all this time. Fragments have lately been appearing and indicate a ritual not so very different from that in use today. The secrets story runs:

> [THE] *true secrets of a Master Mason were lost, and that therefore certain substituted secrets were adopted to distinguish the Master Mason until the genuine secrets might be discovered. Those secrets were lost for a period of nearly 500 years, and were recovered in the manner which has just been explained to you.*

The compression is signposted by the word *true,* used in the same mistaken way as *genuine,* and by the timing error of 500 years. However, the compression error appears before the Sussex.

---

[1] 'Discovery of manuscript at Freemasons' Hall could reveal hidden secrets', *Freemasonry Today*, 6 June 2013.

Carlile

Richard Carlile's 1825 exposure is the first example we have of a Royal Arch ritual after the union. Carlile (1790-1843) was not a Mason but an important journalist and commentator. He is most famous for his publication of Paine's *Common Sense*, *Rights of Man* and *Age of Reason* in sections, making them each available to those who could not afford to buy the complete book at one time. His journal *The Republican* was the first to report the Peterloo Massacre.

Peterloo Massacre, 1819, Richard Carlile, Manchester Libraries.

He campaigned against child labour, for equality of the sexes and for birth control, supported movements against wage cuts and wrote, reminiscent of modern times:[1]

> *Oh! England, to what wilt thou come! Formed by nature to contain a race of men, who might live in the most polished state of society, and command the respect of all the inhabitants of the earth, yet still the most miserable! 'Tis misrule, fatal misrule, that keeps the better half of*

[1] *The Republican*, volume 1, reprint Hard Press, 2017.

thy children in a state of wretchedness, and starvation, whilst the few squander thy produce.

Carlile was imprisoned twice for his activism but his journal outsold the *Times* and his *Manual of Freemasonry* came to be used as a ritual text. Its third degree reads in part:

Brethren, these substituted secrets being regularly imparted to me, I as the humble representative of King Solomon, and as the Master of this lodge, do ratify and confirm, that these substituted secrets shall designate you and all master masons until further time and circumstances shall restore the genuine ones.[1]

In his description of the Royal Arch, following the ceremony of the veils, he refers to the discovery made by the sojourners:

These three mysterious words, [JAO, BUL, ON] *in a triangular form,* [TOGETHER ARE] *the long-lost sacred word of the Master Mason and is too incomprehensible for individual expression but in reward for your industry and zeal, you will now be put in possession of a full explanation of this the Grand Omnific Royal Arch Word.*[2]

This is ridiculous. The word of a Master Mason, a trade certification and nothing more, has become sacred. We must be crystal clear that it isn't, and never was. Whether or not *Jabulon*[3] (as *Jaobulon*) first surfaces in Carlile, *Jabulon* is not the Master Mason's word and never has been. The M-word has been modified in various Craft rituals but it is still the origin of the only Master Masons' word in use.

---

[1] *Manual of Freemasonry,* Traffic Output Publication.

[2] An oddity that something too incomprehensible for individual expression can all the same be explained fully as a reward for industry and zeal.

[3] No one knows where *Jabulon* sprang from. Theories of origin are unconvincing and do not explain how the word came into use. Tydeman said it is a compound word made up of יָה (*Yah*) referring to Yahweh, בעל (*bul*) meaning on high and און (*on*) meaning strength; a little contrived perhaps. Arturo de Hoyos says *Jabulon* was he who found a gold plate engraved with the name of God in the ruins of an ancient temple. Mackey says that *Jabulum* is a corruption of *Giblim.*

Jabulon is just as obviously not one of the sacred names of God. It is only the confusion between the two legends, enabling *Jabulon* to appear disguised as the weird chimera of a sacred Master Masons' word, that hides the fact. What Sandbach refers to as *an excess of misplaced zeal* has in his words *allowed what is only a recognition word to be referred to as if it were a divine name.*

The misguided attempts to give each of the three syllables a religious meaning further compounds the error, leading to silly interpretations which have caused a lot of unnecessary fuss. The suggestion that *ON* stands for Osiris, and that *BUL* stands for Ba'al is ludicrous. There is no evidence to support it and it is a pretty wild idea that late eighteenth century Masons were familiar with Hebrew, Phoenician and Egyptian.

William Finch

While in jail Carlile collected together all contemporary writings available to write his *Manual of Freemasonry*. One text we are assured he had in his possession is William Finch's *Masonic Treatise* of 1802.[1] Finch wrote that King Solomon ordered Hiram to be re-interred, informing the brethren:

> ... *at the same time that by his untimely* [DEATH] *the* [SECRET] *of a Master Mason was lost till future ages should discover* [IT], *but as a reward to them for their fidelity and exertion, the first casual Sn. T. and W. that should occur among them at his raising should be adopted as a substitute till the right was found.*

Again we see the compression, taking us further back.

John Browne

Browne's 1798/1802 *Masonic Key* was written in cipher, but as deciphered by David Slater, the third tracing board reads in part:

---

[1] *Masonic Treatise*, 1802, Onondaga and Oswego Masonic District Historical Society, transliterated Alex Horne, Grand Lodge of British Columbia and Yukon, 1956.

King Solomon ordered the same fifteen loving Brethren to go and raise him to a more decent interment knowing him to be worthy of it, at the same time informed them that by his untimely death the secrets of a Master Mason was lost but, as a reward for their fidelity, the first casual Sign, Token and Word that should occur at the opening of the grave and our Grand Master uprising should be adopted in their room until further ages should discover the right.[1]

John Knight

The earliest instance of the compression I have found appears in a manuscript from Redruth in Cornwall, which Piers Vaughan suggests is an Antient (Atholl) ritual.[2] In 1791, Knight was MEZ of the Druids Chapter of Royal Arch Masons No. 79, a chapter seemingly meeting within a Craft lodge, normal in Atholl working. Part of his catechism runs:

Z. *From whence came Joshua?*
J. *From Babylon.*
Z. *Where going?*
J. *To Jerusalem.*
Z. *What should induce him to leave Babylon and go to Jerusalem?*
J. *To assist in clearing away the rubbish from the building of the first temple in hopes of finding the SW of masonry.*
Z. *Was the SW lost?*
J. *It was.*
Z. *How came it to be lost?*
J. *By the death of our Grand Master HAB.*

Possibility or probability

The *Sheffield MS.* shows no sign of the compression. As a Royal Arch ritual, it is concerned only with the *Sacred Name* legend. There

---

[1] 'Revisiting John Browne's Ciphered Masonic Works', *AQC* 132, 2019.

[2] *Early Ritual of the Holy Royal Arch*, Thomas Smith Webb Chapter of Research No. 1798, New York, 2004.

is no sign of it either in Preston's work, concerned only with the Craft and the *Master Mason's Word* legend. Sheffield and Preston describe rituals in use by members of the Premier Grand Lodge, so the possibility, even probability, arises that it was in Atholl lodges that the sin of compression was first committed. Perhaps it happened this way:

Phase one

> Until at least 1767, the third degree in all lodges was solely concerned with the Master Mason's word – that after the death of Hiram Abif the word previously used as a 'certificate' of professional ability was replaced by an M-word; in French exposures to de-risk the possibility that Hiram had given the old word away; in English exposures as a result of the rule of three.

Phase two

> The Royal Arch appeared during the 1750s and slowly grew in popularity. Its legend was the loss and re-discovery of the sacred name. The absence of any narrative or ritual connection between Craft and Royal Arch may well account for Heseltine's remark that the Royal Arch was part of Masonry but had no connection with Grand Lodge. Far from being hypocritical, Heseltine was accurately describing the situation at the time of the Premier Grand Lodge:[1] it was concerned only with the Craft.

Phase three (a)

> From 1751, the number of Atholl lodges grew in England and Wales. There is a dearth of exposures from the 1760s until Knight in 1791, but it seems quite possible that the Atholls amended the two legends, compressing them into one, since they viewed the Royal Arch as an integral part of Craft Freemasonry.

---

[1] One might, with equal truth, say that *The United Religious, Military and Masonic Orders of the Temple and of St John of Jerusalem, Palestine, Rhodes and Malta* are part of Masonry, but have no connection with Grand Lodge.

Phase three (b)

From the evidence of Preston's work during the period from 1772 to 1816, those lodges owing allegiance to the Premier Grand Lodge made no change to their third degree, still focused on the *Master Mason's Word* legend. From the evidence offered by Francken and the *Sheffield MS.,* the chapters attended by Premier Grand Lodge Masons remained focused on the *Sacred Name* legend. The fact that the Royal Arch was held distinct from the Craft no doubt inhibited change.

Phase four

Towards the end of the eighteenth century, when Preston's influence was in decline, Craft exposures start to appear, based on Knight's Atholl ritual, all with the compression in place.

Phase five

Leading up to 1813, the two grand lodges sought a merger, obviously requiring an agreement over the Royal Arch; the sub-text being the insistence by Duke of Sussex on de-Christianisation. Atholl companions had little difficulty with this,[1] but it was impossible for the Premier side. The solution was the wholesale adoption of the Atholl ritual, made easier by the many exposures leading up to 1813. The Atholls wanted the Royal Arch as the fourth degree; the Premiers would not go that far; the Duke still wanted his de-Christianisation and so the fudge occurred – the word *including* getting them off the hook.

Phase six

Eventually the fudge came under pressure, and a series of vain attempts took off to justify the connection between the (Atholl) third degree and the (Atholl) Royal Arch. Being wedded to the compression and its incoherence, none can succeed.

---

[1] The religious element in today's Royal Arch is somewhat forced. It is irrelevant to the sojourners' story and comes out mainly and often uncomfortably in both the bible extracts and the lectures, written by the Rev. George Browne in 1834/5.

Ninth essay: what to do

The only truly successful way out is to decompress the narrative, but I am told by a brother who is a deep sea diver that decompression can take a long time, and that the longer a diver is down, the longer it takes to decompress. We have been underwater for over two hundred years.

Brother Fraser being prepared for a dive in search of WWII bombs.

We can of course do nothing, but this will not reduce the number of Masons sceptical of the Royal Arch, nor will it eliminate the statements and edicts likely to damage the reputation of UGLE.

Disentanglement

A simple action is the alteration of the *Preliminary Declaration* (it was only preliminary) to read:

> *The United Grand Lodge of England recognises and practises only the three degrees of the Craft and the Royal Arch, which it refers to as 'Antient Freemasonry.'*

This obviates the need to defend the indefensible and rids us of the fudge, both consummations devoutly to be wished, but it does not provide a reason to join the Royal Arch. For this we have to disentangle the two legends, first by removing the phrase added to both Craft and Royal Arch:

> *... until time or circumstances should restore the genuine.*

We cease to refer to the Master Masons' word as sacred and make plain its function as certification. We cease to refer to the sojourners' discovery as the long lost word of a Master Mason, make plain that what they find is the sacred name. Given that the loss of the name is known to be historically untrue, we might take a leaf from the Royal & Select Masters' book and have the sojourners' discover its pronunciation.

The issue for UGLE

It is wrongly supposed that when King Cnut (990-1035 CE) faced the incoming tide, he was arrogantly showing that he was greater than nature. The opposite is true; he was demonstrating that even a great king must accept his inferiority to the Almighty.

> *Let all men know how empty and worthless is the power of kings, for there is none worthy of the name, but He whom heaven, earth, and sea obey by eternal laws.*[1]

The Duke of Sussex was implacably opposed to any extension

---

[1] *Historia Anglorum,* Henry of Huntingdon (*c.* 1088-1157), trnsl. Diana Greenway, Clarendon Press, 1996.

beyond the Craft. In this, his action resembled the faulty interpretation of Canute's paddling, for it must have been obvious that new orders were inevitable. David Harrison's *The Lost Rites and Rituals of Freemasonry* describes many failed Masonic experiments[1] with intriguing names. Those that survived, including the Mark, the Knights Templar and the Rose Croix, were cold-shouldered by the Duke to the detriment of today's United Grand Lodge of England.

The dues gathered by Supreme Councils, Great Priories, and Imperial Conclaves would have assisted the Grand Lodge in its straightened financial situation today. The Royal Arch is the only source of incremental funds and re-Christianising it would further reduce the number of exaltees.

Nevertheless, with amendments to the sojourners' tale and an additional story concerning the pronunciation of YHWH, we could still 'spiritualise' the temple, even without a Christian interpretation, even using John Bunyan's *Solomon's Temple Spiritualized* as a guide.[2] When you think about it, Bunyan's subtitle, *Gospel light fetched out of the Temple at Jerusalem,* is not a bad summary of the *Sheffield MS.*

We would, of course, be seeking secular rather than gospel light, but even this would re-establish a connection between the third degree and the Royal Arch. The Craft would remain an allegory using the building of a physical temple to teach moral values, while the Royal Arch would become a set of symbols yielding spiritual lessons, perhaps something like this:

---

[1] Lewis Masonic, 2017. Among those he mentions are *The Rite of African Builders or Architects, The Order of Xerophagists, The Rite of Elus Coens, The Rite of Philalethes,* as well as the famous *Rite of Strict Observance.*

[2] First published 1688. Reprint Curiosmith, 2010.

Acceptance	Few will see the end.	Love patience and live in the present.
Compassion	Many trades must work together.	Value empathy and concord.
Comprehension	Design and techniques change.	Seek enlightenment with evidence.
Consciousness	Perfection must be normal.	Take responsibility for your actions.
Doubt	Buildings have collapsed.	Stay open to the possibility of error.

A debate on the spiritual lessons in Freemasonry would be enlightening and clarify what we stand for.

The third degree

In disentangling Craft ritual, changes would be needed only in the third degree, the 'odd one out' of the degrees. In the first two, the supreme being is referred to in geometrical terms, the *Great Architect* and the *Grand Geometrician,* names in keeping with the importance of mathematics in early eighteenth century Britain. Newton's *Principia Mathematica* had shown how planetary motion could be explained and predicted by mathematics.

Since few people at the time doubted that the world was god-created, a description of how the world worked was a description of how God created it, a study of God's mind. Recall the retrospect:

> *... you were led in the second degree to contemplate the intellectual faculties and to trace them in their development through the paths of heavenly science even to the throne of God himself.*

The third degree uses no mathematical terms and has no geometrical title for its supreme being. Its ancestry is very different from the first two.

Noah

Anderson in his 1723 edition of *Constitutions* says that Noah:

> *… was commanded and directed by God to build the great Ark which tho' of wood, was certainly fabricated by geometry and according to the rules of masonry.*

and that:

> *Noah and his three sons Japhet, Shem, and Ham, all masons true, brought with them over the flood, the traditions and arts of the Antediluvians.*

The connection between Noah and Masonry was common enough in the eighteenth century. Scott's 1754 *Pocket Companion and History of Free-masons* borrows from Anderson:

> *The first piece of masonry that we know of immediately under divine direction was the Ark, wherein Noah and his three sons, Shem, Ham and Japhet, all masons true, were preserved from destruction … They brought them over the flood, and afterwards communicated to their children, geometry and the art of building.*[1]

The *Graham MS. 1726*

The necromantic style in which Noah is raised by his sons in the *Graham MS.* is similar to the way Hiram Abif is raised by the trusty fellow crafts in the modern third degree.[2] The sons sought knowledge their father had not confided before his death:

> *… Shem, Ham and Japheth went to their father Noah's grave to see if they could find anything … for I hope everyone will agree that all things needful for the new world were in the ark with Noah.*[3]

---

[1] *Printed for Brother Jonathan Scott at the Black Swan in Duck Lane.*

[2] Douglas Knoop writes: *The tradition associating Ham with necromancy survived as late as the 16th century, when it was found in an English work, Reginald Scott, 'Discoverie of Witchcraft' (1586).* 'The Mason Word', 1938 Prestonian Lecture, *The Collected Prestonian Lectures, 1925-1960*, Lewis Masonic, 1984, QC Lodge 1965.

[3] The Grand Lodge of Iowa offers a complete version online.

They agreed that even if they found nothing useful:

> *... the first thing that they* [FOUND] *was to be to them a secret.* [THEY] *most firmly believed that God was able to and would also prove willing, through their faith, prayer and obedience,* [TO MAKE] *what they found as valuable to them as if they had received the secret straight from God.*

and nothing is what they find:

> *... except the dead body almost consumed,* [THEY TOOK] *a grip at a finger which came away, and so on from joint to joint to the rest to the elbow. So they raised up the dead body and supported it, setting foot to foot, knee to knee, breast to breast, cheek to cheek and hand to back, and cried out, 'Help O father! ... Help us now for our earthly father cannot,' and so laid down the dead body once more, not knowing what to do. So one said, 'Here is yet marrow in this bone,' and the second said, 'but a dry bone,' and the third said, 'It stinketh'...*

Genuine?

Part of the attraction of the Graham lies in its use of the phrase *entered, passed and raised,* seemingly referring to a third degree four years before Prichard. Some consider the *Graham MS.* to be of seventeenth century origin and evidence of a third degree at a remarkably early date, although Herbert Poole, in introducing the MS. to *Quatuor Coronati* Lodge, said:

> *The document is so revolutionary in the way in which it cuts across so many firmly established notions, that it may be a very long time before we are able to form any adequate judgment as to its real position and, one may fairly say, the truth about certain matters which have, so far, never been called in question.*[1]

Another MS., The *Rite Ancien de Bouillon,* professed to be the ritual of a London lodge founded in 1732 and meeting at the Ben Johnson's Head tavern in 1748. Claims were made that the rite

---

[1] 'The Graham MS.', *AQC,* Vol. 50, 1937.

originated in Jerusalem during the time of Godefroid de Bouillon (1060-1100), first ruler of the (Christian) Kingdom of Jerusalem. It contains three degrees, the first two having what Pierre Nöel refers to as *des particularités notable* while the third contains innovations *qui évoquent furieusement* the Royal Arch.[1] The Bouillon is now considered a fake. Pick & Norman wrote:

> *There are to be found in the catechisms of the 1720s, slight indications of the esoteric knowledge now communicated to Installed Masters. Some confirmation of this may be sought in two documents, unfortunately neither very satisfactory.*[2]

Babel

Even if the *Graham MS.*[3] likewise turns out to be untrustworthy, the Noah legend may still be an ancestor of the Hiramic legend. Indeed, it might even have been a competitor as Knoop & Jones write of the possibility of yet another in the legend of the Tower of Babel.[4] In an unlikely passage, Genesis 11: 1-9 reads:

> *Now the whole world had one language and a common speech. As people moved eastward, they found a plain in Shinar* [MESOPOTAMIA] *and settled there* [AND] *said, 'Come, let us build ourselves a city, with a tower that reaches to the heavens, so that we may make a name for ourselves …' But the Lord came down to see the city and the tower the people were building. The Lord said, 'If as one people speaking the same language they have begun to do this, then nothing they plan to do will*

---

[1] 'Le Rite Ancien de Bouillon', Pierre Nöel, *Le Blog Maçonnique, Hiram.de, June 2018.*

[2] *Pocket History of Freemasonry,* Fred L. Pick and G. Norman Knight, Frederick Muller, 1953. The other document is *L'Ordre des Francs Maçons Trahi.*

[3] Acaster is convinced that it is genuine. He writes: *There are three other shorter texts known which closely resemble parts of Graham. Each one seems to have been accessed from separate, perhaps original, versions of the main question and answer parts.* As an aside, he also sees elements of the Mark in it, particularly the disagreement over wages and Solomon's dodgy resolution of it. 'The Noah Legend and the Graham MS.', E. John T. Acaster, *AQC,* Vol. 131, 2018.

[4] *The Genesis of Freemasonry,* Douglas Knoop & G.P. Jones, Manchester Univ. Press, 1947.

be impossible for them. Come, let us go down and confuse their language so they will not understand each other.' So the Lord scattered them from there over all the earth, and they stopped building the city.

The prevention of people working co-operatively is a strange aim for gods or men, and just as peculiar to modern ears is the supposed moral of the story, that mankind should not aspire beyond its proper place.[1]

Tower of Babel, by Lucas van Valckenborch, 1594, Louvre Museum.

The Minor's degree

The legend of the Tower of Babel is the narrative of the curious *Minor's Degree* which appears as an appendix to *Hiram*. Unlike the *Asociación de Jóvenes, Esperanza de la Fraternidad*[2] first established in Cuba, these minors are postulants, seeking to prove themselves

[1] Something like this appears in our ritual: *distinctions among men are necessary to preserve subordination.*

[2] Association of Youth, Hope of the Fraternity.

worthy of initiation. The ritual concerns the *first lodge held,* meeting on *the pleasant plain of Babylon called Shinar,* where its members sought to build a:

> *... stupendous edifice ... an hundred and one years after the flood.*

Nimrod was their Grand Master, seen as a king who rebelled against God. He ducked around God's confusion of their language by teaching the brethren to converse in signs, and thereby they made the plain of Shinar *far more splendid than all other parts in the magnificence of its buildings.*[1]

What might have been

There are at least three competing sources for the legend in the third degree. In another world, the third degree might have centred upon Noah & the Ark or Nimrod & the Tower of Babel, and not on Hiram Abif & the Temple of Jerusalem. In our world the Hiram legend won out but even so Hiram's death, a key component of the legend today, was not initially part of it.

The third degree as we see it today has no unique claim to authenticity. Its ritual and narrative might so easily have been different. It has been the subject of many changes since its inception, and one more, even a return to its eighteenth century format, cannot be proscribed.

---

[1] A more appropriate moral would be that of overcoming every difficulty, divine or otherwise.

Bibliography

Ahiman Rezon, Laurence Dermott, 8th edition, revised Thomas Harper, 1813.

Babylonian Chronicles, British Museum, B.M. 219.01.

'The change of words in the 18th century', David West, *Masonic-research.com.*

Comment on Poole's paper on the *Graham MS.*, W.J. Williams in *Quatuor Coronati* Lodge, *AQC, Vol.* 50, 1937.

'Compatibility', *Understanding the Royal Arch*, Richard Sandbach, Lewis Masonic, 1992.

Deism at the time of the founders of the Premier Grand Lodge, David West, Hamilton House, 2nd edition 2018.

'The Desired of all Nations in Haggai 2:7', Frank W. Hardy, *Historicism*, No. 12, Oct. 1987.

'Discovery of manuscript at Freemasons' Hall could reveal hidden secrets', John Hamill, *Freemasonry Today*, 6 June 2013.

Duncan's Masonic Ritual and Monitor (1866) online at sacred-texts.com.

The Early French Exposures, ed. Harry Carr, *Quatuor Coronati* Lodge, 1971.

The Early Masonic Catechisms, Douglas Knoop, G.P. Jones, & Douglas Hamer, Manchester University Press, 1943, *Quatuor Coronati* Lodge, 1975.

Early Ritual of the Holy Royal Arch, Piers Vaughan, Thomas Smith Webb Chapter of Research No. 1798, 2004.

English Masonic Exposures 1760-1769, A.C.F. Jackson, Lewis Masonic, 1986.

'Evolution of the Hiramic Legend in England and France', Joannes Snoek, *Heredom* 11, 2003.

'Evolution of the Royal Arch Ritual', Keith Tallon, *The Masonic Study Society*, 2016.

Fields of Blood, Karen Armstrong, The Bodley Head, 2014.

Francken Manuscript 1783, Henry Andrew Francken, Kessinger Reprints.

'Freemasonry and Christianity', H.B. White, *Freemasons Magazine and Masonic Mirror*, January, 1868.

Freemasonry: a French view, Roger Dachez & Alain Bauer, Westphalia Press, 2015.

Freemasons' Book of the Royal Arch, Bernard E. Jones, Harrap, 1957.

The Genesis of Freemasonry, Douglas Knoop & G.P. Jones, Manchester University Press, 1947.

'The Graham MS.', Herbert Poole, *AQC*, Vol. 50, 1937.

The Graham MS., online at Grand Lodge of Iowa.

'Henry Andrew Francken & his Masonic Manuscripts,' John Acaster, *World Conference on Freemasonry, Fraternalism and History*, May 2015. Re-published in *Heredom*, The Scottish Rite Research Society, online.

Hiram: or the grand master-key to the door of both antient and modern free-masonry, A member of the Royal Arch, 1766, reprinted Gale ECCO Print Editions.

Historia Anglorum, Henry of Huntingdon, trnsl. Diana Greenway, Clarendon, 1996.

A History of God, Karen Armstrong, Random House, 1999.

'The Lectures of English Craft Freemasonry', P.R. James, *AQC*, Vol. 79, 1966.

'The Legend of Hiram Abif', Jerry Marsengill, *Transactions of A. Douglas Smith, Jr. Lodge of Research*, October, 1988.

The Lost Rites and Rituals of Freemasonry, David Harrison, Lewis Masonic, 2017.

Masonic Legends, David West & Matthew West, Hamilton House, 2017.

Masonic Treatise, William Finch, 1802, transliterated Alex Horne, 1956, online at Onondaga and Oswego Masonic District Historical Society.

Manual of Freemasonry, Richard Carlile, 1825, reprint Traffic Output Publication.

The New Jewish Encyclopedia, ed. David Bridger, Berman House, 1976.

'The Noah Legend and the Graham MS.', E. John T. Acaster, *AQC*, Vol. 131, 2018.

Peerings from within the Royal Arch, E. John T. Acaster, Provincial Grand Lodge of East Lancashire.

'Peterloo', Richard Carlile, *The Republican* Volume 1, Reprint Hard Press 2017.

The Pocket Companion and History of Free-masons, a book printed for Brother Jonathan Scott at the Black Swan in Duck Lane, 1754.

Pocket History of Freemasonry, Fred L. Pick & G. Norman Knight, Muller, 1953.

'Provincial Warrants', T.M. Carter, part II, *AQC*, Vol. 42, 1930.

'Revisiting John Browne's Ciphered Masonic Works', David Slater, *AQC* 132, 2019.

'Le Rite Ancien de Bouillon', Pierre Nöel, *Le Blog Maçonnique*, June 2018.

Rite Ancien de Bouillon, John T. Thorpe, Leicester Lodge of Research 2429, 1926.

Royal Arch: The Fourth Degree of the Grand Lodge of the Antients, Yasha Beresiner, Batham Royal Arch Lecture for 2000.

Sheffield MS., Sheffield Masonic Library, online at SCRIBD.

A Shorter History of Goats, Devils and Freemasons, David West, Hamilton House, 2018.

Solomon's Temple Spiritualized, John Bunyan, 1688, reprint Curiosmith, 2010.

'The Third *Francken MS.* of the Rite of Perfection', John Hamill, *AQC* Vol. 97, 1984.

William Preston and his work, Colin Dyer, Lewis Masonic, 1987.

Illustrations

In Praise of Bells

Dick Whittington on Highgate Hill listening to Bow Bells

In Praise of Bells

The Folklore and Traditions of British Bells

JOHN CAMP

ROBERT HALE · LONDON

First published in Great Britain 1988

Robert Hale Limited
Clerkenwell House
Clerkenwell Green
London EC1R 0HT

British Library Cataloguing in Publication Data
Camp, John
In praise of bells : the folklore and
traditions of British bells.
1. Bells—Great Britain
I. Title
789′.5′0941

ISBN 0-7090-3277-3

Photoset in North Wales by
Derek Doyle & Associates, Mold, Clwyd
Printed in Great Britain by
St Edmundsbury Press, Bury St Edmunds, Suffolk
Bound by WBC Ltd.

Contents

By the same author

Oxfordshire and Buckinghamshire Pubs
Discovering London Stations
Discovering Bells and Bellringing
Portrait of Buckinghamshire
Bellringing
Magic, Myth and Medicine
Holloway Prison
The Healer's Art
One Hundred Years of Medical Murder
Buckinghamshire County Guide

Illustrations

All illustrations by Jack Peppiatt

Acknowledgements

The writing of this book was made much easier by the number of specialists who kindly supplied me with information. I am particularly grateful to Reg Darvill (late of St Albans) for allowing me to plunder his library of books on bells and for giving me access to his collection of *Ringing World* back numbers. My thanks also go to Alan Frost RIBA for information on church towers and other matters, to Andrew Wilby and William T. Cook MA for details of the history of the Ancient Society of College Youths, and to Edward Barnett for information on the Royal Cumberland Youths. I am also obliged to Mrs J. King for information regarding the Ladies' Guild.

Others whose brains I have picked include Mrs Hazel Basford for her notes on Quex Park, Mrs Angela Clark for information regarding the Skinners' Day tradition at Tonbridge, Stephen Coley for the Devon 'Pixies' Revenge', John Ketteringham for details of Lincoln Cathedral bells, Ken Goodall and Vic Cox for adding to my knowledge of handbell history, William Stewart of Lossiemouth for material on 'Lady Gordon's bell' and Lloyds member Don Oakley for information on the Lutine Bell. Thanks also to David Thorne, editor of *The Ringing World* and to Alan Hughes of the Whitechapel Bell Foundry. I am also grateful to Roy Judge for allowing me to see his thesis on the May Day customs at Magdalen College Tower, Oxford.

My thanks go also to Jack Peppiatt for his splendid illustrations.

Introduction

The first thing to be said about this book is that it is not primarily concerned with the art of bellringing – known to dedicated ringers as 'The Exercise'. Nor, indeed, is it solely concerned with church bells, though, as they are the most historic and also the most nostalgic bells, they feature in this book to a large extent.

But other kinds of bells exist and, though they may not be as rich in legend and tradition as those associated with churches, they have their place. School bells, ships' bells and railway-signal bells all have their traditions, to say nothing of the haunted bells that are reported from time to time in the kitchens of Victorian mansions. There is also a section on handbells and a recollection of the great days of handbell concerts in Manchester during the second half of the nineteenth century. After a lapse, handbell concerts are returning.

Again, even when people indulge in their hobby of change-ringing and method-ringing, it is not confined just to church towers. Secular towers exist and have their own tales to tell, like the famous Quex Park tower in Kent and the bells hung in a tower on a farm in Oxfordshire. Legends and traditions centre not only on the bells but on the towers containing them. Many towers, both religious and secular, are detached from the main body of the building. They may be tall and handsome, as at Evesham, or squat and flat on the ground as at East Bergholt in Suffolk.

Not surprisingly there are endless folk-tales and legends concerning bells in medieval times, not a few involving Satan himself. There are bells that are said to ring in rivers or under the sea, and even tales of bells ringing underground. Bells have been used to cure madness and to bring criminals to justice. It has also happened that bells have killed people, and not just in the fictionalized manner described by Dorothy Sayers in *The Nine Tailors*, where a man is 'deafened to death' when he is locked in a belfry. (In Suffolk, in the eighteenth century, a man is said to have committed a murder and immediately followed it by ringing a three-hour peal in his parish church!)

Many legends, especially those dating from medieval times, are found in the same form up and down the country. It is pointless to repeat them all, and only the most interesting are quoted.

There is a section dealing with the literature of bells, ranging from nursery rhymes and doggerel to the imaginative versification of Longfellow, and from the simple words on boards in most belfries to the splendid prose of John Bunyan in which he describes his reluctant withdrawal from his lifelong hobby.

There are stories of Big Ben, the bells of St Paul's and other cathedrals, and a chapter dealing with the ancient ringing societies and their traditions. There is also mention of the modern ringing societies and their annual outings. Technical terms are kept to a minimum and are used only when they are needed for a fuller understanding of how bells are hung and how they produce their sound.

Bellringing has played a big part in social history, and the former enmity existing between ringers and clergy is not entirely ended. Even the very architecture of churches was changed in the latter half of the nineteenth century by the behaviour of ringers in their tower – changes such as removing the floor of the ringing-chamber so that the ringers would have to ring from ground level in full view of the congregation.

If, as a result of reading this book, you develop an interest in ringing, it is the simplest thing in the world to do something about it. At the next practice-night at your church (something of which most people are only too aware!) climb the spiral stairs to the ringing-chamber and ask what is happening. You will be made most welcome. You will NOT be asked to start ringing immediately, as some folk imagine, for bellropes and wooden stays are far too costly to be in the hands of complete novices. You will first be taught how to 'handle a rope' – with an experienced ringer by your side – and then be gradually introduced to the art of ringing. It is not physically demanding but needs a clear head and a certain aptitude for simple arithmetic. Even if you do not develop an ambition to be a ringer, it is hoped that your interest in bells will be stimulated, and that you will enjoy reading this book as much as the author enjoyed writing it.

JOHN CAMP
Wingrave, Bucks

1
A Ring of Bells

The oldest English church bell at Caversfield in Oxfordshire dates from 1219

Although this book is mainly about the history and folklore of bells in Britain, it may be of interest, as a preliminary, to sketch in something of the early history of bells as noted in other countries, particularly in the Far East.

There is every reason to believe that more than 4,000 years ago bells were used by the Chinese in worship and as a form of communication. Both handbells and the larger temple bells were in use, the big bells being struck externally with a hammer, indicating their development from the primitive gong. (The gong itself has a history going back to the flat pieces of wood or metal struck together to produce a signal.)

In the Middle East the bells referred to by early writers were almost certainly tiny spherical bells, totally enclosed and known as 'crotals'. Small bells like these were suitable for adorning ceremonial garments, and a very early mention of them is found in the Old Testament. In Chapter 28 of Exodus, vv. 33-4, we read that Aaron was required to have robes ('ephods') adorned with purple and scarlet pomegranates, with small golden bells between them. According to the Jewish historian Flavius Josephus, small crotals were used by King Solomon (a man full of good ideas) when he installed them to frighten the birds from the roof-top gardens of his palace. King David is also associated with bells, but more musically, for a medieval manuscript shows him playing a tune on a gallery of bells mounted on a frame.

The Ancient Egyptians used bells to announce various feasts and characteristically had them buried with the dead to enable them to summon servants in the next world.

One of the most practical devices involving bells was used in 42 BC. at the siege of Lycia, when Brutus ordered that nets containing little bells be floated over the surface of the moat surrounding the town so that he would be warned immediately should anyone try to leave by water. It seems very likely that small crotals have long been used as adornment for both man and beast, and as far back as Assyrian times the harness of horses was decorated in this way.

But not all ancient bells were small and spherical. Obviously such bells could not produce much noise, and something more sonorous was needed. The Greeks and Romans had large bells similar in shape to those in use today. They were hung at the temple doors in Roman times to signal the various religious services (the Hindus did the same), and a very large bell was installed in most Roman towns to inform the plebs when the public baths opened. Only the deaf remained dirty.

As early as AD 180 we meet possibly the first occasion in which a bell was used in a mechanical instrument. This was a form of time-measuring device known as a clepsydra based on the flow of water. At certain intervals, carefully regulated, the water caused a bell to ring. Unfortunately we have no detailed knowledge of this instrument.

For some curious reason we find very little evidence regarding bells in Europe until well after the arrival of Christianity. Then, however, the ringing of bells became an integral component of church services and religious life generally. Indeed, it was not long before Christianity had produced a patron saint for bellringers for certain anatomical and somewhat bloodthirsty reasons. This was St Agatha, a well-proportioned virgin and martyr living in Catania, Sicily, in AD 250. Little is known of her but legend has it that she was tortured and then stoned to death, her breasts being severed from her body. The shape of her breasts being not unlike the shape of bells, she was immediately adopted as the patron saint of both bellfounders and bellringers.

One of the earliest references to bells in Europe is made by St Gregory of Tours (538-93), a bishop and historian. He mentions small bells used on clothing and harness but also remarks on the much larger bells hanging in churches and sounded by an internal clapper, adding that a cord was sometimes attached to the clapper. This description marks the fundamental difference between the evolution of bells in the Orient and in the Western world. In the East the bell remained a hollow, straight-sided instrument sounded externally, producing a single sonorous tone but with no distinctive note. In the West development was different, bells evolving in the shape of an inverted cup sounded by a clapper inside. In Europe early bells have been found made from two bent pieces of metal attached at the top and sides. A handle was provided at the top for attaching a rope, and the whole thing was often bronzed over to produce a sweeter sound, though by our standards today this must have been harsh.

Small bells of some 8 inches in height would have been carried by the early missionaries to signal their approach. Mystic qualities have been attributed to such bells, and it is not surprising that over fifty of this kind have been found in Ireland, preserved as holy relics. So valuable and sacred were they assumed to be that they were frequently used as legal title-deeds in the conveyance of land or property. Handing over the ancient family bell conferred the legal right to bequeath the property to a relative.

Many of the Irish bells have been put in the safe keeping of museums in Dublin and Belfast. By far the most important is the bell in the Royal Irish Academy in Dublin, said to have been carried by St Patrick himself. Though long acknowledged as the patron saint of Ireland, Patrick was born in Gloucestershire about AD 390. He was educated in France and later in Rome, and about 430 was sent to Ireland by Pope Celestine to convert the Irish from druidism. St Patrick's bell (*Clog-an-Phatraic*) was buried with him when he died in 460. A century later the bell was removed from the tomb by St Colomoille and given a magnificent outer case of silver, gold and precious stones infinitely more spectacular than the primitive-looking iron bell which it enshrines.

Another bell dating from St Patrick's time is the Bell of Blood (*Clog-na-Fola*) presented by a saint to a church in Connaught. It is said to have mysterious powers and is able to restore lost or stolen property to its rightful owner. If property had been stolen and various suspects identified, each man in turn was required to take hold of the bell and swear to his innocence. If the real thief handled the bell his face would become contorted and repulsive and would so remain until the stolen goods were returned. So powerful was the mystique surrounding the Bell of Blood that as late as 1850, when a group of vagabonds were due to be tried for robbing a house, every item was returned the day before the trial when a rumour circulated that the Bell of Blood was to be used.

In Wales a few ancient bells have been found dating mainly from the sixth century but there seem to be no legends directly attributed to them, nor are they endowed with magical powers. A sixth-century bell was found at Llangwynodl, in Powys, and at Llangenau, near Brecon, a bell of similar age, once covered in bronze, has been excavated. Both are handbells and may well have been used in funeral processions to drive evil spirits away. Curiously enough a detailed study of the shape and

'Tapping' small handbells in medieval times

substance of these bells indicates that both came originally from Ireland.

The large tower bells which eventually were installed in churches in Britain seem to have evolved from the bells in the famous round towers found all over Ireland. Larger than handbells but small by modern standards, being about 16 inches in height, such bells were hung at the top of round towers to warn of pirates and marauders. Later these bells had ropes attached which enabled them to be rung from ground level, so allowing a warning to be sounded but at the same time offering a quick escape by the ringer.

A more peaceful tale of a bell is that told by the Venerable Bede regarding the death of St Hilda of Whitby in AD 680. Just before she died, says Bede, 'This nun of a sudden heard the well-known sound of a bell in the air, which was used to awake and call them to prayer when any one was taken out of this World.' This appears to be a clear reference to what later became known as the 'passing bell', which will be dealt with later in this book.

By the year 750 bells had begun to be hung in church towers. In later centuries it was to become a much more secular activity.

As bells became larger, the specialist art of bellfounding came into its own. It is known that St Dunstan (*c.*925) was an early bellfounder and contributed much to the art during the tenth century. Church bells became popular about this time due to a change in the Saxon law. It was decreed that a churl could be promoted to the rank of thane if he had an estate of 500 acres or more and a church with at least four bells on his land. It was about this time that the ringing of the *couvre-feu* or curfew was also made a legal requirement, and it was thus in existence before the arrival of William of Normandy, in 1066, and not introduced by him as often stated.

England has no small bells as ancient as those of Ireland. The oldest bell in a church, though undated, is almost certainly that hanging in the pretty riverside church of St Lawrence at Caversfield, Oxfordshire. It is known to have been given to the church by Sir Hugh Gargate in 1219, though there is evidence to indicate that it was already in existence some years before its presentation. The oldest church bell in England bearing positive evidence of its age is at Lissett, Yorkshire. Here we find a bell with a date in Roman numerals MCCLIIII (1254) The numerals are upside-down. Another early bell, also dated, is at Cold Ashby, Northamptonshire, inscribed '1317', again in Roman figures. At Duncton, Sussex, we find a curiosity in the form of a foreign bell dated 1369 but cast in Holland.

Just over a century later, in 1483, the importation of bells was forbidden, no doubt as an early protectionist or anti-European measure. Henry VIII later banned the export of bells and bell-metal except under licence. After his death the law seems to have been largely neglected, though it was not officially repealed until the eighteenth century, in the reign of George III.

A set of bells (from three to twelve) in a church tower, tuned so that each is one musical interval apart from its neighbour and capable of being rung in turn, is called a 'ring' of bells. Strictly speaking, it should not be called a 'peal', as this is the sound the bells make when rung in a regulated sequence.

One of the earliest known rings of bells hung in an English church was at Croyland Abbey, Lincolnshire, where six bells were given to the monks in 984. As was the custom of the time, the bells were officially baptized and given names. From lightest to heaviest (or treble to tenor) the bells were named Baga, Pega, Tunkatellum, Belerene, Bartholomew and Beladine. A few years later an even larger and more sonorous bell was added named Guthlac, tuned to the other bells. The harmonious sound of these bells ringing in sequence was commented on by many writers of the day, and even the historian Thomas Fuller, writing six centuries later, remarked that the deep tone of Guthlac had once been hailed as a cure for a headache. (Many writers since have attributed the reverse effect when describing the ringing of bells over a long period.) However, this unusual form of therapy did not last very long, for in 1091 a fire destroyed the abbey and its bells with it. Today the rebuilt abbey church remains and has a mainly eighteenth-century ring of six, still with a bell called Guthlac, one of the dedications of the church.

Whilst on the subject of ancient bells, it may be of interest to sketch in the derivation of various names connected with bells and ringing. The word 'campanology' is often used by non-ringers to indicate the art of bellringing. Some writers claim that the word originates from the Italian district of Campania where, about AD 400, it is said that the bishop, Paulinus, first introduced the sound of bells in the Christian religious service. This seems most unlikely, for Paulinus, a prolific writer on church history, makes no mention of bells or ringers anywhere in his books, which is odd to say the least. Ringers themselves rarely call it 'campanology' but refer to bellringing as 'The Exercise'.

Other words found in ancient writings are: *cymbalum* and *campanella* for cloister bells, *nola* for a small bell and the Greek *krotalon* for a small spherical bell or crotal. As has already been mentioned, the Gaelic for 'bell' is *clog*, and this has a close affinity with the French *cloche*, the German *glocke* and the Scandinavian *klokke*.

The Roman word *tintinnabullum* was used to describe the sound of any bells ringing, and an adaptation of this word was used by Fabian Stedman (of whom more later) when, in 1668, he wrote the first book dealing with the supremely English art of change-ringing. He named it *Tintinnalogia*.

2
Bellfounding and Hanging

Shaping the clay mould or cope of a bell

When Croyland Abbey lost its bells in the great fire of 1091, the monks soon began the task of rebuilding. The replacement of the seven great bells was far beyond their scope and it was decided to incorporate into the new building a small tower capable of housing two bells. They were provided by Fergus of Bolton, a tinsmith and metal-worker who was the first English bellfounder to be mentioned by name. Until that time the technique of casting and hanging bells had been known only to monks and lay brothers, and it was not until some centuries later that bellfounding became established as a secular trade and founders marked their own products. The first full-time established bellfounder seems to have been

Roger de Ropeford of Exeter who was working in that city in 1284.

From the eleventh century the practice of bellfounding was carried on by itinerant journeymen, usually with an apprentice, who travelled from parish to parish casting new bells and repairing old ones. They had mobile foundries and furnaces and dug large pits in which the shape of the bell could be contained and the molten metal added. After the bells were cast and hung, these pits were usually filled in again and forgotten. Over the years interest in industrial archæology has resulted in many of these old pits being rediscovered. In 1970 the demolition of a church in Exeter revealed the pit where the original bell was cast for the Norman tower of 1150. In the years between, the half-remembered existence of these pits produced a kind of folk-memory giving rise to many legends of 'buried' bells in parishes up and down the country.

During the history of bellfounding many experiments have been made with various metals, including gold, silver, aluminium and zinc, to produce a suitable 'mix'. The normal constituents of bell-metal in Britain is seventy-seven per cent copper and twenty-three per cent tin, giving an alloy known as bronze. This basic mixture has been in use for many centuries though the proportions differ slightly for small bells and handbells and also with foreign founders. Experiments have shown that the addition of gold and silver to a bell would have much the same effect as the increase in the proportion of copper and would impair the sound of the bell. Despite this, many legends persist of wealthy donors insisting on gold and silver being added to the bell-metal to produce a 'sweter' note. It does not work.

There is an entertaining legend concerning the use of silver in bells dating from the first days of Christianity in Devon. The West of England, in those far-off days, was very much under the control of pixies, and many believe that to this day the Cornish 'piskie' may still exert an influence. The coming of Christianity was not welcomed by the pixies. Nor was the building of churches, which they considered a threat to their existence. In particular they hated the sound of bells, equivalent to putting garlic in front of a vampire. At Ottery St Mary, in Devon, they watched while the foundations of the church were dug but apparently took no action despite their disapproval. However, they soon discovered that the church was to have a ring of bells and that these were to be cast at the Exeter foundry.

The pixies thought that silver and copper were both ingredients of bell-metal and knew that these ores had to be dug out of the earth. Accordingly they ordered the 'little people' who live below ground to impede the mining of these metals in every way possible. For a time they were successful but eventually sufficient silver and copper were extracted, the pits were dug and the casting of the bells began. The pixies thereupon put into operation plan No.2. This was to extract the dew from flowers and sprinkle it on the cooling bell-metal, so causing the bells to crack. But the flowers found out about this plan and, presumably already converted to Christianity, added nectar to the dew and so averted the catastrophe.

Pixies are nothing if not stubborn, as any Westcountryman will tell you. When the day came for the bells to be taken from the foundry at Exeter to the church at Ottery St Mary for hanging, the pixies put plan No.3 into operation. The party of carriers, led by Brother John of Exeter, found themselves confused in their direction and 'pixillated' and were led across country towards the sea. It was only when Brother John stepped on a thorn at the cliff edge and exclaimed 'God bless my soul!' that the men came to their senses and discovered their danger. The bells were eventually hung in the church of St Edward the Confessor at Ottery with no further misadventures.

But the pixies were only biding their time. In 1454 they struck again when a new ring of bells was due to be dedicated on Midsummer's Day. When the ringers arrived in the morning, they found that the ropes had been inextricably tangled together during the night. Only after prayers had been said and the power of holy water invoked were the ropes able to be separated and ringing to commence.

This time the pixies almost gave up. But they let it be

known, by means of communication peculiar to pixies, that as time meant little to them they would not interfere again for another 500 years.

Evidently with this warning in mind, in 1954 a group of Ottery parishioners resurrected the legend and put on a play to signal the anniversary, entitled *The Pixies' Revenge*. This was performed annually by the local schoolchildren until it lapsed in 1971. More recently it has been revived, and it is now given each year by the Cubs and Brownies of the town. So far there seems to have been no attempt at sabotaging either the bells or the ringers, though the pixies are an excuse when someone goes wrong while ringing.

Apart from the standard form of bell-metal used in Britain, other metals have occasionally been employed in bellfounding. Several rings of steel bells have been cast and are in use at Bassaleg in Gwent, Birmingham, Hale in Cheshire and Waddesdon in Buckinghamshire, to name only a few. A ring of what are termed 'ceramic' bells are in use at Liss, Hants.

One of the problems of the early founders was to prolong the life of the bell and to stop it cracking at the point where it was regularly struck by the clapper. Turning the bell was a difficult and expensive job, and in any case, once the bell was cracked, its tone was impaired. From the fifteenth century onwards attempts were made to solve the problem by altering the shape of the bell and thickening and widening the mouth. It is for this reason that medieval bells are longer and more straight-sided than later bells, and this may be seen in the ancient bells at Lissett, Claughton and Caversfield.

About this time, too, bellfounders ceased to be peripatetic and established themselves in permanent foundries in the larger towns and cities, usually near the church. In Salisbury, for example, Culverhouse Street was originally Bellfounders Street, and in many towns there exists a Foundry Lane near the church. In York Minster there is a famous window depicting the various processes of bellfounding in medieval times. It was installed in the church in 1308 by Richard Tunnoc, a bellfounder and citizen of some importance. Yet another connection with bellfounding in York is an ancient medieval cross of stone with a bell on one side and a furnace on the other, and it no doubt marks the grave of an early founder.

After the Reformation there was a lull in the art of bellfounding for about a century. Then, for reasons which will be explained later, (see p.45), both founding and ringing saw a great revival after 1650. A few sixteenth-century firms did survive, or even begin founding, notably the Newcombe family of Leicester who were in business in 1506, and William Knight at Reading in 1518.

Most famous of all was the Whitechapel Bellfoundry in London established by Robert Mot in 1570. Tradition has it that he originally came from Kent, where his father had started a highly successful scrap-metal business as the result of the removal and sale of bells at the dissolution of the monasteries. Young Robert came to London and for a time did founding of various types, including casting cannon for use against the Armada in 1588. After Mot's death the business changed hands several times though continuing to cast and found bells. The names of the proprietors changed through the years from Lester & Pack, Pack & Chapman, Chapman & Mears and Mears & Stainbank.

It is the oldest continuous private company in the world and during more than 400 years of non-stop production has supplied bells to many of the City of London churches including the famous Bow Bells of St Mary-le-Bow, Cheapside, the 'Oranges and Lemons' bells of St Clement Danes and the bells of St Michael's, Cornhill. The most famous bell produced at Whitechapel is undoubtedly Big Ben in the clock-tower of the Houses of Parliament which they re-cast in 1858 after an unfortunate first attempt by the opposition firm of Warner & Co of Stockton-on-Tees. (See p.163).

Though in continuous production, the Whitechapel Foundry moved to a site opposite the original one, in 1738, and took over the old Artichoke Inn. During its long history it also acquired other foundries, which it usually closed, including the Gloucester foundry of the Rudhall's, that of Robert Wells in Wiltshire and the well-known foundry of John Briant in Hertford town. Today the Whitechapel Foundry is in the safe hands of Mr Alan

Working on the rehanging of bells at Intwood in Norfolk in 1987

Hughes and his family and may be visited by parties after prior notice has been given.

The only other foundry casting church bells in Britain today is Taylor's of Loughborough. Though claiming a connection with the fourteenth-century foundry at Leicester, the name of the present firm began in 1782 when Robert Taylor established a foundry at St Neots, Cambridgeshire. After moving his business about the country for some years and establishing foundries in Devon and in Oxford, he finally settled in Loughborough in 1840. His only surviving son, John Taylor, built the foundry buildings in the town that we see today.

Though the Whitechapel Foundry has a longer and more continuous history, the firm has changed hands several times. Taylor's, on the other hand, though having a shorter history, can claim a far longer association with one family than can Whitechapel. Taylor's foundry also has the honour of having made the heaviest bell in England which can be used for full-circle ringing – the 82-cwt Emmanuel tenor bell of Liverpool Cathedral. For various technical reasons the foundry has also specialized in carillons and has many such instruments for use at home and overseas. Like the Whitechapel Foundry, Taylor's may be visited by prior application. It also has a very interesting bell museum open to visitors in which the whole history and art of bellfounding may be traced back to the thirteenth century.

Rudhall's of Gloucester, later swallowed up by the Whitechapel Foundry, produced many great bells between 1684 and 1830, including the bells of London's St Martin-in-the-Fields with its ring of twelve. Two of the best-known West Country founders were the Purdue and Bilbie families of Somerset. At the other end of England Miles Graye of Colchester was a famous seventeenth-century founder. At Stamford may be seen the grave of Toby Norris, a noted seventeenth-century ringer and founder with a plate of bell-metal cast in his own foundry as headstone. Some small foundries lasted well into the twentieth century, such as Henry Bond at the Burford foundry in Oxfordshire.

Probably the most recent firm to take up the challenge

of casting church bells was the Gillett clockmaking factory originally established in Croydon, Surrey, in 1844. In 1877 Arthur Johnson, an enthusiast of metal, joined the company, which as Gillett & Johnson began casting church bells. Perhaps because of more modern technology in the early years of the century, the foundry produced many bells and carillons for overseas including the 74-bell carillon of New York's Riverside Church. In 1957 Gillett & Johnson were taken over by a large engineering combine and reverted to making clock machinery. Today it is once again a private company, but no longer engaged in founding church bells.

The technicalities of bellfounding are complex, and it is not intended to describe them in this book. It is enough to say that, when preparing to cast a bell in a foundry, a 'core' is built on the foundry floor exactly the size of the inside of the bell. Over this is placed the 'cope', which is a larger metal cone the same shape as the outside of the bell. With cone and cope securely clamped into position molten bell-metal is poured from the top to fill the space between. Any lettering required on the outside of the bell will have previously been done in relief on the inside of the cope. Once the whole thing has become cool, the cope is lifted off and the new bell taken off the core. It is then tuned by various electronic devices to the desired note.

A bell, when struck, does not give out just one note but a series. The main note is known as the fundamental and has a note an octave higher called the nominal and a note an octave below called the hum-note, which persists long after the other notes have died away. The notes in between are known as 'partials', and it is one of the duties of the tuner to ensure that the fundamental sounds true and that the partials are controlled.

Normally, the more metal there is in a bell the deeper its tone. This has occasionally been a source of friction when a supposedly generous donor, wishing to present a new bell or bells to a church, has discovered that the cost is rather greater than he could afford. A good example of this is seen at Glastonbury where a bell cast and donated in 1776 bears the inscription:

Our tones would all have been much deeper
If contributions had been greater.

But the art of casting a bell, complex as it is, is only part of the story. The bell must be transported from the foundry to the church and there hung in the belfry with its companions, in a massive frame. Each bell must be anchored to a wooden wheel and the rope attached to the wheel let through the floor into the ringing-chamber below.

Most foundries employ their own expert staff for performing this work, though there are various firms which specialize in hanging though not bellfounders themselves. Probably the best known of these is run by the White family of Appleton, a village just across the river from Oxford on the road to Swindon. They will undertake to lower a ring of bells from a tower, send them to Whitechapel or Loughborough for attention and then re-hang them in the tower when the work is done. For many years the Whites were blacksmiths in the village and keen ringers in many Oxford churches, a city known for the multitude of churches and a paradise for all ringers.

On 4 March 1818 a ring of six bells, removed from a London church when it was demolished, was presented to Appleton church by the local squire, Robert Southby of Appleton Grange. Later the ring was augmented to eight in 1854 and finally to a ring of ten in 1861. But it was the original gift of six bells in 1818 that has always been considered a red-letter day in the history of the village, and every year since there has been a commemoration of this event, generally on the Saturday nearest 4 March.

On that day ringers descend on Appleton from every corner of England, and ringing continues all day, one pub remains open from morning until night, and in the evening there is a ringers' dinner at which over a hundred may be present, amongst whom will be found many of the elite of the ringing fraternity. The day would not be complete without a rendering of the March the Fourth song:

May friendship and freedom this day much abound
May mirth and good humour go jovely around;

May the young and the old, the grave and the gay,
Remember that this is our March the Fourth Day.

In this present year which we now all have seen,
The number one thousand, eight hundred eighteen,
The six well-tuned bells that by Southby were given
Rang their first merry peal, our hearts to enliven.

Then come all you aged and witness the scene:
Bring your sons and your daughters to dance on the green;
You are heartily welcome to take of the fare
Which will drive away sorrow and banish all care.

So fill up your bumpers, and this toast be given:
'Here's Southby for ever, may his soul rest in Heav'n'
For his bounteous hand it has made us all sing:
'Old England for ever – and God Save the King.'

In 1854 another verse was added:

But when thirty-six years had quite altered the date,
The peal of six bells was transposed into eight.
For a treble and tenor were put up quite right
By that friend of all ringers, the famed Alfred White.

Alfred White himself lies buried in Appleton churchyard in a grave whose headstone depicts a ring of ten bells, and his family still continue in their work.

In more spacious days the hanging of new bells in a church was the occasion for much ceremony and merry-making. On arrival the bells were left standing on the floor of the church near the tower so that the congregation could have a good look at them – a once-in-a-lifetime opportunity for many people. Occasionally this caused confusion – and continues to do so, for only recently, when the bells were on show in this manner in a London church, an elderly lady was heard to ask the verger how often the bells were taken down for dusting!

During this period the bells may be blessed and dedicated, though no longer christened with the names of saints and adorned with christening robes as was the custom in medieval times. Before the dedication the bells were often subjected to what has been described as a 'profane baptism'. The treble or smallest bell was upturned and filled with beer or other liquor, which was distributed amongst those present.

The traditional jollifications associated with new bells is well depicted by that gentle cleric Gilbert White of Selborne. He describes the hanging of a re-cast ring at Selborne parish church in 1745 in these words: 'The day of the arrival of this tuneable peal was observed as a high festival by the village and rendered more joyous by an order that the treble bell be fixed, bottom upwards in the ground and filled with punch of which all persons shall be permitted to partake'.

The final journey of the newly cast bell is its hauling up into the tower. It is carefully lifted through a trapdoor in the floor of the ringing-chamber, then up through another trapdoor in the ceiling into the belfry itself. Specialist bellhangers supervise the work, then attach the bell to its wheel and finally fit the whole assembly in its frame with the other bells. Each bell is made to swing at right-angle to its neighbour to cancel out the stress of several tons of bell-metal swinging at the same time in one direction, for damage to the tower could easily be caused. Some new frames now being fitted are made of steel rather than timber to improve rigidity, though in coastal towns there can be the problem of rust on the frame, with constant need for maintenance as a result. However, there are some ringers who still prefer the massive timber frames which have been common in belfries for centuries and which, say these enthusiasts, may even help to improve the standard of ringing. But this is a contentious point and has no place in this book.

3
Bell Inscriptions

Inscribing reversed wording on the inside of the cope

The inscriptions found on bells are a study in themselves and tell us a great deal about the beliefs and traditions of the old foundries. They also make an important contribution to social history and often provide a fascinating glimpse of local events.

The early founders did not mark their names on their bells but tended to inscribe their own individual trade mark or logo. From this many may be traced but a clue also lies in the style of the lettering used, usually written in flowery Latin, for the dedication of the bell or religious text. Many Latin words were abbreviated, and sometimes only the initial letter was used. The words on the bell are often divided from each other by stops, varying from foundry to foundry and sometimes in the form of the grotesque faces seen on the misericord seats in many cathedrals.

From the sixteenth century the custom of naming a bell had ceased and the inscriptions began to be written in English in normal script, presumably for a wider readership. As the example from Glastonbury indicates, many of these inscriptions were to the point, especially those dating from the eighteenth century or before. The capacity for ringing to induce a thirst is all too apparent in this message from a bell in Warwickshire:

> Harken do you heere
> Our claperers want beere.

'Claperers' in this context seems to be a synonym for 'ringers'.

The cost of providing bells was always a problem, and a compliment to the donor was sometimes included in the bell inscriptions when it was cast. An inscription acknowledging a generous donation may be found at Bath:

> All you of Bath that hear me sound
> Thank Lady Hoptons hundred pounds.

A rather more restrained comment is found on a bell in Sussex which says:

> At proper times my voice I'll raise
> And sound to my subscriber's praise.

The standard of grammar on many bell inscriptions is poor, and the sentiments are often banal. One rather charming example of a couplet evocative of seventeenth-century rural speech is on a bell in Worcestershire:

John Martin of Worcester he made wee
Be it known to all that do wee see. 1675.

Many tenor bells carry inscriptions that remind us how finite we all are, and do so in somewhat depressing terms:

Unto the church I do you call
Death to the grave will summon all. (1745).

This is found at Amersham, Buckinghamshire, but is a sentiment repeated on countless tenor bells up and down the country. A more exhilarating message is that inscribed on the old 'morning bell' at St Ives, Cambridgeshire, which says: 'Arise and go about your business', while at Owmby, Lincolnshire, there is another 'financial' comment – whether it is in gratitude or criticism is rather hard to determine, for it says tersely: 'This peal repaired 1811. The bishop gave fifty pounds.'

Towcester (Northamptonshire) has a bell with the slightly gruesome legend:

Pull on brave boys I'm metal to the back
But will be hanged before I crack.

At Blewbury, Oxfordshire, definite signs of frustration may be seen on one of the bells. This was cast by a part-time founder at nearby Cholsey who was really the village blacksmith, with little knowledge of bells. He cast a bell three times for the church at Cholsey, but each time it cracked when struck. He succeeded at the fourth attempt, and the bell says briefly: 'Nil Desperandum'.

In contrast to this terse comment is what must be one of the longest bell inscriptions in existence. It is found at Brixton, Devon, and recounts the history of one of the six bells: 'In the year 1740 John Lord, zealous for the promotion of Campanalogia, caused me to be fabricated and placed in this tower. Sixty years I led the peal when I was unfortunately broken in the year 1800. I was cast in the furnace, refounded in London and returned to my former station. Reader, though shall also know a Resurrection. May it be unto eternal life.'

Though the tenor bell, being the largest, is often selected for religious texts and forewarnings of doom, the fact that it is the smallest, or treble, bell that sounds off first when ringing starts has resulted in many cheerful inscriptions. One found very frequently on the treble is:

I am the first and tho but small
I will be heard above you all.

An alternative couplet found almost as frequently remarks:

I mean to make it understood
That though I'm little yet I'm good.

Perhaps the most cheerful of all is found at Northenden, Manchester, which says quite simply: 'Here goes, my brave boys.'

In some instances we find that the inscription on the bell names both the dedication and the founder, as at Halton Holgate, Lincolnshire: 'IHC campana beate Marie Johannis Potter Fecit' 'Jesus Christ. The bell of the Blessed Mary. John Potter made me.' (The letters IHC representing 'Jesus Christ' often precede bell inscriptions in Latin.)

Other bells have wording in memory of the donors or those intimately concerned with the church. One such is at Barton-in-Craven, Yorkshire, where the translation from the Latin reads: 'St John the Baptist pray for the souls of John Pudsey, Knight, and Mary his wife.'

Both the above are pre-Reformation inscriptions, but later in the century inscriptions slowly became to be written in English. A very early one, found at St John's Church, Stamford, Lincolnshire, says: 'Richard Snawdon, Parson. Anno 1561.' This is particularly interesting as it is one of the earliest examples of the use of the word 'parson' for a priest. Another sixteenth-century inscription in English is on a bell in the church of St Peter with St James at Nottingham. Surprisingly, this bell was given by a lady who took in washing – she was evidently very well paid for it, for she also left money for the following inscription to be placed on it:

Ave Maria of your charitie
pray for the soul of Margere Dubbleday.'

She left more money for the bell to be rung every weekday morning at 4 a.m. presumably the time when she got up.

Though the transition from Latin to English took place over some years, it is perhaps surprising that there is only one recorded example of an inscription in Norman French. The bell is in Shropshire at Bitterley, near Ludlow, and reads in translation: 'The Lord Jesus and St Anne by the ordinance of Alice Sturye whom God pardon in his great mercy.' The bell is late fifteenth-century and, as is sometimes found in pre-Reformation bells, the letter 'S' is reversed throughout the inscription.

Another oddity occasionally found is the inscription printed on the bell upside-down. This is so on a bell in the church at South Luffenham in Leicestershire. The right way up it says: 'Hew Watts made me 1563.'

Lincolnshire, the source of so many interesting bells and legends, produces a very strange inscription on the treble bell at Witham-on-the-Hill, given to the church of St Andrew by a certain William Augustus Johnson. It dates from 1831 and shows that Mr Johnson was certainly no royalist. Unlike most donors he specifies on the inscription the occasions on which his bell must not be rung:

Twas not to prosper or hate
William Augustus Johnson gave me;
But peace & joy to celebrate
And call to prayer to heav'n to save ye;
Then keep the terms and e'er remember
May 29th ye must not ring;
Nor yet the 5th of each November
Nor on the crowning of a king.

29 May, it will be remembered, is Oak Apple Day, formerly celebrated as the birthday of Charles II.

A curiosity found on some bells is an 'alphabetical' inscription. Parts of the alphabet are printed, usually in the correct order but rarely completely. Whether this is a lack of inspiration on the part of the founder or some sort of code is not known. There is a good example on a bell in St Mary Magdalen, the parish church at Geddington, Northants:

ABCDEF GHIKLM NOPQRS

Perhaps even stranger than an 'alphabet' inscription is that on a bell at Pucknowle, Dorset, which apparently in English, has no punctuation or spacing and reads as follows:

HETHATWILLPURCHASHONOURSGAYNEMVSTANCIENTLATHERSSTILMAYNTAYNE

The bell historian J.R. Nichols says he has been informed that 'lather' is an Old English term meaning 'to make a noise'.* This, however, seems to throw little light on the matter.

At St Benedict's, Cambridge, there is an amusing inscription in doggerel verse recounting the history of a bell and with it the names of the churchwardens involved:

John Draper made me 1618
as plainly doth apeare
this bell was broake and cast againe
wich times churchwardens were
Edwarde Dickson for the one who stode
close by his tacklin
and he that was his partner then
was Alexander Jacklin.

This is obviously not a very high standard of versification, but typical of the era when English inscriptions were coming into fashion.

During the eighteenth century, when competition between foundries was brisk, some founders did not hesitate to advertise themselves on their bells and occasionally to decry the work of other founders. In 1783 the Chepstow foundry of Evans & Nott was asked to take down and recast a bell in the parish church of Blackwell (now in the county of Avon) made some years earlier by Bilbie & Boosh in the same county. They did the work but could not resist inscribing on the bell the couplet:

* *Bells thro' the Ages.*

Bilbie and Boosh may come and see
What Evans and Nott have done by me.

Another example of what the advertising world calls 'knocking copy' is found at Badgworth, Somerset. This is the work of Rudhall's, the famous Gloucester foundry, and pokes fun at another foundry whose bell they had to recast:

Badgworth ringers they were mad
Because Rigbie made me bad
But Abel Rudhall you may see
Hath made me better than Rigbie.

Other inscriptions record important historical events such as 5 November (noted on many bells), and in Wiltshire one bell says: 'I was cast in the yearre of the plague, warre and fire 1666.' A rather chatty inscription at Tadcaster goes as far as to express surprise: 'It is remarkable that these bells were moulded in the Great Frost of 1763.'

It certainly is!

From the eighteenth century onwards it became fashionable for bells to be inscribed with the dates of naval and military victories, and at Worcester a ring of eight bells records the victories of the Duke of Marlborough during the reign of Queen Anne. Two bells are dedicated to the Queen and Marlborough, the others to the battles of Blenheim, Barcelona and Ramillies, and Generals Menin, Turin and Prince Eugène. The bells were installed between 1706 and 1712.

A somewhat premature account is found on a bell at Ashover, Derbyshire, which was recast and rehung after Napoleon's abdication and imprisonment on the island of Elba in 1814. It says: 'This old bell rang the downfall of Buonaparte and broke 1814.' That it broke after announcing this news may possibly be an example of divine retribution in view of what was to happen. As every schoolboy knows, Napoleon returned from Elba early in 1815, collected an army during the famous 'Hundred Days' and finally faced Wellington on the field of Waterloo, with results well known to posterity.

The tenor recast for 'Boston Stump', Lincolnshire

An interesting series of inscriptions celebrating the end of the Great War is found on the third, fourth and fifth bells in the north-west tower of Westminster Abbey. They are:
3rd bell: 'Faith 1919. Thanks be to God which giveth us the Victory.'
4th bell: 'Ruth 1919. There is none other that fighteth for us.'
5th bell: 'The Lord of Hosts is with us. 1919.'
The ring of ten bells which includes the above was recast and rehung by the Whitechapel Foundry in 1971.

Though church bells are associated mainly with ecclesiastical history, it is as well to reflect that history is being made around us every day and that bells may make a comment on this as much as anything else. Britain's close association with the United States of America and the presence in Britain of a large number of US Air Force personnel are underlined by a ring of bells in the parish church at Eriswell, Suffolk, a well-known American base. The five bells, cast by Taylor's of Loughborough, were presented to the church by the US Air Force in 1958, and the inscriptions on the bells form a series of rhyming couplets:

1. 'Americans gave me.'
2. 'John Taylor made me.'
3. 'God protect those who fly.'
4. 'May Anglo-American friendship never die.'
5. 'May this bell forth tell
   Glory to God in Eriswell.'

Whatever may happen in the future, these bells will for ever remain a reminder of the American presence in Suffolk in the years following World War II.

With America still in mind, it is pleasant to learn of the existence of a bell recording the first landing on the Moon. Particularly interesting is the age of the donor. It is at Ingoldmells in Lincolnshire, where the bells were recast and augmented in 1970. One bell is inscribed: ' "Guthlac" This bell was cast in the year during which Man first set foot on the Moon. The gift of Eric William Stow in his fourteenth year.'

Despite the increasing pace of modern technology and

the coming wonders of which we may only guess, there is at the same time a growing interest in the past and its customs and traditions. This may be seen everywhere, from the renewed use of leeches in medicine, through the recruitment of horses for transport in the Army and the current vogue for the works of Helen Ashton, Sax Rohmer and 'Sapper'. It should therefore come as no surprise to discover that the tradition of naming and baptizing bells is being revived. When a new ring of fourteen bells was installed at Canterbury Cathedral in 1981, the bells were named after important people in Canterbury's history. They included: Ethelbert, the first Christian king of Kent in 597; Augustine, the first Archbishop of Canterbury in 602; Alphege, an archbishop murdered in 1012; Lanfranc, the first Norman Archbishop of Canterbury 1067, and Thomas, in memory of St Thomas à Becket, murdered 1170.

The revival of the ancient custom of naming bells after saints may be seen again at the new church of St Benedict just outside Northampton. Here six light bells have been so named and were dedicated in July 1987. One bell, given by an anonymous donor, is named after St Ragener, a local Saxon martyr, while another, dedicated to St Cecilia, was given by a parishioner in memory of his mother.

Some people, especially the elderly, see in this renewed interest in the past an indication proving that the old methods were probably the best after all. Whilst this view is in contrast to the modern attitude so often encountered, that any change must of necessity be an improvement, it underlines the fact that most customs and traditions were almost certainly based on actual events and lay only just below the surface in the collective folk memory.

4
Ringing the Changes

Ringers' Jacks at (left) *Beccles and* (right) *at Hinderclay*

The long tradition of ringing church bells in Britain, dating from Saxon times, was to undergo a fundamental change about the middle of the seventeenth century. Many bells having been destroyed or lost after the dissolution of the monasteries by Henry VIII between 1536 and 1539, they were gradually being replaced when the process was interrupted yet again by the Commonwealth which, under Cromwell, banned all churches from having, or ringing, more than two bells, as this was considered a form of frivolity. The Civil War also resulted in more bells being removed from churches to be melted down for cannon. In 1635 the church tower at Deddington, near Banbury, collapsed, bringing the bells with it. They were left on the ground for some time until sold to Cromwell's New Model Army for a considerable sum. The proceeds of the sale went to buying beer for the villagers, so earning the village its title of 'Drunken Deddington'. The church now has a ring of eight bells and has long lived down its reputation.

In re-hanging its new ring of bells, Deddington, like many other churches at the time, did so with a difference. Prior to the Reformation, bells had been hung in the church tower, each with a three-quarter wooden wheel or even a half wheel, with a rope running round the perimeter of the wheel through a hole in the belfry floor down to the ringing chamber below, where it ended in the multi-coloured and fluffy 'sally'. Though this allowed each bell to be rung in turn, the interval between the sound of each bell could not be accurately controlled. After the Civil War, as bells were gradually re-hung, various bellhangers continued to experiment by attaching the bell to a whole wheel. The result of this was dramatic: it was discovered that the swing of each bell could be controlled with such precision that it could ring immediately before or immediately after its neighbour according to the amount of 'pull' exerted on the rope.

With a ring of six bells, for example, which could normally be rung from treble to tenor (1-2-3-4-5-6) the variation of the pull on the rope could cause some bells to change places, resulting in the ringing order of, say, 2-1-4-3-6-5. At the next pull on the ropes the bells could be made to alter their order of ringing again, and each alteration was called a 'change'.

The number of changes possible on a given number of bells is surprisingly large. On six bells the number of changes possible without repeating a sequence is 720, on seven bells 5,040, and on eight bells the number rises to 40,320. On twelve bells the possible changes run into several millions, and it has been calculated that, if rung non-stop by a band, they would take some thirty-six years to complete.

The possibilities presented by controlled change-ringing were noted by many ringers, of whom the most famous is Fabian Stedman, a Cambridge printer and keen ringer. In

Bell mounted on a wheel and frame for ringing

1668, after many years of experiment and calculation, he published the first-ever book on change-ringing called *Tintinnalogia* and followed this nine years later with another book, *Campanologia*. In these two books Stedman laid down certain rules for ringing changes, including, for example, the stipulation that a bell may change places only with the bell ringing immediately before or behind it. He also took sequences of changes and grouped them into methods according to the 'work' of each bell. Without going into the details of change-ringing too deeply, the diagram below may give an indication of how the bells change their places in the ringing, and the No.5 bell is marked to show what its 'work' is. In the method shown the No.6 bell, the tenor, rings last at every change, and this is known as ringing 'behind'.

```
1 – 2 – 3 – 4 – 5 – 6
2 – 1 – 3 – 5 – 4 – 6
2 – 3 – 1 – 4 – 5 – 6
3 – 2 – 4 – 1 – 5 – 6
3 – 4 – 2 – 5 – 1 – 6
4 – 3 – 5 – 2 – 1 – 6
4 – 5 – 3 – 1 – 2 – 6
5 – 4 – 1 – 3 – 2 – 6
5 – 1 – 4 – 2 – 3 – 6
1 – 5 – 2 – 4 – 3 – 6
1 – 2 – 5 – 3 – 4 – 6
```

Like the No.5 bell, each bell has its allotted path. This pattern of changes is part of the method known as Grandsire (pronounced 'grandser'). Stedman gave his 'methods' names, such as Cambridge and Norwich, usually based on the first town in which they were rung. Understandably enough, one of the earliest methods is known as 'Stedman'. He also defined a 'peal' as a sequence of 5,000 or more changes.

A peal of over 5,000 changes takes about three hours to ring. It requires concentration and a good memory, though by remembering the work of your own bell in accordance with the above diagram it is much easier than one might think. The longest continuous peal by one band was rung at the Loughborough Foundry campanile in July 1963, when a band of ten rang 40,320 changes in just over seventeen hours. One ringer who took part, when asked how he coped with hunger, thirst and other bodily functions, replied tersely: 'Just will-power.'

Gargantuan as this sort of thing may be, most ringers content themselves with ringing quarter-peals, if they indulge in method-ringing at all, for this is not the only system, interesting as it may be.

Another way of ringing is known as 'call-changes'. In this the ringers begin by ringing in the normal sequence of 1 to 6 and continue that sequence until the captain calls a 'change'. He may call '3 to 4' (for example), indicating that those two bells should change places in their order of ringing. They will then continue to ring that sequence until the captain calls another change, and will continue ringing the new sequence until he calls again.

Call-changes are extremely useful in teaching people to ring. They also have the advantage of enabling the listener in the street or outside to assimilate and recognize the sequence in which the bells are being rung before it changes again. Method-ringing, with a new change at every pull of the rope, may seem something of a jangle to the non-ringer and is not always appreciated.

In both kinds of ringing the smooth sequence of the bells is of great importance. The interval between the sound of one bell and the next is only a split second but this should be constant for all bells. So often two bells seem to ring almost together, and there is an appreciable gap before the next bell rings. Smooth, continuous ringing is known as 'good striking' and traditionally is the main objective of the dedicated ringer. It is no use learning complicated methods if your striking is not good, and you will soon be advised of this fact by the tower captain. In the West Country good striking is very highly prized and many consider that good striking on call-changes is far more enjoyable than method-ringing. Striking competitions between teams of ringers have long been popular in Devon and Cornwall and have now spread to the rest of the country.

Before any ringing can start, the bells must be swung

from their normal mouth-downwards position until they are upside-down. The bell is swung in a wider and wider arc until it is in the 'up' position, where it is held very carefully and allowed to rest on a short piece of wood, fixed at one end, which keeps it just off centre and therefore almost upright. A stay attached to the wheel stops the bell going over past the upright position, for by doing this it would wind the rope up round the wheel and might entangle the ringer.

If the bells are rung for morning service and will be needed again for evening service they may well be left in the 'up' position in between, to avoid the chore and sometimes the cacophony that results when the bells are all rung up. When the bells are in this position, the situation is potentially dangerous, and it is extremely unwise for anyone to go up into the belfry and stand near the bells. Just touching a bell may cause it to tip over. Even a footstep has been known to do this. Anyone standing under a tenor bell, which may weigh a ton, is in danger of being crushed to death as has happened in the past. For this reason two precautions are taken. Firstly it is a tradition that, if the bells are 'up', the bell-ropes are looped over themselves in a special way in the ringing-chamber, and secondly all doors to the tower and ringing-chamber are locked. Even in the ringing-chamber a danger exists under such conditions, for a non-ringer pulling a rope when its bell is 'up' may cause the bell to turn over, so causing the rope to whip and thrash about uncontrolled in the room and cause injury to the astonished visitor.

Before any ringing starts, the wise tower-captain will ensure that everyone present is accounted for and that nobody has gone up into the belfry to examine or service a bell or fittings. But accidents still happen. In Wiltshire a vicar decided to show the children of his Sunday School what the church bells were like. He had a key to the tower and to the ringing-chamber, but unfortunately on that Sunday afternoon the bells were 'up', and when the good vicar put his hand lovingly on the tenor bell, it immediately turned over, crushing a child to death. At Great Linford in Buckinghamshire the sight of blood spiralling down the bell-rope soon after ringing began was the first indication that a check of the belfry had not been made. In Stoke-on-Trent a similar accident occurred when a keen ringer decided to oil the bearings of a bell before practice one night but omitted to tell any of the team where he was.

Despite these tragic events there appears to be only one example of a belfry ghost. This was in a church in Devon where, in the seventeenth century, a man was crushed to death by the tenor bell. His grieving widow, who did not like ringing anyway and said he had devoted far too much time to it, forecast that he would haunt the belfry to discourage future ringers and perhaps save a few marriages. Whether or not this form of campanological marriage-counselling was of any value is not known. What *is* known is that at various times strange knockings have been heard from the belfry while ringing is in progress, and certain ringers claim to have seen a shadowy figure climbing the ladder up to the bells.

Accidents may well happen in the ringing-chamber itself without there being any fault on the part of the ringer. The stay or slider may break and wind up the rope round the wheel. The situation beloved by generations of cartoonists may well then come about, of the ringer being hoisted aloft by the rope. It is said to have happened at High Wycombe, Buckinghamshire, when the man ringing the 1½-ton tenor was carried upwards when the stay snapped, breaking his two wrists on the ceiling and knocking him out. He then fell to the floor, breaking both legs. (The problem of getting the injured man down from the tower via a very narrow spiral staircase has itself become something of a legend in the district.) In a situation of this kind the experienced ringer will immediately let go of his rope and make for the wall of the chamber. The damage done by a flailing rope can be immense, which is the reason why it is also a tradition that every learner has an experienced ringer behind him in case he or she should lose control of the rope and possibly get a leg or arm tangled in it.

However, one legend that has no basis in fact is that used by Dorothy L. Sayers in her detective novel *The Nine Tailors*. In it she describes how, in a Fenland church, a man was murdered by being locked in a belfry for three hours while a peal was being rung. Medical opinion is that, though a man might be deafened or even driven mad by such treatment, death would be most unlikely to result.

Something that may cause damage, and which is certainly frightening, is the fairly rare situation of the clapper flying off. When this happens, it produces a very loud and startling noise followed, on occasion, by the pointed end of the clapper appearing in a shower of plaster through the ringing-chamber ceiling. In 1986, at All Saints Church, Worcester, the clapper of the tenor came off towards the end of a peal attempt. Said the tower-captain later, in an interview demonstrating characteristic British phlegm: 'We understand that such occurrences at All Saints are quite common. It is only 200 years since another peal came to grief when the tenor clapper fell out.'

At Nantwich, Cheshire, a fatality occurred when a new bell was being installed. The parish register records:

> Jan 22nd 1714. Mark, son of Mark Topham,
> Kill'd by the 4th bell clapper.

A very serious incident took place in Liverpool in 1810. On 11 February that year ringing was taking place in the church of St Nicholas when stones began falling into the ringing-chamber. Within minutes the entire tower had collapsed, killing twenty-two of the congregation instantly.

Despite the heaviness of many bells, the tenor always weighing most, they are not very difficult to ring, and comparatively little strength is required. Many young girls and women are now found ringing regularly, for most modern bells turn on ball-bearings. As explained above, the bells have to be 'rung up' before ringing can start, and usually a man, or sometimes two, is required to ring up a really heavy tenor. But once the bells are swinging, it needs only a very light pull on the rope to keep them moving.

Most ringers limit themselves to ringing one bell, but there have been exceptions, and ringers have been known to ring two bells at a time, one with each hand. The record for this sort of thing seems to be held by a certain George Smith at the Church of St James in Clerkenwell, London, who chimed eight bells at a time one day in 1865, using thumbs, fingers and feet to hold the ropes. Admittedly this was not full-circle ringing but 'chiming', a method where the bell is moved just enough to cause the clapper to hit the side and sound.

Not satisfied with this he went on to chime ten bells at once at St Martin-in-the-Fields the following year.

Despite occasional eccentrics like George Smith, the average ringer is sober enough and dedicated to his hobby, but occasionally even the most down-to-earth ringers go over the top and do things like trying to ring five or six quarter-peals in one day in different towers.

Usually ringers care a great deal for tradition, and it is not unusual for several members of the same family to be ringers and carry this down from generation to generation. At Barrow-on-Humber we find a ringing tradition in the Crowder family going back to 1760. In Lincolnshire the Holmes family of Edenham can trace a ringing history of six generations and, perhaps the most remarkable of all, the Truss family of Marlow, Buckinghamshire, can claim a continuous ringing history of 300 years, from 1593 to 1893. In the same county the six sons of Robert Gibbs of Winslow rang the New Year in together on no fewer than forty occasions during the eighteenth century. A record of another kind is that held by Canon R.J. Peyton-Burbery at Brading, Isle of Wight. He learned to ring at twenty years of age but did not manage his first quarter-peal until his ninetieth birthday, in 1971.

The decor in any ringing chamber includes the noticeboards and peal-boards. Ringing, as has been demonstrated, is not without risk, as early notices indicate. This one is in the tower at Stamford:

All you that do intend to ring
You undertake a dangerous thing.

Many ringing-chambers have rules, often in rhyme, governing the conduct of those present and aiming to minimize accidents. At the parish church of Southill, Bedfordshire, is found the following notice:

> He that wears Spurs, or Hat, or Cap or breaks a stay
> Or from the floor does by a bellrope sway,
> Or leaves his rope down Carless on the floor,
> Or nuisance makes within the belfry door,
> Shall sixpence forfeit for each single crime,
> 'Twill make him carefull at another time.

A very ancient set of rules is found in the ringing-chamber of the church at Drewsteignton, Devon. After listing the penalties payable for various belfry misdemeanours, it concludes:

> Who will not to these rules agree
> Shall not belong to this belfrie.
> John Hole, Churchwarden.

If you abided by the rules and rang properly, there were definite compensations, mostly of a liquid kind, represented by the barrel of beer kept in most towers until early Victorian times. The beer was drunk from leather jugs or 'jacks', and some were very large. If the ringing-chamber had no barrel on tap, the 'jack' was taken from house to nearby house and refilled to its capacity of about three gallons. It was customary for notable bigwigs to present jacks to the ringers inscribed with the appropriate wording, no doubt to ensure that their name went down to posterity. An example is the 22-gallon 'jack' presented to the ringers of Lincoln Cathedral by Alderman Bullen in 1782. He was also a brewer. At the same time it must be stressed that, although a good deal of drinking went on in most towers, anyone with his head fuddled with beer would have difficulty in finding his way through the complications of a method, even one as simple as Grandsire. This danger is pointed out in what must be one of the most entertaining bits of doggerel concerning ringing, found on a ringers' jug at Beccles, Suffolk. Dated 1827, it says:

When I am filled with liquor strong
Each man drink once, and then ding dong.
Drink not too much to cloud your Knobbs
Lest you forget to make the bobbs.

The 'bobbs' referred to relate to an occasional variation in the path of the bell, which is necessary to ensure that all the desired changes are rung. The ability of apparently simple folk to memorize complicated methods is akin to those darts players in country pubs who, after several pints of best bitter, are still capable of adding and subtracting the score in their heads without reference to the board or using the chalk.

It is obvious that the large quantity of beer imbibed must have created a strain on the bladder and is the reason why some chambers carry a board warning of 'untrussing on the leads' as in most churches the roof is easily accessible from the ringing-chamber. At Brington, Northants, nobody could misinterpret the message written on a board. It says simply:

Anyone caught pissing here
Shall fourpence pay and then be clear.'

Just what is going to be cleared is not specified.

Noise and bad language were also frowned upon in most towers, such as:

If you chance to curse or sweare,
Be sure you shall pay sixpence heare.

York Minster, as mentioned, has a medieval stained-glass window depicting the work of the bell-foundry. Another more modern reference to ringers is found at Ripon Cathedral where a beautiful window records the ringing of a peal in 1886 as part of the city's celebration of the thousandth year of its charter. At St Albans is another very interesting 'ringing window' showing members of the band ringing a peal in August 1945 to celebrate the end of World War II. The window was designed by Martin Webb, himself a St Albans ringer.

Much more common in ringing-chambers than quaint boards warning of penalties or dangers are those prosaic boards giving details of quarter-peals and full peals. (For some unknown reason nobody ever seems to ring a half-peal!) These are a traditional method of recording ringing achievements and, though less entertaining than the boards carrying warnings, are nevertheless often of great interest historically.

In Norwich the church of St Peter Mancroft has two important peal-boards. One is the first record of a peal of 5,040 changes rung in 1715. The second is a large board decorated with bells and angels bearing the following inscription:

> On the 26th of August 1718 was rung that harmonious peal called Grandsire Triples which have been the study of the most ingenious men of this age who delight in the art of variation, but all their projections have proved errors until it was undertook by John Garthon who with long study and practice having perfectly discovered those intricate methods which were hidden from the eyes of all ringers in England, the extent of this peal being 5,040 changes have often been rung with changes alike, but the first time it was rung true was in three hours and a half without any changes alike, or a bell out of course, by these men, whose names are under written against the bells as they rung.

James Brooke	Treble	Henry Howard	5
John Briggs	2	Wm. Callow	6
Wm. Palmer	3	Tho. Melchior	7
Robt. Crane	4	Tho. Barrett	Tenor

St Peter Mancroft also has a parchment in the church with elaborate illustrations dating from 1716 listing the rules of membership of the Norwich Scholars Purse Society or Benefit Society, an organization that controlled ringing in the city for many years.

Still in Norwich, but this time at the church of St Giles, is a board commemorating the death of a seventeenth-century ringer. It is on the wall of an aisle and not in the ringing chamber:

Near to this place John Webster fell
Beloved by all who knew him well:
The most ingenious noted Ringer
St Giles sixth bell he round did bring her.
He closed the Peal, struck with his Bell,
Ceasing the same, down dead he fell.
November 17th 1670.

A later tribute to a well-known ringer is found on a tablet in the ringing-chamber of St Mary's, Brinkley, Cambridgeshire:

IN MEMORY OF GILBERT SYMONDS WHO DIED JUNE
ye 29th MDCCLVIII aged 63 years.
Here lieth one Who in ye time of Life,
Loved good Company well and hated Strife,
Was a Companion Good to those he knew,
And often would put forth a Jest or two.
Took such delight in ringing a bell
That in ye Art but few could him Excell.
All things below with him are done and past,
Death took him off, his knell is rung at Last.

It is not uncommon for epitaphs to ringers (frequently termed as 'ingenious') to be found in country and even city churchyards. In the churchyard of St Nicholas at Nuneaton, Warwicks, is found this tribute:

Here lieth a ringer
Beneath this cold clay,
Who rang many peals
Both serious and gay.
Through Grandsire and Trebles
So well could he range
Till death called a 'bob'
And brought round the last change.

The ringer was David Wheway who died on 13 October 1828; most ringers will be familiar with the terms used.

In a Yorkshire churchyard is found a quaint early nineteenth-century epitaph to two young brothers, one of whom died as the result of a belfry accident, the other perishing at sea:

These 2 youths were by misfortun serounded,
One died of his Wound and the other was Drownded.

Entering a ringing-chamber and watching the ringers at work is a real lesson in concentration. The sallies fly up and down as each bell speaks, the eyes of the ringers are everywhere watching the other ringers' ropes, and now and again the captain will call an instruction to remind a ringer of a change in the sequence or to put him right if he has gone wrong. Apart from their value in allowing a tight hold of the rope to be taken, the multi-coloured sally is also a sign of the position of the bell itself and when it is going to ring. The sight of two sallies coming down at the same level is usually an indication that two bells are going to ring at the same moment – not the object of the Exercise! This sort of noise, unavoidable when teaching people to ring, is probably the reason for the occasional anti-ringing feeling that exists. Attempts to ban ringing are sometimes encountered and are dealt with later in this book. (see p.80).

Perhaps the attitude of the average ringer to his bell may best be summed up in the words of a Buckinghamshire farmer and ringer at Ludgershall. He said: 'I like to think of a bell as a lady. Handle her with care, treat her with respect and she will always respond.'

Enthusiasm for ringing, whether or not the bell is treated as female, can lead to some odd situations. In 1986 the *Liverpool Echo* informed its readers that a Mrs Stephanie Lindhorst-Jones, described as 'a teenage bride', was claiming unfair dismissal from her place of employment because she refused to work on Sundays. Her reason for so doing was because she was a regular Sunday service ringer at her parish church. At the industrial tribunal that was held, it was decided that this was a legitimate excuse. She was given her job back and awarded £1,120 compensation. If not the start of a tradition, this case can certainly be regarded as a precedent.

Another precedent, which again may prove to be the beginning of a tradition, is concerned with the re-decoration and general maintenance of ringing-chambers. Most ringers are at work during the week, and Sunday ringing and practice-night leave little time for attending to belfry matters. This is very often seen to by ringers who may be at home during the day or by the wives of male ringers who, unlike the seventeenth-century Devon ringer's wife, are not actively engaged in dissuading their spouses from pursuing their hobby. In 1987, for the first time, young offenders sentenced to do work under the Community Service scheme re-painted and re-decorated the woodwork in the ringing-chamber and belfry of their parish church. This, however, is not the only occasion in which crime and campanology have come together.

In the parish church of St Mary Magdalen at Debenham, Suffolk, there is a peal-board recording the ringing of a 'long peal' of 10,080 changes by a band of eight local ringers on 16 March 1767. It is a fairly heavy ring at Debenham, the tenor bell weighing over 21 cwt, and it took just over six hours to ring. They began very early in the morning, the tenor bell being rung by a local lad named James Wilson. Around midnight the previous night a young girl had been brutally attacked and murdered twenty miles away, at Bury St Edmunds, and it was James Wilson who was identified as the murderer. At his trial he used as alibi his taking part in the peal at Debenham, and the jury agreed that he could not have made the journey between Bury St Edmunds and Debenham in the time stated. He was acquitted and went on to become one of the best-known ringers in the Eastern Counties. It is said that on his deathbed he confessed to the murder and explained that after the deed he rode his horse non-stop for twenty miles to be at Debenham in time for the ringing to start. Unfortunately all the Assize records of the old Norfolk Circuit at the time of the trial have vanished and we cannot, therefore, adduce the evidence submitted by either side. The legend still persists, however, as visitors to Debenham will discover for themselves.

The sometimes unhappy relationship between ringers and the clergy is dealt with in a later chapter (see p.117), but at least one cleric (and a non-ringer at that) took a great interest in bellringing at a time when it was far from usual for a parson to do so.

In 1862 the incumbent of St James' Church, Hull, the Reverend William Knight, wrote a poem of thirty-three verses relating an incident concerning the local ringers. The poem begins:

> One Tuesday night not long ago
> My mind to disencumber
> I took a solitary walk
> Upon the banks of Humber.

On his journey he became aware that the bells of the parish church were ringing and he knew enough about the subject to recognize that the ringers were trying for a quarter-peal. All was going well, he says, when suddenly one of the ringers went wrong and the peal attempt came to a jangling halt.

> And now a silence intervened
> And all was still and quiet;
> 'Dear me' I thought 'how sweet the calm
> That supercedes a riot!'

He then goes on to relate how, with perhaps a certain lack of tact for a clergyman, he entered the church, climbed the low spiral stairs to the belfry ('Kept bending – bending – bending') and enquired of the ringers what had gone wrong. Though all looked embarrassed, none of the eight would admit an error, and the worthy cleric, unwilling to believe that a ringer would ever tell a lie, ends his poem with the following somewhat sarcastic stanza:

> And now from henceforth be it known
> Whene'er a peal turns lame,
> The Ringers never are at fault
> The Bells are all to blame.

That verse could well be reprinted and hung in many a belfry!

5
The Common Bell

Passing bells calling for prayers for a departing soul

The sound of bells ringing, especially church bells, has a profound effect on most people. The emotions aroused may be grave or gay, fill us with foreboding and thoughts of death, provide good cheer as they ring for a wedding or, at times, arouse the feeling known as *hiraeth* by the Welsh – the longing of the traveller for the sights and sounds of his homeland.

For many small boys the tinkling of a bicycle bell remains an exciting sound likely to stay in the memory for life, and even today similar feelings are aroused by the chimes of the ice-cream van, even if they insist on mauling Neapolitan airs or operatic arias.

Bells have been with us a very long time and there has

always been a reason for ringing them, usually associated with religion. They were used by the early missionaries to announce their presence and to ensure good audiences for their sermons and evangelical efforts. Very small bells were first used in early church services in Britain not so much to summon the faithful to prayer but to mark the focal points of the Mass, a tradition that persists in some Roman Catholic and High Anglican churches to this day. As churches became established and monasteries were built, it became customary for large bells to be installed. Legend insists that the first bells of this kind were hung in the trees of the churchyard, and that towers were later provided for the church as a permanent home for the bells under one roof.

In the monasteries the ringing of the great bells was performed largely by the lay brothers who also had other duties to do in and around the church or chapel.

One of the earliest references to ringing for a solemn occasion is in the legend that the bells at Tintagel rang for the death of King Arthur at Camlan in AD 537. Another early reference is found about 750, when Egbert, Archbishop of York, ordered in his book *Excerptions* that all priests should ring the bells of their church at stated times each day, namely at 9 a.m., noon, 3 p.m., 6 p.m. and 9 p.m. to remind the public of the monastic duties of the day. St Dunstan drew up similar rules, and so did Archbishop Lanfranc of Canterbury in 1068. In some churches a single bell was rung before the service started, to warn the faithful to begin praying. Very common was the custom of ringing several times on the tenor bell if a sermon was to be preached, though whether this was intended as a warning or an attraction is not known. A more useful form of ringing began at eight o'clock each morning in some cities so that those who had clocks could regulate them and those without knew that another working day had begun. At Lincoln in 1270, which was then a busy inland port, early ringing was sometimes performed by local sailors.

Both the Reformation and the Commonwealth saw a significant reduction in church bellringing, and the Calvinists, in particular, abhorred ringing as being a mark of 'popery'. The Anglican Church was far less hostile, and though many bells were removed at the dissolution of the monasteries, it was ordained that every place of Anglican worship should have at least 'one proper bell properly ornamented' which should be rung for morning and evening prayer. An inscription on one bell in Essex cast during the Commonwealth says: 'Lord by thy Might, keep us from Pope and Hypocrite.'

When bellringing had once again come into its own after the Restoration and ringing became normal for church feasts, there also arose a demand from the public for the bells to be rung on family occasions, such as births, marriages and deaths, for which the ringers were paid. Marriages were the most popular reason for ringing, funerals the most interesting. Not every baptism calls for the church bells to be rung, but practically every church wedding does. This remains one of the very few occasions on which the ringers are still paid, though in most towers the earnings go into the 'belfry fund' which exists to pay for items such as new ropes, cleaning materials for the ringing-chamber and general maintenance of bells and belfry. As most church weddings are on a Saturday afternoon, it is not always easy to persuade the ringers to oblige, and most ringers feel that it is only right that ringing should be paid for and come out of the large sum spent on 'white weddings' these days.

One curious custom connected with ringing for a wedding and found in the North of England was to toll the tenor bell as the happy couple left the church to signify how many children they were likely to have. It would be interesting to know who it was who decided this figure!

The ringing of a bell, usually the tenor, at or before the time of death is a very ancient custom which has sometimes caused a degree of confusion, if not despair. This surrounds the ringing of the 'passing bell' when someone was obviously dying but had not yet departed this life. A church regulation in the time of Elizabeth I has this to say about it: 'Item, that when anye Christian body is in passing, that the bell be tolled, and that the curate be speciallie called for to comforte the sicke person; and after the time of his passinge to ring no more, but one short peal and one before the buriall and another short peal after the buriall.' In this context it should be remembered that the use of the word 'peal' (sometimes 'pele') does not refer to a peal of 5,000 changes or more but to a very short series of changes, often muffled, known to bellringers more usually as a 'touch'. The 'passing bell' is obviously the bell referred to by John Donne in the famous phrase from his *Devotions*: 'And therefore never send to know for whom the bell tolls; it tolls for thee.' This is a clear indication that the bell was tolled when a person was thought to be dying, and could not have improved the morale of the person concerned, nor that of the family.

The Elizabethan edict made it quite clear that a priest *must* be summoned on such occasions, and in 1526 we find an entry in the accounts of St Mary Woolnoth, a City of London church now no more, paying the parish clerk for summoning the priest and doubling the fee if the occasion was at night. The reason for ringing the 'passing bell' was said to be to alert others to the imminent death of a villager or acquaintance and to ask for prayers. Another very ancient belief was that it frightened away evil spirits who cannot stand the sound of bells of any kind. Whatever the reason, it seems to have attracted a certain amount of unpopularity and almost died out during the eighteenth century. One writer has expressed his dislike of the custom in the following words:* 'It is to be hoped that this ridiculous custom will never be revived, which has been most probably the cause of sending many a good soul to the other world before its time: nor can the practice of tolling bells for the dead be defended upon any principle of common sense, prayers for the dead being contrary to the articles of religion.' In 1874 in Northamptonshire one old lady heard the passing bell rung for her but determined to outwit the pessimists – and recovered!)

Despite this outspoken and somewhat odd opinion, ringing a bell for funerals and burials still continues. The 'death knell', rung after the person had died, was always tolled on the tenor. Sometimes it was rung while the coffin was on its journey to the church, and always during the

* Quoted in W. Andrews, *Anecdotal History of Bells* (1895).

graveside burial service. Indeed, so important was this tolling considered that a code of ringing was devised to impart information to those attending or listening. The bell was tolled nine times for a man, six for a woman and three times for a child. In some churches the age of the departed was announced by the appropriate number of strokes. This tradition is still alive and encountered in rural parishes, though the 'code' varies from place to place.

One common variation is three chimes for a man and two for a woman, whilst in another parish it is six for a boy and five for a girl. At Marsham, Norfolk, an even more complicated set of codes was in use, requiring the tenor to be tolled nine times for a married man, eight for a bachelor, seven for a married woman, six for a spinster, four for a boy and three for a girl. These were known as 'knocks for the dead'.

Because they provided information, the notes of the bell were called 'tellers' on these occasions. This was often corrupted to 'tailors' and this is the derivation of *The Nine Tailors* the title of Dorothy L. Sayers' famous mystery novel concerned with ringing.

An odd use of the death-knell found in some churches before the Reformation was to ring it on Christmas Day to announce the death of Satan on the coming of Christ. At Dewsbury, Yorkshire, this custom has persisted and the tenor bell is tolled once for every year since the birth of Christ. Legend has it that the custom was initiated by a local baron, Thomas de Sothill, in the fourteenth century, to expiate a murder he had committed. Locally it is held to mark the death of Satan and is known as 'The Old Lad's Passing Bell'.

Those closely associated with a particular church or cathedral sometimes left legacies to pay for the bells to be rung on the anniversary of their death. This pre-Reformation custom seems to have existed at first mainly in East Anglia, and in 1501 a priest of King's Lynn, Norfolk, left three acres of land to provide revenue for ringing on his 'year day'. In Suffolk, at Bury St Edmunds, in 1463, a parishioner left money for the bellman to go ringing through the town on the anniversary of his death, and in 1477 at the church of St John the Baptist at Peterborough the ringers were paid 14 pence to ring for the anniversary of the death of a certain Abbot Genge.

Perhaps the oddest bequest of this kind is found at Bath, where in 1813 Thomas Nashe, married for many years to a notorious shrew, left £50 in his will to the abbey ringers for them to ring 'a muffled and funereal peal' on the anniversary of his wedding, and on each anniversary of his death to ring 'merry mirthful peals to commemorate my happy release from Domestick Tyranny'.

Occasionally one meets the case of a too-enthusiastic ringer letting his hobby take the place of his civic duty. In 1625 Richard Copcutt, an enthusiastic ringer of Islip (Oxon) left 8 shillings a year as a bequest to the ringers, but also left his wife and six children unprovided-for and on the parish. The bailiffs were not amused.

A bequest from a modern lover of bells has created a new ringing tradition. In the Suffolk village of Rushmere St Andrew lived Dr Victor Poll, whose chief delight was listening to the church bells. When he died in 1986 at the early age of thirty-nine, he left provision in his Will for the bells to be rung in his memory for an hour, morning and evening, on Midsummer Day.

An example of handbells being rung at a death is found on the Bayeux Tapestry, where the funeral of Edward the Confessor is depicted with two boys carrying small bells accompanying the bier. Chaucer, too, seems to be referring to a small handbell in the *Pardoner's Tale*, when he says:

> And as they sat they herde a belle clynke
> Before a corse was carried to the grave.

The association of bells and death is found in the ancient rite of excommunication which requires the use of bell, book and candle. In this sombre ritual the bell is considered to be a symbol of death, the book is the Book of Life, and the candle signifies the soul.

One important bell apart from those in the tower is the smaller one known as the Sanctus bell. This was usually housed above the chancel in a small turret with a rope going down below, so that the server could ring it when the priest intoned the words '*Sanctus, Sanctus, Sanctus*'. The bell was tolled three times, mainly to advise those outside the church that an event of the greatest importance was taking place within. Many village churches still have a Sanctus bell which continues to be used in much the same manner. In some places it is also used as a 'sermon' bell. In Commonwealth times the 'sermon' bell was not used to give notice that a sermon would be preached at that service, but was rung at the moment in the service when the sermon was due to begin. This enabled those who disagreed with church ritual to remain outside and enter the church only in the certainty that they would hear an edifying discourse.

Though the Sanctus bell was officially banned after the Reformation, its use was revived in 1630 by Archbishop Laud of Canterbury as part of his attempt to combat Calvinism. Some clergymen who obeyed this new rule found themselves at odds with their flock who apparently had no desire to hear the bell rung again. This happened at the Suffolk village of Long Melford, where the rector was attacked by a mob on the way home from church, and beaten on the head with a frying-pan while the crowd jeered, 'Here is your Sanctus bell.'

Another use of the Sanctus bell in the eighteenth century was to advise the faithful that Communion could be taken at that service. On such occasions it was rung thirty-three times to represent Our Lord's age at the time of his crucifixion.

The semi-religious use of the curfew-bell was probably introduced by Alfred the Great as a means of ensuring that fires were put out by nightfall, as an obvious safety device. The law was re-imposed by the Conqueror, who gave it the Norman name of *couvre-feu*, probably with the more potent reason of stopping nocturnal plottings or meetings directed against the invaders. The ringing of the curfew-bell was eventually ended in the reign of Henry I, though in many places it continued as a safety measure and in the fifteenth century we find many instructions to parish clerks in the City of London and surrounding areas to ring the bell in the evening. It became a tradition, though not a legal requirement, and varied from parish to parish.

Chaucer mentions it in *The Miller's Tale*, and Shakespeare, though he talks of it in four plays, attributes a different time on each occasion. The tradition of the curfew-bell seems to have lingered for many centuries, and as late as 1713 there is an instruction to the parish clerk of Barrow-on-Humber to ring for the 'corphew' during the winter months.

With its sombre connotations of doom and the ending of life it is not surprising that the tenor bell played a big part in the execution of criminals.

In 1605 a certain Robert Dawe of the City of London presented a large bell to the church of St Sepulchre, together with an annual fee of £1.6.8d, for the sexton to toll the bell each time a party of felons left Newgate Gaol to be hanged at Tyburn. Considering the number of offences that merited the death penalty in those days, it is not surprising that these 'hanging parties' were quite frequent and greeted by the populace as a hugely entertaining spectacle attended by men, women and children. The night before the executions the parish clerk of St Sepulchre's would stand outside the prison ringing his handbell and intoning: 'You prisoners that are within, who for wickedness and sin after many mercies shown to you are now appointed to die tomorrow in the forenoon; give ear and understand that tomorrow morning the greatest bell of St Sepulchre's parish shall toll for you from six till ten, in order and manner of a passing bell, which used to be tolled for those which lie at the point of death, to the end that all godly people hearing that bell, and knowing it is for you going to your deaths, may be stirred up to hearty prayer to God to bestow his grace and mercy upon you while you yet live.' There was certainly no question of 'for whom the bell tolls' on these occasions.

Having delivered himself of this homily, the clerk was then invited to enter the prison, stand outside the condemned cell and recite:

All you that in the condemned hold do lie,
Prepare you for tomorrow you shall die;
Watch all, and pray, the hour is drawing near
That you before the Almighty must appear;
Examine well yourselves, in time repent,

That you may not to eternal flames be sent.
And when St Sepulchre's bell tomorrow tolls,
The Lord above have mercy on your souls.

Next morning the prisoners would be loaded onto a cart, each given a nosegay, while the chaplain prayed in a loud voice: 'All good people pray heartily to God for these poor sinners going to their deaths and for whom this great bell doth toll.'

It was once the custom to use church bells as a warning or tocsin in times of danger. At the Church of St Michael at Oxford the bells were chimed during the frequent disturbances between Town and Gown and in earlier times had been used when the tower was being besieged. Those on top of the tower hurled stones and other items down on the attacking troops whilst those inside the church prayed for deliverance. In many places a bell was used as a fire-alarm, and in Sherborne Abbey there is one such bell formerly used in this way bearing the legend

Lord, quench this furious flame,
Arise, run, help and out this flame.
J W I C 1652

Another way of sounding an alarm was for the bells to be rung backwards, from tenor to treble, though it is not easy to find recorded instances of this practice. It is mentioned by Tom Ingram in his entertaining book *Bells in England*. The more common method of sounding an alarm was for the bells to be sounded at exactly the same moment. This was known as 'firing' the bells and is still occasionally done at times of national rejoicing.

There has been a long tradition of ringing for military and naval victories, as has been seen by the list of Marlborough's exploits recorded on the bell at Worcester. The records of Peterborough Cathedral note that 5 shillings were paid to the ringers on 7 June 1665 for 'ringing the great bells at the overthrow of the Dutch Fleet.' At Brixton, Devon, a new bell was given to the parish church by the squire to celebrate the naval victory over the French off Flamborough Head in 1779.

Needless to say, church bells were rung throughout Britain to celebrate the end of hostilities in both World Wars. In between, on 29 September 1938, nine towns in England rang bells to signal the signing of the Munich Agreement and Chamberlain's famous phrase 'Peace in our time'. Ever forward-looking, the ringers of Liverpool had rung their peal the day before!

Political events were also commemorated by ringing – such as the Gunpowder Plot on 5 November 1605. The accounts of St Margaret's, Westminster, note a payment of 10 shillings to the ringers that same year for ringing 'at the time the Parliament House should have been blown up'. They were certainly quick off the mark. In some areas the custom of 'firing' the bells (the old method of alarm) is still used on Guy Fawkes Day and is known as 'Shooting Old Guy'. This also happens at Harlington, Bedfordshire, where the ringers are rewarded with pork pies and beer. This kind of loyalty is commendable though it may depend both on one's political views and on one's religion.

A more recent event was marked by the ringers of St Nicholas-at-Wade in Kent in June 1986, when they rang a half-muffled quarter peal in memory of the nuclear disaster at Chernobyl. Another 'disaster' for many people, but on a less serious scale, was the closure of the GWR workshops at Swindon in March 1986 (the 150th anniversary of the formation of the company) which prompted a half-muffled peal from the ringers of Swindon.

There are countless instances of bells being rung to announce royal births, coronations and deaths or even a royal visit. An example of this long-standing tradition is found in 1532 at Waltham Abbey, whose accounts record that when Henry VIII visited there the ringers were paid one penny 'for the ringing of the prince his coming' – a seemingly paltry amount for such an important event. Even so, it was an improvement on the ringers of Lambeth who had refused to ring at all when Henry visited there in 1517 and the embarrassed clergy were forced to fine the ringers 2s.6d. for their obstinacy.

Bells were rung on the accession of Edward VI, Mary

Tudor and Elizabeth I and even on the appointment of Oliver Cromwell as Lord Protector in 1653, and have been rung at all coronations since.

One man who must have been deeply affected by bells was the Prince Regent, later George IV, when in 1817 they tolled for the death of his only daughter, the Princess Charlotte, and her stillborn child. Almost exactly a year later, in November 1818, another muffled peal was rung for the Prince Regent's mother, the old Queen Charlotte, who died at Kew. There was joyous ringing in May 1819 when the Prince Regent's brother, the Duke of Kent, won what has become known as 'the royal stud race' and sired the infant girl who, though it was not realized at the time, was to become Queen Victoria.

The Duke of Kent had lived in some style overseas with his mistress, the attractive French Madame de St Laurent, and on his recall to England to marry the German princess selected for him he did not change his mode of living. Like all his brothers he rarely bothered to pay any bills, believing that the honour of supplying the needs of royalty was reward enough for the tradesmen concerned. When he died at Sidmouth, muffled bells were rung to signal the departure of the coffin for Windsor. It was also the signal for the infuriated tradesmen of Sidmouth to line the route and block the way with carts, agreeing to allow the cortège to continue only after their bills had been settled. The result was a near-riot on the road from Sidmouth to Honiton and the coffin had to be taken back to Sidmouth. There the local Yeomanry were called out and later that night, under cover of darkness, the procession once more set out for Windsor. It took four days, resting at night in a local churchyard where muffled bells were rung, to reach Cumberland Lodge where it lay in state. Whilst this was happening and funereal peals were being rung, the old King George III, the Duke's father, died a mile away in Windsor Castle, requiring further muffled peals to be rung. At last, on 14 July 1821, the bells of every church in the kingdom announced the coronation of the Prince Regent as George IV.The occasion was marred a little by the eccentric behaviour of his wife, Queen Caroline, who attempted to get into the Abbey by every possible means though barred by her husband. She had earlier been tried, in 1820, for her unseemly behaviour, and acquitted, a result which created other reasons for joyful ringing. Only three weeks after her husband's coronation Caroline was dead and more muffled ringing took place. With a royal birth, six royal deaths, one royal trial and a coronation, the Abbey ringers must have worked very hard during the period 1817 to 1821.

Church bells were frequently used for secular reasons, and the bell normally employed for this purpose was known as 'the common bell'. In 1552 at Moulton, Northants, instructions stated that a special bell, sometimes called a 'mote' bell would be rung to gather together the inhabitants of the town to hear any important announcements. Nottingham had a 'common bell' as early as 1315. In many instances the bell so used was eventually removed from the church and performed its function from the town hall, thus entirely severing its connection with religion.

Another custom which has become almost entirely secular is the Pancake Bell rung on Shrove Tuesday and, in some parishes, associated with a pancake race by young women round the churchyard. The Shrove Tuesday bell was originally a summons to parishioners to eat their last good meal before Lent began, and the pancake is a relic of this tradition. Probably the best-known Pancake Race is that taking place each year at Olney, Bucks, which is reputed to date from the fifteenth century.

Olney is a small, pleasant town, famous mainly for two eighteenth-century residents, the poet Cowper and the reformed slave-trader John Newton, who became rector of Olney in 1764. Between them they wrote the very large number of hymns known collectively as *The Olney Hymns*, many of which are still sung today. Cowper, in a letter to a friend, once wrote that, 'Occurrences here are as rare as cucumbers at Christmas', but one occurrence in the town was the annual Pancake Race on Shrove Tuesday. On that day the housewives of Olney would prepare their pancakes, assemble near the church and, on the sound of a bell, race up the High Street and back to the church, each carrying her pancake. The first to arrive with her pancake still intact was the winner, and another bell would be rung to signal this.

The custom of the Pancake Bell and race (said to have begun in 1445) lapsed during World War II but was revived in 1948 amidst much publicity. It came to the notice of the American town of Liberal, in Kansas, which had also been celebrating Shrove Tuesday for some years in a similar way. Today the two towns have a Pancake Race at exactly the same time and over a virtually identical course, and it has become much more a contest between Liberal and Olney than between the respective housewives. In Olney, for reasons best known to the organizers, the race is judged by churchwardens dressed in costumes fashionable during the Napoleonic Wars. After the race is over a short service is held in Olney church and the bells rung again. In the church visitors may see the unusual sight of frying-pans stacked around the font while some of the Olney hymns are sung, of which perhaps the best-known is the ever-popular 'Amazing Grace'.

The Pancake Bell was once rung in many English towns, including Chesham (Buckinghamshire), Hoddesdon (Hertfordshire), Stamford (Lincolnshire), and Oakham (Leicestershire), but latterly, except at Olney, seems to have fallen into disuse. However, in the present climate of reviving everything that reminds us of the past, it may well once again become a feature of English rural life, albeit a somewhat self-conscious one.

Another bell connected with food is the now long-forgotten 'Pudding Bell'. This was rung in some parishes when the congregation was leaving the church after morning service and was intended as a warning to the lady of the house, or the cook, to put the pudding on the hob ready for dinner. Even more ancient was the Oven Bell, which was rung to advise villagers that they could bring their dough up to the manor-house and bake it in the huge ovens in the kitchen.

In the Fen District, church bells were rung some hours before the time of the meeting of the local 'jury' who controlled matters relating to agriculture and draining, and was known as 'the Dykes and Drains Bell'. Audible

Nightwatchmen guarding plague-infected houses to stop the occupants escaping

for many miles over the flat countryside, it gave plenty of notice that the 'jury' was to meet later that day.

As we have seen at Bath, people have left bequests for bells to be rung for many strange reasons. Often it is to give thanks for deliverance from some peril, such as being lost in a storm or fog, when hearing the church bells, they were put on the right path. Incidents of this kind are found all over the country, a well-known one being at the pretty hilltop village of Wingrave, in Buckinghamshire. In 1786 the wife of a wealthy landowner, a Mrs Elizabeth Theed, was lost in a violent storm while making her way from the nearby hamlet of Rowsham across the fields to Wingrave. Then, in despair of surviving her ordeal, she suddenly heard the sound of Wingrave bells above the fury of the storm and found the right direction. In thanks she gave three fields to the parish church of SS Peter and Paul and ordered that on the patronal festival of the church each year the bells should be rung, and at the next service the floor of the church should be spread with hay from the fields. This custom is still observed annually at Wingrave, the hay being 'danced' into the church by the local Morris men while the bells ring. There follows a short service at which the story of the hay is recounted.

Just over thirty years earlier there had been a similar incident at Twyford, in Berkshire. In 1753 a Mr William Davis, described as 'a man of standing and substance', had lost himself in a fog off the Bath road whilst returning from Reading. Hearing the bells of Twyford church ringing, he immediately changed direction, so avoiding falling into the unseen chalk-pit that gaped before him. The grateful traveller left the sum of 20 shillings for the church bells to be rung annually in the morning and evening of 7 October, the anniversary of his escape.

In North Wales the church bells were rung as a sign of alarm if a climber was missing, and to alert the rescue team, and in Essex, one of the earliest ringing societies was formed as a result of a ringer being lost. This was at Saffron Walden, in 1623, when a band of ringers agreed to ring should anyone be lost in the dense woods that covered this part of the county in the seventeenth century. In Shropshire, at Church Stretton, the custom became established too late, after a villager had lost himself in a storm on the Long Mynd and perished as a result. His family left money for a muffled peal to be rung on the anniversary of this sad event, and it is known today as 'The Dead Man's Peal'.

In Lincolnshire 10 shillings was left to the ringers annually by a man lost on the moors, known as the Corringham Scroggs, for the bells to act as a guide to other wayfarers during the winter months.

Even at sea ships have been saved from wreck by the ringing of church bells. This happened at Burgh-le-Marsh, also in Lincolnshire, when the tenor bell of the parish church alerted the captain of a passing ship that his navigation was at fault and that he was heading for the rocks. Once safely ashore, the captain donated a silken bell-rope for the tenor. He also presented to the church an acre of land at Orby, the rent of which was to be given to the ringers for ringing on the anniversary of the event. This land is still known by the name of Bell-Acre.

Another reason for ringing associated with a lucky escape is that which commemorates Oak Apple Day. This was the day in 1651 when the young Charles II had to climb into an oak tree after the Battle of Worcester to hide from the enemy. He succeeded, and fled to France, to return as king at the Restoration in 1660. Oak Apple Day is celebrated on his birthday, 29 May. This custom seems almost to be dead everywhere, though Christina Hole mentions it as surviving at Wishford, in Wiltshire. Here the custom is associated with the collecting of oak branches from Grovely Woods nearby, and there is a grand procession round the village accompanied by the ringing of the church bells.*

A tragic event, as distinct from a lucky escape, is found at Wells Cathedral and some parish churches when the bells are rung half muffled for Holy Innocents' Day on 28 December.

In Kent there is an interesting ringing tradition based on Tonbridge School, a large boys' public school founded by a member of the Skinners' Company about 1560. On

* *English Custom and Usage* (Batsford, 1941.)

Skinners' Day representatives from the Company visit the school, and boy ringers were paid to awaken the school staff and members of the Company that morning. The bells were rung at 7 a.m. but the boys who were not ringing went bathing in the river and an hour or so later assembled outside the inn in Tonbridge where the representatives of the Skinners' Company were staying. They cheered and shouted and stopped only when the Master of the Skinners' Company, arrayed in his dressing-gown, came to the balcony and made a short speech. In the evening the bells were rung again, as a summons to dinner. The processions and much of the ceremonial are now no more, though the ringers still act as an alarm clock on Skinners' Day.

There are not many other bell traditions connected with education but one of the oldest is found at Oxford. Here the six-ton bell 'Great Tom' of Christchurch College is still rung 101 times at five past nine each evening. Formerly it was chimed to correspond with the number of undergraduates in residence, and each of them had to be back in college by the final stroke.

A character in C.P. Snow's novel *The Masters* remarks that nine English traditions out of ten date only from the latter half of the nineteenth century. Certainly many were revived during this period, just as the present obsession with what is termed 'nostalgia' is reviving many other traditions. But one tradition regarding bellringing is hidden in past history, and its origins are difficult to unravel.

This is the tradition of ringing, and choral singing, from the top of Oxford's Magdalen Tower, at dawn on May Morning. There are many theories about how it began, and the different opinions of various historians make research difficult and the true facts almost impossible to ascertain. The several legends have been examined and discussed in an informative treatise by Roy Judge.*

According to him the story began in 1484 when the manor of Slymbridge, Gloucestershire, was owned by the Earl of Berkeley. At this time Magdalen College was being

* *Folklore*, volume 97,i. (1986).

built, and the Earl agreed to donate the sum of £10 annually for prayers to be said for the repose of his soul when the time came. The manor of Slymbridge later passed to Henry VII but the money continued to be paid and prayers said.

The Bell Tower of Magdalen was completed in 1504 and the bells were hung the following year. When the King died in 1509, a requiem Mass was said and undoubtedly the bells would have been rung muffled. Henry died towards the end of April, and the funeral was held at the beginning of May, which might be the reason why the tradition continued on 1 May.

What is very difficult to discover is the reason why the singing was done from the *top* of the tower. Richard Parson, writing at the end of the seventeenth century, described the location as 'well established', and a contemporary writer, Anthony Wood, refers to it as done 'according to ancient custom'. As the tower had been in existence for less than 200 years when he wrote this, 'ancient custom' seems a slight exaggeration.

From about this time there seems to have arisen a curious custom involving the 'jangling' of the bells. This tradition was mentioned by John Pointer when he wrote in 1749: 'Custom on all Commemoration Days to have the Bells rung in a confus'd Manner and without any Order, this being the Primitive Way of Ringing.'

By the turn of the century the religious connotations of the ceremony seem largely to have been forgotten, and though the choristers of Magdalen continued to sing their *Hymnus Eucharisticus* from the top of the tower on May Morning, they did not do so without opposition from the plebs below. They were subjected to rude and blasphemous singing, and the sounding of trumpets, horns and rattles, together with the beating of drums or any clangorous object. The enraged choristers retaliated by smuggling rotten eggs up to the top of the tower and pelting the crowd below. How this disgraceful situation was partly resolved is described by the Reverend John Bloxham, Fellow of Magdalen, writing in 1844: 'There are some now living who remember the mode of singing the hymn at an early period of this century as irreverent. The principal function of the choristers seemed to be to throw down rotten eggs on the people below. Old Munday, the principal Porter, tried to remedy this by standing at the bottom of the Tower staircase and tapping the pockets of the choristers, as they passed him, with the Tower key.'

Another memory of those days, with its curious combination of singing and ringing, is provided by J R Green writing in 1901. He was a chorister in the late 1840s, and one cannot help feeling that his own memories are bathed in a somewhat nostalgic glow: ' ... the sun was fully up, surplices were thrown off, and with a burst of gay laughter the choristers rushed down the little tower-stair, flung themselves on the bell-ropes, "jangling" the bells in rough mediaeval fashion till the tower shook from side to side. And then as they tired, came the ringers; and the jangle died away into one of those peals, change after change, which used to cast such a spell over my boyhood.'

The origin of jangling the bells seems as difficult to discover as the custom of singing from the top of the tower, and in 1872 Henry Bramley, a noted Oxford historian, wrote that it was 'a very interesting survival of a remote past grafted from some Pagan rite'.

The May Morning ringing has been carried out by experienced ringers since the day in 1883 when a too-enthusiastic chorister grabbed the rope of a bell that was 'up' and nearly strangled himself. The whole thing has become a huge tourist attraction, and folk-dancing, barber-shop quartets and other forms of jollifications even today compete with the choristers and ringers. As Roy Judge remarks: 'It has great goodwill and a considerable potential for enjoyment.'

As has been often remarked, our school days are governed by bells. Indeed, a school bell in Lincolnshire dated 1713 carries the inscription: '*Magistro et Discipules Sono*' ('I sound for master and pupils').

Tradition being a living and constantly growing thing, it is pleasant to note a new 'tradition' established at Beaudesert Lower School in Leighton Buzzard, Beds. When the original Victorian school was demolished in 1981 and the new school opened, the head teacher, Mr

Will Holm, decided it would be pleasant to have something from the old school gracing the new one. He chose the old school bell, which, after cleaning and refurbishing by the local Rotary Club, was presented to the school and now hangs in the entrance-hall. The children were fascinated by it and all wanted to ring it. Mr Holm therefore instituted the custom that on the last day of each summer term every child who was leaving to go to the middle school in September would be allowed a ring on the bell. All children at the school, therefore, ring the school bell once during their time there. Though this may remind us of Mr Sam Goldwyn's remark to his writers that what he wanted were 'some new clichés', it is a genuine example of a tradition in the making.

One bell curiosity comes from Winstone, Gloucestershire. Here in November 1986 a quarter peal was rung to mark the retirement of circuit judge Anthony Bulger QC from Gloucester Crown Court. The band of six ringers consisted of two magistrates, two police officers and two solicitors. The local Press had a field-day with jokes about 'going to a peal'!

Apart from the extraordinary request of the misogynist Thomas Nashe of Bath, one of the oddest reasons for ringing is due to the ordinary Englishman's love of fiction. In 1741 the reading public were eagerly awaiting the final instalments of Samuel Richardson's novel *Pamela* – the first true novel in the English language. At Upton, near Slough, when the bells of the old church were rung to signal that the final instalment had been delivered to the local bookshop, near riots took place and the entire company of would-be readers repaired to the Red Lion to find out how the book ended. Sir William Herschel, the celebrated astronomer and discoverer of Uranus, lived nearby and did not approve at all. He described it as "the naïvest reason ever put forward for the ringing of bells".

Since that time many reasons have been put forward for ringing, and today's ringers still look for events to celebrate just as they did in the early years of change-ringing. In May 1987, for example, a quarter-peal rung at St John's Church, Darlington, gained the unusual distinction of being not only recorded in the pages of *The*

Ringing World but also reported nationally. The occasion was the baptism of little Nicola Bell, known as 'the miracle baby'. Her mother, Deborah, had suffered a brain haemorrhage and was kept on a life-support machine only until the child in her womb was mature enough to be born. The quarter-peal was also in thanksgiving for Deborah's life and in recognition of the devotion shown by the staff of the Maternity Unit of Middlesbrough General Hospital.

A less pertinent reason for ringing was given by the ringers of Rothwell, Northants, in 1960, when they rang a peal 'to commemorate the 100th anniversary of Fydor Dostoyevsky's return to St Petersburg after ten years' exile in Siberia'. It is unlikely Dostoyevsky was a ringer.

One of the most pointed reasons for ringing was seen at Hereford in 1871, when a local innkeeper lost his licence. The aggrieved publican, who was also a ringer, gathered a band of friends and in retaliation proceeded to ring the church bells nonstop during the 'permitted hours'. Said the *Ledbury Free Press*, with righteous indignation: 'This is the grossest belfry outrage we ever heard of.' The protest was effective, for the licence was soon restored at a hastily convened meeting of the licensing justices.

Through the centuries many other people have attempted to silence bells in Britain. One of the earliest objectors to bells, and in fact to any form of 'noise' during a service, was the Cistercian monk Abbot Aelred who wrote in 1146: 'Why such organs and so many cymbala in the church? What with the sound of the bells, the noise of the cymbala and the united strains of the organ pipes, the common folk stand with wondering faces, trembling and amazed.'

The traditional ability of bells to disperse storms and bad weather is dealt with later in this book, (see p.87), but the reverse of this belief is seen in an incident during the Commonwealth. In 1656, when the church at Withycombe Raleigh, Devon, was almost demolished in a violent storm, one parishioner, John Childley, wrote to Oliver Cromwell himself requesting a ban on all ringing, which, he claimed, had resulted in an Act of God by attracting the storm and so destroying the church.

In 1724 a Dr Martin Howard, living at Hammersmith, which was then a village west of London and now part of the metropolis, objected to the tenor bell being chimed at 5 a.m. as an alarm-clock for those who had to go to work. A wealthy man, he promised to provide a clock and cupola at his own expense if the chiming stopped. His offer was gratefully accepted.

In Carlisle in 1745 the cathedral ringers were misguided enough to ring for Bonnie Prince Charlie when he came through the city. Their celebrations were destined to be short, and the corporation, loyal to George II, imposed a ban on ringing at the cathedral for the next 180 years. Fortunately the ban was not upheld that long.

Ringing in cities seems to have upset many people. In 1796 the rector of St Peter's in Lincoln was petitioned 'to take steps to prevent the ringers of the church from ringing so frequently for gentlemen coming to town and on other business'.

Opposition to the ringers themselves, rather than ringing, was a feature of clerical life during much of the nineteenth century. But still in this century opposition to bells continues, sometimes from unexpected sources, as in 1935 when Fleet Street journalists tried to stop ringing at the nearby church of St Bride's on the pretext that it was disturbing their concentration. Nothing happened at the time but their wish was granted in 1941 when the church was bombed. About the same time as this was happening in London, the traditional ringing-in of the New Year was stopped at York Minster when hooligans began throwing bottles at the windows. After a ban of nearly fifty years ringing in the New Year began again in 1985.

The advent of World War II brought about the longest ban on ringing ever known in Britain. When the sirens announced the outbreak of war at 11 a.m. on Sunday 3 September 1939, they precipitated chaos and misunderstandings within minutes. There was a blue and cloudless sky and no apparent enemy in sight, and in any case nobody had the slightest idea what to do. Fortunately the 'all-clear' was sounded within minutes and it proved later to have been a false alarm. Not the least of the confusion in the weeks that followed was created by the Control of

Noise (Defence) Order, which most people thought meant a ban on all bellringing. Though church bells were specifically exempted from the Order, this had not been made clear. However, one unfortunate cleric in Lincolnshire was imprisoned for twelve days for allowing ringing, but the sentence was quashed on appeal.

Once the situation was understood, ringing began again during 1940, though with sadly depleted bands, until the episode of Dunkirk in May of that year. There British and other forces were evacuated by a flotilla of little ships – an event surprisingly referred to as a 'victory' by the British ever since. After Dunkirk it was confidently expected that the Germans would very soon mount an invasion of the south of England by sea and air. Great thought was given as to how warning of such an event might be given immediately throughout the land. At a meeting at Tunbridge Wells between General Ironside and General Home, it was decided that church bells would be rung to signal an invasion and for no other reason. Accordingly, on 13 June 1940, a new Control of Noise Order came into force, and on the following Sunday, for the first time in a thousand years, not a single church bell was heard in the land.

This Order created more problems than it solved, for it had not been thought through with any detail. One immediate query was – who was going to ring the bells when the invasion came? The Home Guard volunteered to do this, until it was pointed out to them that only experienced ringers could make the bells sound and that it might be highly dangerous for any untutored ringer to try. In this connection the redoubtable Dorothy L. Sayers, who had established herself as something of an authority on ringing since the publication of *The Nine Tailors*, wrote the following letter to the *Daily Telegraph*: 'I have been waiting, fascinated, for someone in authority to realize that to order a completely raw hand to run along and ring a church bell is rather like ordering him to run along and milk a savage and reluctant cow; the net result would be much the same, except that the bell can kick much harder than the cow.'

The Home Guard could not do the job, and how could

the local band of ringers be assembled quickly when many of them were working miles away? Another problem was that, when the ban was suddenly imposed, without warning of any kind, ringing had been going on in some towers, and the bells had been left in the 'up' position. As they could not be left like this for the duration of the war, and as they would undoubtedly sound as they were 'rung down', a general dispensation to do this had to be obtained after the ban had been imposed. As the government did not think fit to make the situation generally known, this created panic in many places and caused the Home Guard to turn out. Again,the government had given no guidance to the public as to what to do when they heard the church bells ring. No information was available until March 1941, when it was decided that the ringing of the bells would be a sign to the Home Guard only that enemy troops had landed nearby. The general public was advised to 'take no notice'!

In the light of this lack of direction and general muddle it is not surprising that there were a few false alarms. In August 1940 the Germans dropped nearly a hundred empty parachutes over the Midlands in order to create a panic and test the reactions of the populace. Some churches rang their bells, and the Home Guard was alerted until it was realized that the parachutes were harmless. Other incidents occurred when imaginative individuals spotted what they thought were parachutists landing, but none of these incidents was confirmed. During the Battle of Britain in 1940, a party of four German civilians in a rowing-boat was intercepted while attempting to land on the south coast, apparently briefed to study troop movements. In a state of near panic, the authorities issued an instruction to signal the 'red alert', meaning 'invasion imminent', and once more the bells rang out and the tireless Home Guard mustered until the scare was over.

Another panic was initiated that same year when, off the Cornish coast, an apparent armada loomed out of the fog heading for the shore. It was, in fact, the local fishing fleet returning early to port after an unexpectedly successful haul, but before this was realized church bells began to ring beween Penzance and Bristol.

The banning of bells in wartime was by no means

popular with everyone, and much correspondence ensued in the national Press about 'the silence that can be felt' – as one correspondent put it. In the House of Lords, in July 1940, Lord Mottistone said: 'We must abandon this faint-hearted policy wherever it is found.' He ended his speech with the somewhat sombre words: 'Let England hear again the bells and let us meet death with a smile if it must come.'

But the ban continued. It was lifted for a few hours on 15 November 1942 to celebrate the victory at El Alamein and also for an hour on Christmas Day that year, and then was finally lifted on 27 May 1943. When the Prime Minister was asked in the House what alternative form of alarm would be used in the event of invasion, he replied, in typically Churchillian style: 'I have every reason to believe that the news will be bound to leak out!'

Isolated examples of attempts to stop bellringing have been seen since the war. One such was the attempt of the Royal Cumberland Youths to ring a peal at St Martin-in-the-Fields on 1 May 1951 as part of the Festival of Britain. Unfortunately it coincided with a May Day rally in Trafalgar Square, and ringing was stopped by the police after ten minutes as it was thought that the speakers could not be heard and this would make the large crowd restless. It is possible, of course, that the crowd would have been even more restless had they heard the message.

On another occasion, at Bishopwearmouth in Tyne & Wear, ringing on practice-night was stopped when the police, investigating a burglary at a shop in the town, found they could not decipher any messages on their portable radios.

One man who was not impressed by the traditional ringing during Christmas was a newcomer to the village of Uffculme, in Devon, in December 1986. He complained to the vicar that the Christmas Eve ringing was disturbing the sleep of his nine-month-old daughter, and much to the rage of the locals the vicar agreed that the ringing should cease. There was an immediate outcry from the village's population of 2,000, one of whom remarked that complaining about the bells was 'like buying a house next to a railway station and then objecting to the trains'. It seems the matter was finally resolved by a national newspaper offering to pay the cost of double-glazing the complainant's house.

But antipathy towards the sound of bells is nothing new. The Eastern Counties has long been a centre for ringing enthusiasts, particularly after changes and methods became popular. One band in Norfolk in the eighteenth century was so keen that they organized a weekly ringing practice at six in the morning, causing a local resident to pen these lines:

> Ye rascally ringers, inveterate foes,
> Disturbers of those who are fond of repose,
> I wish for the peace and quiet of these lands
> That ye had round your necks what ye pull with your hands!

6
Magic Bells

The devil steals a bell from the ruins of old Halvergate church, Norfolk

For many centuries bells of all kinds have been credited with magical properties. In medieval times, as we have seen, the sound of bells was reputed to cure the mentally unstable, to force criminals to confess, to confuse and rout an enemy and generally to dispel evil spirits. This last attribute may be clearly seen in the use of the 'passing bell' and the 'death knell' before and after death.

St Patrick claimed to be able to banish imps and goblins by throwing his small bell into the air but, as with many stories from Ireland, this must be treated with a degree of scepticism.

A very common belief was that the sound of bells could dispel storms and bad weather. In 1493 Wynkin de Worde,

Caxton's partner, wrote in *The Golden Legend*: 'The evil spiryte that ben in the regyon of th'ayre doute moche when they here the bells rongen when it thondreth, and when grete tempeste, and outrages of whether happen to the ende the fiendes and wycked spirytes should be abashed and flee and cease the movynge of the tempest.'

Though de Worde's narrative was printed at the end of the fifteenth century, it was an amalgam of stories from a thirteenth-century manuscript, so the superstition regarding bells and storms was already very old. Even so, there were those who proclaimed their disbelief in the tradition, none more loudly than Bishop Latimer. This extraordinary champion of the Reformation (who once preached a sermon on playing-cards, showing how 'trumps' could get one to heaven) derided what he described as 'this foolery': 'You know, when there was a storm or fearful weather, then we rang the holy bells; they were they that must make all things well; they must drive away the devil! But I tell you, if the holy bells would serve against the devil, or that he might be put away by their sound, no doubt we should soon banish him out of England; for I think that if all the bells in England should be rung together at a certain hour, there would be almost no place but some bells might be heard there, and so the devil should have no abiding place in England.'

From the bishop's comment that there was scarcely anywhere in England outside the range of church bells, it must be assumed that most churches at the time had bells, though monastic bells had been silenced at the Reformation. There are many notes in church accounts authorizing payment to ringers at a time of storm, as found at Sandwich, Kent, where the 1464 entry states: 'For bread and drink for the ringers in the great thunderying'. At one time old St Paul's Cathedral, in London, had a special fund to pay the ringers 'for ringing the hallowed belle in great tempeste or lightenings'.

Just how the sound of bells was able to dispel storms is not known but presumably it was thought to be due to the sound rising and causing an atmospheric disturbance above the steeple. Long-lived though this belief was, by the seventeenth century it had little credibility left and some clerics were even of the opinion that bells in their steeples actually attracted storms. In 1650 the Reverend Thomas Fuller, later to be famous for his *Lives of the Worthies of England,* said it was untrue that church bells were proof against lightning and went on to quote a tale that during a violent storm in the Channel the only churches struck along the south coast were those whose bells were ringing at the time. Yet despite the views of such eminent divines as Latimer and Fuller the belief continued well into the nineteenth century, for there is an account in the *Torquay Directory* as late as 1870 of the church bells being rung at Dawlish to dispel lightning and thunder.

If church bells were capable of dispelling the evil sprites that caused storms, they were also efficacious against those elements causing illnesses and plagues. This is seen on the inscription of a bell at Christchurch, Dorset, which translated from the Latin, says: 'May the Festal Lamb be near at hand that He may of his goodness put plagues to flight.' Again this was a belief that took a long time to die, and as late as the end of the nineteenth century a bell at Grimsby, Humberside, was cast with the legend: 'With my voice I praise the Lord for pestilence vanished.' The ringing of handbells during the Great Plague of 1665 may well have been an injunction to 'bring out your dead' but may also have been a method of trying to dispel the fatal vapours that were causing the epidemic.

Another piece of magic attributed to bells is their ability to ring themselves without human agency, or to be heard over a wide area as a sign of some important happening. There is a strong tradition that 'magical' ringing was heard in 1253 when the Bishop of London was travelling through Northamptonshire on his way to visit the famous Bishop Grosseteste at Buckden. Suddenly the travellers heard the sonorous note of a great bell, though there was no convent or monastery within many miles. On arrival at Buckden they found that the Bishop had died at the precise moment they had heard the bell. Other travellers in the area, it seems, had also heard the bell, including a hunting-party lost in the forest who were thus guided back to the town.

Only two years later, in 1255, another example of 'miraculous' ringing took place at the burial of Little St Hugh, said to have been murdered in Lincoln by the Jews. An old ballad relates:

> And a' the bells of Merrie Lincoln
> Without men's hands were rung;
> And a' the books of merrie Lincoln
> Were read without men's tongues;
> And ne'er was sich a burial
> Sin Adam's days begun.

The North of England provides us with another example of bells with magical attributes, this time associated with Durham Cathedral. In 1429 most of the building was destroyed by fire whilst the monks were at their midnight devotions. The monks prayed to St Cuthbert, who is enshrined in the cathedral, and though most of the building was destroyed, the tower and its bells remained intact. Every year since, on the anniversary of the event, choristers climb the tower to sing a *Te Deum* in thanksgiving.

Apart from their ability to ring on their own, bells also seem to have the capacity to punish wrongdoers. A very early example of this comes from South Wales and concerns the Glamorgan monk St Illtyd, reputed to be a kinsman of King Arthur, and a soldier before entering the church. He foundered a chapel in Glamorgan for which he obtained a small bell for the roof with which to call the faithful to prayer. A local chieftain stole the bell and took it across the Severn to England, carried by a horse. But in its new setting the bell refused to ring and a string of disasters struck the chieftain. In despair he put the bell once again round the neck of the horse, which immediately set off, without bidding, across the Severn back to Wales. Reaching Glamorgan, it suddenly stopped, lowered its head and allowed the bell to fall to the ground. The village was Llantwit Major, near the coast, and here St Illtyd established his new church.

Another version of this story says that a bell was being sent by St Gildas to the bishop of St Davids in

Pembrokeshire. The way led past St Illtyd's chapel, and the saint expressed his great admiration for the bell. When it finally reached St Davids, the bell refused to ring and the bishop, taking this as a sign, returned it to St Illtyd for his new church. St Gildas features in another legend concerning a bell. This time he gave a small bell to one of his monks and sent him to Cornwall on missionary work. He was to stop when the bell began ringing of its own accord, which it did when the monk reached a village near Falmouth where he established a chapel.

There are several stories concerning miraculous bells in Wales, most of them recounted by Giraldus Cambrensis, the twelfth-century historian. In one of them a man who had offended the local prince was confined to a castle near Brecon. His wife was the owner of a small bell, said to have belonged to St David and therefore miraculous, which she offered to give to the prince in return for her husband. The prince agreed, took the bell but refused to release her husband. He hung the bell on view on a wall of the castle. That very night the entire village and the castle with it were mysteriously engulfed in flames. The only survivors were the prisoner, his wife and the section of the castle wall bearing the bell.

North Wales, too, has its stories of bells. During the reign of Queen Elizabeth I the bishop of Bangor (a man who lived permanently beyond his means) decided to augment his income by selling the cathedral bells to France. They were duly taken down and loaded on a ship, and the vessel set sail. Within two hours, and whilst still in sight of the coast, the ship founded in a flat calm, taking the bells with it and leaving no survivors. At exactly that moment the rapacious bishop was struck blind!

Another very well-known example of retribution exacted by a bell is described by Robert Southey in his epic poem 'The Inchcape Rock'. The poem begins:

> The Abbot of Aberbrothok
> Had placed the bell on the Inchcape Rock;
> On a buoy in a storm it floated and swung
> And over the waves its warning rung;
> When the Rock was hid by the surge's swell
> The mariners heard the warning bell;

And then they knew the perilous Rock
And blessed the Abbot of Aberbrothok.

The poem goes on to relate how a well-known pirate of the area named (inevitably) Ralph the Rover, stole the bell from the rock and hurriedly left Scottish waters to plunder and pillage elsewhere. He at length returned to Scotland but in the area near the Inchcape Rock his ship was caught in a storm. Having no bell on it, the Rock was unrecognized and Ralph the Rover and his crew perished in the ocean. The dramatic end is described by Southey as follows:

But even in his dying fear
One dreadful sound could the Rover hear,
A sound as on the Inchcape Bell
The Devil below was ringing his knell.

Wordsworth, too, has a poem about a miraculous bell, this time concerning the medieval St Catherine and her handmaiden, improbably named Mabel. This is yet another of the many legends recounting how a saint was to carry a silent bell until it began to ring on its own. This it did in the area round Ledbury, Herefordshire, where the saint, acting on her divine briefing and no doubt with Mabel's help, built herself a chapel.

Bells ringing on their own have not always been benign but occasionally a sign of displeasure. In a short treatise on miracles published by the Catholic diocese of Westminster in 1825, there is an account of how some robbers, pillaging a church while the villagers were asleep, decided to ring the bells as an act of bravado. To their consternation, once the bells had begun to ring they would not stop, neither could the thieves detach themselves from the ropes and they were thus forced to be carried up and down until the villagers came and apprehended them.

Probably more common than any other tradition concerning bells is their association with water – either drowned in the sea or vanishing into a river. In many of these tales it is related how the bells can be heard ringing beneath the water, something which appears to be a physical impossibility. Yet the tales are numerous and still believed.

One such legend combining retribution with underwater ringing comes from Cornwall – like Wales, a source of many strange stories. The picturesque little town of Boscastle has no bells, but in the Middle Ages a peal of four was ordered from a foundry in Holland. The bells were stored on the deck of the ship to make the journey, which was calm and uneventful. When the north Cornish coast was reached, the pilot from Boscastle came aboard and, being a religious man, gave thanks loudly to God for the safe arrival of the bells. The captain, however, was anything but religious and insisted that the bells had arrived without mishap entirely because of his faultless seamanship and that God had nothing to do with it. Immediately a storm arose and the bells slid off the deck into the sea. To this day Boscastle folk maintain that in stormy weather the bells can be heard ringing under the water. That church still has no bells.

Another story of bells sliding off a ship into the sea comes from Whitby. In 1539, during the dissolution of the monasteries, the abbey bells were dismantled and sold to the King against the wishes of the local people. They, too, were carried on the deck but only two miles from shore the bells slipped from the deck into the sea, from where they can be heard ringing to this day.

Stolen bells can also cause trouble, especially if tactless remarks are made, as is demonstrated by this incident from Wiltshire. At a remote village church the single bell was stolen by Satan and dropped into the nearby river. Holy incantations on the part of the rector and some physical effort with ropes by the villagers succeeded in raising the bell to the surface. At this point the rector, overcome with excitement, cried out: 'In spite of all the devils in Hell, here comes our old bell!' Immediately the ropes broke and the bell sank back into the water.

There is a rather similar incident from Knowlton, in Dorset, but in this case no tactless remark. The locals tried three times to pull the bell out of the river but each time they were unsuccessful. A local rhyme runs:

Medieval bells lost at sea outside Boscastle harbour on their way over from the Netherlands

All the devils in Hell
Could never pull up Knowlton's bell!

In the Tintagel area of Cornwall we meet another of the many legends that abound, this time centred on the ruins of the chapel of St Nectan. The saint had a small bell mounted on the roof of the chapel which could be heard at sea and served as a warning to sailors of the rocks below. When he was dying, he ordered that the bell be taken down and thrown into a small stream whose waters immediately boiled until the bell had sunk out of sight. With his last breath St Nectan said that England was fast becoming irreligious and that the bell would ring again only when the true faith had been restored to the country. A century or more later some local workmen attempted to find the bell by diverting the stream. As they worked, a bell began ringing and a ghostly voice intoned: 'The child is not yet born who will recover this treasure.' The work stopped forthwith and the bell remains silent and submerged.

A Scottish legend manages to combine several magical attributes in one bell – that of St Fillan in Perthshire. In 1778 the rector of the village published a book describing how, in earlier times, the single church bell had been immersed in a holy pool which gave it special powers. It was kept on a tombstone in the churchyard and much used to cure cases of insanity and epilepsy. The procedure was to bring the bell into the church overnight, where it was securely bound with ropes. In the morning the patient was brought to the church, and the bell was untied and placed on his head. Unfortunately there is no record of the success or otherwise of this treatment, though presumably it was at least as effective as John Wesley's injunction, in his *Primitive Physik* of 1749, to cure a madness by filling a hat with snow and putting it on the victim's head. The bell also had other 'magical' properties including the ability to ring loudly if illegally removed from its tombstone site and to continue ringing until replaced.

While the use of bells to dispel epidemics is well authenticated, there are few instances of a bell being used on individual patients. Oddly enough, the ability to cure has been given to the ropes by which the bells are rung rather than to the bells themselves. It was once thought that a bellrope brought from the church and tied round the belly of a pregnant woman would ease the birth. Alternatively the woman would climb up into the ringing-chamber where the rope would be tied to her skirt (or her shoe) and the bell chimed three times. This, too, would ensure a satisfactory delivery. It was also a well-known fact that the oil from the bearings of the bell and its wheel was a standard remedy for bronchitis and related troubles if smeared on the chest.

Common around the coasts of Britain, but particularly from East Anglia, come stories of villages engulfed by the eroding sea. Probably the most famous of these is the Suffolk village of Dunwich which, from the fourteenth century, has slowly been engulfed by the ever-creeping tide. During the nineteenth century the pace quickened and one by one each house, the village shop, the inns and finally the church all disappeared beneath the waves, the spire being visible until 1919. Inevitably there exists a legend that at certain times the bells of Dunwich church can be heard ringing under the waves. There is a similar story concerning a former coastal village near Blackpool in Lancashire, and another from Kenfig in Glamorgan.

Most stories of drowned bells are apocryphal, though plentiful, and stories about them persist. An incident of a rather different kind was recorded in 1976 when the 'peal' page of *The Ringing World* listed the names of those who had rung a full peal at the church at Derwent Woodlands, Derbyshire. Local ringers soon advised the magazine that this could not possibly be, and must be a hoax, as the parish of Derwent Woodlands is now at the bottom of a reservoir, though the bells were removed before the valley was flooded. Those reported as having rung this peal were not amused, nor was the editor of *The Ringing World*, who has suffered from many hoaxes of this kind in the past.

Not only do legends persist of bells ringing under water but there are many stories of them ringing below ground. It is possible that such tales arise from the dim folk-memory of the itinerant medieval bellfounders digging pits in a field in which to cast their bells. The original pits were deep and in many instances have remained with the name of 'bell field' or 'bell acre' and the added embellishment of the sound of bells being occasionally heard. Another source of such legends may well be due to some bells being dismantled by the monks at the time of the dissolution of the monasteries and buried.

Earthquakes and landslides also account for legends of subterranean bells still heard ringing, as at the former village of Fisherty Brow in Cumbria. Centuries ago, it is said, a landslide engulfed the village one Sunday during what must have been a very moving sermon. Local children were once bidden to put their ears to the ground on Sunday mornings to hear the lost church bells still ringing. There is a similar story concerning the village of Hadstock, in Essex (though here the village and its church have been rebuilt), and at Roxby, Lincolnshire, a huge mass of stones is said to mark the site of a former church whose bells can still be heard.

At Raleigh, Nottinghamshire, an entire village is said to have been swallowed by a landslide and until the middle of the nineteenth century all the villagers would gather at the site on Christmas morning to hear the 'magic' ringing of the bells.

Some buried bells are said to have been the result of criminal action by Satan himself, as at the Norfolk village of Halvergate, where a fire destroyed the former church and left only the bells intact. They were valuable items and it was proposed to sell them, but unfortunately the parson and churchwardens could not decide how the proceeds should be divided. While the argument was raging, the Devil arrived and made off with the bells. Hotly pursued by the parson, who was evidently learned enough to know the appropriate Latin prayers against devils who stole bells, Satan dropped them into a boggy field, where they sank out of sight. They have never been seen since. The field is to this day known as the 'bell-hole'. There are almost identical tales of bells buried in marshland from Berkshire and Shropshire.

One very strange story comes from Trevethin, Gwent,

where in the eighteenth century a child was taken up into the belfry to be shown the bells. Unfortunately they were in the 'up' position and, when the boy attempted to push one, it turned over and crushed him to death. The offending bell was taken down and buried without ceremony in a field near the church. For many years after, it was strongly believed that every time a child died in the village the bell could be heard tolling.

Not all ghostly ringing is the province of church bells. Now and again we encounter apparently supernatural ringing in houses, usually in Victorian dwellings where a system of bells in the kitchen was used as an indication that assistance was needed in the upper floors. The well-known expert on the supernatural, Mr Harry Price, tells of an incident in Earl Street, Westminster, of bells in the kitchen ringing so loudly and continuously that it sent a maid into convulsions. The sound of handbells ringing was also noted at the famous hauntings of Borley Rectory, Essex, in the 1920s.

Perhaps the best-authenticated example of this kind is that which occurred in Suffolk at Bealings House, near Woodbridge, in 1834. Here, on Sunday 2 February of that year, the bells in the servants' quarters began to ring in what has been described as a manner 'both protracted and frenzied'. The owner of the house was Major Edward Moor, a Fellow of the Royal Society and one unlikely to be taken in by any kind of hoax. The ringing began while he was at church, but at first only intermittently and by one bell. The same thing happened on the Monday. On Tuesday the manifestations began in earnest, and Major Moor, who later wrote a book on the subject,* came home to hear that all the bells in the kitchen had been ringing violently at intervals for some hours. He went into the kitchen after ensuring that the rest of the house remained unoccupied and recorded: 'I was intently looking at the bells and suddenly five bells began ringing violently; so violently was it that I should not have been surprised if they had been shaken from their fastening.' The bells

* *An Account of the Mysterious Ringing of Bells at Great Bealings, Suffolk* (1834).

continued to sound daily until on 27 March, after fifty-four days, they ceased as suddenly as they had begun.

One well-known legend in Britain is concerned with sleigh bells, even though it does not originate here but abroad and has gained its fame through a theatrical production. This is *The Bells* – the Victorian melodrama made famous by the performance of the young Henry Irving, in London, in 1871.

The play itself, said to be based on a true story, was the product of two French writers and was first produced under the title of *Le juif polonais,* in Paris in 1869. It was not well-received and in the following year was purchased by the American impresario, Colonel Hezekiah Bateman, who mounted the piece at the Lyceum Theatre, London, in 1871 with Irving in the lead. As was the custom in those days of giving theatrical value-for-money by presenting a double-bill, it was to follow a dramatization of scenes from *Pickwick,* in which Irving played Mr Jingle.

The story concerns a certain Matthias who, with his family, keeps an inn in a remote part of Alsace. One evening the sound of sleigh-bells across the snow heralds the arrival of a tall and sinister looking Polish Jew who seeks accommodation for the night. Matthias is suspicious that he will not be paid, but the Jew shows him a purse full of gold that he carries on his belt. Matthias agrees to give him a bed, but while he sleeps kills him with an axe and disposes of the body by throwing it into a nearby quarry. As a result of the theft, Matthias and his family prosper but the innkeeper is haunted by the sound of sleigh-bells approaching which perpetually reminds him of his crime. On the eve of his daughter's wedding to the local chief-of-police, Matthias dreams that he has been forced to confess and is about to be hanged. With a loud cry of 'Take the rope from my neck', the murderer leaps from the bed and falls dead before his frightened family.

Irving was determined that every detail of the production should be dramatic and had had a hoop made mounted with bells almost exactly like the bell-harness worn by horses. During his electric performance as Matthias, the bells were carried across the stage behind the backdrop, simulating the sound coming from a distance, approaching and then fading away again.

The Bells was an outstanding success at the Lyceum due to Irving's quite extraordinary performance, and London society flocked to see it. It ran for 151 nights – a very long run for those days – and was given at Sandringham before members of the royal family at the command of Queen Victoria. Later it opened Irving's highly successful American tour. In later years the famous critic James Agate was to remark 'If our young playgoers saw Irving in *The Bells* today, they would burst like electric-light bulbs!'

Successful though the play was, it unfortunately caused the ruin of Irving's marriage. On the first night there was the usual back-stage party which he and his wife attended and where he was complimented on his bravura performance. On their way home by cab, the excited actor told his wife that this was a turning-point in his career and that his future on the stage seemed secure. He was brought down to earth with a jolt when Mrs Irving merely asked 'Are you going to go on making a fool of yourself like this for the rest of your life?' Irving stopped the cab, got out and walked away. He never went home again and did not speak to his wife for the rest of his life.

On the twenty-fifth anniversary of the first night of the play Irving was presented with a two-foot high silver bell designed by Sir Alfred Gilbert RA. The year before, he had been knighted – the first British actor to receive this honour, but the ceremony must have given him painful memories of that fateful evening so many years before. Irving died while on tour in 1905 and was still playing in *The Bells* a few days before his death. In this century the play had a successful revival in the 1920s, with Sir John Martin-Harvey, originally a member of Irving's company, playing the part of Matthias.

Whether caused by magic, divine retribution or mere coincidence, an odd incident at Newmarket the day after Derby Day in 1872 must be mentioned. A local horse, Cremorne, had won the Derby at Epsom and as a result there was great jollification in the town, which included the ringing of the bells of All Saints Church in Newmarket. Though the Suffolk town has been intimately concerned with horse-racing since 1619 and has been the headquarters of the Jockey Club since 1792, not every resident is of a 'horsey' disposition, and many were unhappy about the church bells being used to celebrate a sporting event. What happened on that occasion is best described by the local paper *The Newmarket Journal*.

> Two very singular accidents occurred in the steeple of All Saints church in this town while the ringers were engaged in ringing peals on Thursday last. It appears that the set had just entered a peal in celebration of the Cottage Flower and Horticultural Exhibition, when the second bell jumped from its hangings, and fell heavily upon the beams and floor supporting the frame. Having recovered from the fright the ringers obtained assistance and replaced the bell, and proceeded with their task which they succeeded in accomplishing and retired for refreshment. They re-assembled in the evening on the occasion of the Cremorne Entertainment and while ringing merrily, a second mishap occurred, the treble bell (eight cwt.) suddenly bounced from its place, and like its neighbour – the second – fell with a crash upon the already damaged floor; but fortunately the massive beams prevented her going down; consequently the ringers below escaped injury and the bell was uninjured. The damage to the bell-fittings and the frame could not be repaired in time to allow of further ringing that day, and the merry peals which had enlivened the town were abruptly terminated.

In the next issue of the *Church Bells* magazine, an editorial commented adversely on the incident: 'Two of the bells fell from their places as if refusing to give forth their tones on such an occasion. Accidental as this may have been, let it be looked upon as a rebuke to the parson and churchwardens for allowing such a shameful desecration of the bells of All Saints, Newmarket.'

In this incident one is forcibly reminded of the view of many good people that the fire which destroyed much of the south transept of York Minster in July 1984 was a 'rebuke' by God to the Church of England for the consecration as Bishop of Durham of Dr David Jenkins, who had recently made remarks casting doubts on literal belief in the Creed.

7
The Poetry of Bells

Churches on London's skyline in the seventeenth century

The fact that in strict campanological terms a bell is said to 'speak' has more truth in it than is popularly supposed. When bells ring in a regular rhythm constantly repeated, it is only natural that eventually words will become associated with the notes and rhythm. From infancy most children in Britain are familiar with the rhyme 'Oranges and Lemons' which tells of the message rung out by the bells of various London churches. Though both words and tune are very old, they did not appear in print until 1874, when they were published, together with Walter Crane's delightful illustrations in *Baby's Opera*, a children's book produced by Frederick Warne & Co. The poem does not begin with 'oranges and lemons' as is usually thought and is a good deal longer than most people realize. As a matter of interest it is given here in full:

Gay go up and gay go down
To ring the bells of London Town.
Bulls' eyes and targets
Say the bells of St Margett's.
Brickbats and tiles
Say the bells of St Giles.
Halfpence and farthings
Say the bells of St Martin's.
Oranges and lemons
Say the bells of St Clement's.
Pancakes and fritters
Say the bells of St Peter's.
Two sticks and an apple
Say the bells of Whitechapel.
Old Father Baldpate
Say the slow bells at Aldgate.
You owe me ten shillings
Say the bells of St Helen's.
Pokers and tongs
Say the bells of St John's.
Kettles and pans
Say the bells of St Anne's.
When will you pay me?
Say the bells of Old Bailey.
When I grow rich
Say the bells of Shoreditch.
Pray when will that be?
Say the bells of Stepney.
I'm sure I don't know
Says the great bell of Bow.
Here comes a candle to light you to bed,
Here comes a chopper to chop off your head.

In several other counties similar rhymes exist purporting to translate the sound of the bells. One example comes from Northamptonshire and is on the same lines as 'Oranges and Lemons':

Pancakes and fritters
Says the bells of St Peter's.
Where must we fry 'em?
Say the bells of Cold Higham.
In yonder land furrow

Say the bells of Wellingborough.
You owe me a shilling
Say the bells of Great Billing.
When will you pay me?
Say the bells of Middleton Cheney.
When I am able
Say the bells of Dunstable.
That will never be
Say the bells of Coventry.
Oh yes it will
Says Northampton's great bell.

It will be noted that the rhyme takes almost as many liberties as were taken with the county boundaries in 1974.

Few of the rhymes said to be sounded by the bells in parish churches seem to fit the rhythm of the bells as they actually ring. At Kettering the bells purport to be saying:

Joe Timms Joe Timms,
Come lend me your limbs
And I'll lend you mine tomorrow.
I love my life
As I love my wife
But I'll neither beg nor borrow.

It seems very difficult to fit this in with the twelve bells of the church of SS Peter and Paul. Much easier, though almost as nonsensical, was a verse once attributed to a Devon church:

My dog bite thy dog's tail,
Thy dog bite my dog's tail.

The best-known bells in the world, those of the Westminster Chimes, traditionally say:

Lord through this hour
Be Thou our guide
And by Thy power
No foot shall slide.

Many children's rhymes are based on bells, perhaps the best-known being:

Ding Dong Bell
Pussy's in the well
Who put her in?
Little Johnny Green
Who pulled her out?
Little Tommy Stout
What a naughty boy was that
To try and drown poor pussy-cat!

Another rhyme used by children when racing each other was:

Bell horses, bell horses,
What time of day,
One o'clock, two o'clock
Off and away.

Apart from the verses said to be sounded by the bells, there exists in addition a large number of rhymes, rarely set down but known in each county, referring to some aspect of the bells. They frequently comment on a happening in the locality based on bells, and sometimes there is a scathing reference to the stupidity of the local community. Here is one from Hertfordshire:

Oh the foolish Welwyn people
Sold their bells to buy a steeple

and another from Lincolnshire:

Owerby's parish, wicked people
Sold their bells to build a steeple.

Verses with an almost identical story are found at Shalfleet (Isle of Wight), Hatton (Lincolnshire) and Stoke Newington (North London).

Back again in Hertfordshire, there is a jingle that seems to refer to the custom of wife-swapping – evidently much older than we think. The verse runs:

Lend me your wife today
I'll lend you mine tomorrow.
No! I'll be like the chimes of Ware
I'll neither lend nor borrow!

For some curious reason the few rhymes found in Scotland all have the same theme and only minor variations to fit in with the name of the town. A typical example comes from Lockerbie:

Lockerbie – a dirty place
A kirk without a steeple;
A midden-hole at ilka door
But a canty set o' people.

There is an almost identical verse relating to Banff, but the verse describing Dunkeld is a little more specific:

Was there e'er sic a parish, a parish, a parish,
Was there e'er sic a parish as little Dunkell?
Where they stricket the minister, hanged the precentor,
Dang down the steeple and then drunk the bell.

In England the Essex village of Ugley is notorious for its unfortunate and highly inaccurate name. It has not been neglected in the kind of rhyme under discussion, one of which says:

Ugley church, ugly steeple
Ugly parson, ugly people.

Not surprising that the former Ugley Women's Institute changed its name to The Women's Institute, Ugley Branch. It is very fortunate for these anonymous rhymesters that 'steeple' rhymes with 'people'!

No such limitations arise in true poetry or literature mentioning bells. Longfellow, in his version of *The Golden Legend* (1851) attributes much symbolism not only to the bells and their equipment but also to the ropes and even to the action of the ringers:

The bells themselves are the best of preachers
Their brazen lips are learned teachers
From their pulpits of stone, in the upper air,
Sounding aloft without crack or flaw,
Shriller than trumpet under the law,
Now a sermon, and now a prayer;
The clangorous hammer is the tongue,
This way, that way, beaten and swung,
That from mouth of brass, as from mouth of gold,
Might be taught the testaments, new and old.
And above it the great cross-beam of wood
Representeth the Holy Rood,
Upon which, like the bell, our hopes are hung.
And the wheel wherewith it is swayed and swung
Is the mind of man, that round and round
Sways and maketh the tongue to sound.
And the rope, with its twisted cordage three
Denoteth the Scriptural Trinity
Of Morals, and Symbols, and History:
And the upward and downward motions show
That we touch upon matters high and low;
And the constant change and transmutation
Of action and of contemplation,
Downward, the Scripture brought from on high,
Upward, exalted again to the sky;
Downward, the literal interpretation,
Upward, the vision and mystery.

Enthusiasm and symbolism such as this are rare, though in 1618 Frater Drabicus wrote a 425-page tract in which he said that the sound of bells on earth proved that Heaven would consist of the non-stop ringing of bells. Few have been able to contradict him on this point.

More symbolism is found in the references to bells which abound in Shakespeare. In *Much Ado About Nothing* (Act III, scene ii) Don Pedro describes Benedick thus: 'He hath a heart as sound as a bell and his tongue is the clapper; for what his heart thinks his tongue speaks.' Again, Hamlet describes Ophelia's deranged mind as: 'sweet bells jangled out of tune' (Act III, scene iii). Othello was rather less complimentary with his anguished cry of 'Silence that dreadful bell!'

The poet Keats seems equally anti-campanological when, in his 'Ode to a Nightingale' he says: 'Forlorn! the very word is like a bell.'

The association of bells and death is again expressed in A E Housman's 'A Shropshire Lad' (stanza xxi) in the haunting lines:

The bells they sound on Bredon
And still the steeples hum.
'Come all to church, good people' –
Oh, noisy bells be dumb;
I hear you, I will come'

The New Year is intimately associated with the ringing of bells, and the feeling of entering a new era is splendidly expressed in Tennyson's 'In Memoriam':

Ring out, wild bells, to the wild sky,
The flying cloud, the frosty light;
The year is dying in the night,
Ring out, wild bells, and let him die.

Ring out the old, ring in the new,
Ring happy bells across the snow;
The year is going, let him go,
Ring out the false, ring in the true.

Ring out old shapes of foul disease;
Ring out the narrowing lust of gold,
Ring out the thousand years of old,
Ring in the thousand years of peace.

Ring in the valiant man and free,
The larger heart, the kindlier hand;
Ring out the darkness of the land,
Ring in the Christ that is to be.

Tennyson is a little gloomier in his poem 'Crossing the Bar' with the phrase:

Twilight and the evening bell
And after that the dark!

In a much lighter vein, and a far lower standard of verse, is the poem by the nineteenth-century Irishman Francis Mahony (Father Prout) on Shandon Bells:

The bell on Inchcape Rock

With deep affection
And recollection,
I often think of
Those Shandon bells,
Whose sounds so wild would,
In days of childhood,
Fling round my cradle
Their magic spells.
On this I ponder
Where'er I wander,
And thus grow fonder,
Sweet Cork of thee;
With thy bells of Shandon
That sound so grand on
The pleasant waters
Of the River lee.

The poem runs to seventy lines, and my own favourite stanza is:

There's a bell in Moscow
While on tower and kiosk O
In Saint Sophia
The Turkman gets ....

This poem was once a favourite with schoolboys who were punished by having to copy out one hundred lines of verse. It has the shortest lines of any poem in *The Golden Treasury*.

Another well-known poem with a bell motif but akin to doggerel is that by William Godwin, friend of Charles Lamb and an eminent writer and philosopher in his time, who should have known better. It is 'The Miner's Dream of Home':

The log was burning brightly
'Twas a night that should banish all sin,
For the bells were ringing the Old Year out,
And the New Year in.

Unfortunately this poem seems to have some affinity with George R. Sims' much-parodied epic 'It is Christmas Day in the Workhouse', and this does little for it.

A contemporary of Godwin, a certain William Bowles, wrote a sonnet on Oxford in which bells are mentioned. The poem is quite dreadful, and the opening lines are:

How sweet the tuneful bells' responsive peal
As when, at opening morn, the fragrant breeze
Breathes on the trembling sense of wan disease
So piercing to my heart their force I feel.

Byron was so disgusted with this poem that he called Bowles 'the maudlin prince of mournful sonneteers'.

Almost as maudlin were the verses written by Cleveland Coxe, Bishop of West New York. He was born in England and in an apparent attack of home-sickness penned the following lines:

The bells and chimes of Motherland
Of England, green and old,
That out from grey and ivied tower
A thousand years have tolled.
How merrily they call afar
To cot and baron's hall
With holly decked and mistletoe
To keep the Festival.

One would certainly prefer the humour of Thomas Hood in his 'Faithless Sally Brown' where he remarks:

They went and told the sexton
And the sexton tolled the bell

or even the sentiments expressed in the famous World War I ditty:

The bells of Hell go ting-a-ling-a-ling
For you but not for me.

A later and more satisfying poet, Ralph Hodgson, mentions bells in his poem in which he attacks those who harm or exploit animals. He says:

T'would ring the bells of Heaven
The wildest peal for years,

If Parson lost his senses
And people came to theirs.

From time to time ringers with literary aspirations produce lengthy poems on the subject of local happenings. The 4 March song at Appleton has already been mentioned but here is an example from Cornwall recounting the prowess of five ringers from Egloshayle:

Come all you ringers good and grave, come listen to my peal,
I'll tell you of five ringers brave that live in Egloshayle;
They bear the sway in any array where'er they chance to go,
Good music of melodious bells 'tis their delight to show.

The foreman gives the sign and then he steps out with his toe,
He casts his eyes about them all and gives the sign to go;
Away they pull with courage full, the heart it do revive,
To hear them swing and music bring – one, two, three, four, five.

There's Craddock the cordwainer first who rings the treble bell,
The second is John Ellery who none could e'er excel,
The third is Pollard, carpenter, the fourth is Thomas Cleave
And Goodfellow the tenor-man who brings them round so brave.

They went out to Lanlivery and brought away first prize,
They came back through St Tudy and did the same likewise;
There's Stratton men, St Mabyn men, St Issey and St Kew,
But these five men of Egloshayle could all the rest outdo.

Now to conclude our merry task the sovereign's health we'll join,
Stand any man who takes the flask and drink his health in wine.
And here's to Craddock, Ellery, and here's to Thomas Cleave,
To Pollard and the tenor-man who ring 'em round so brave.

The people all for miles around do tell o'er hill and dale,
The fame of these five ringers who live in Egloshayle.

The poem dates from about 1810, and memorials to the five ringers still stand in the churchyard of Egloshayle, now a suburb of Wadebridge.

As mentioned earlier, ringing competitions based on good striking have long been common in the West Country, and a rhyme from Devon, 'The Bell Ringing', describes such an event:

Chorus:
'Twas in Ashwater Town, the bells they did sound,
They rang for a belt and a hat laced with gold,
But the men of North Lew rang so steady and true
That there never was better in Devon I hold.

1. One day in October neither drunken nor sober
O'er Broadbury Down I was wending my way,
When I heard of some ringing, some dancing, some singing,
I ought to remember that Jubilee Day.

2. 'Twas misunderstood for the men of Broadwood
Gave a blow on the tenor should not have been there,
But the men of North Lew rang so faultlessly true,
A difficult matter to beat 'em I swear.

3. They of Broadwood being naughty, they said to our party
We'll ring you a challenge again in a round,
We'll give you a chance at St Stephen's by Launceston,
The prize to the winner a note of five pounds.

4. When the match it came on at good Callington
The bells they rang out o'er the valley below,
The old and young people, the hale and the feeble,
They came out to hear the sweet music flow.

5. They of Broadwood once more were obliged to give o'er,
They were beaten completely and done in a round,
For the men of North Lew pull so steady and true
That no better than they in the West can be found.

Poems on ringing composed by local ringers are not so easily found today, though examples appear from time to time in the magazine *Ringing World*. One modern example is worth quoting, however, not the least of its interest being that it was written by an eighty-eight-year-old ringer from Oxfordshire who had been ringing since he was thirteen. It is a fairly long poem but one verse will suffice to demonstrate the mental agility of this very old man which remained after a lifetime of ringing:

In times of joy and gladness they have always played a part
In sorrowing times their muffled notes have smoothed the aching heart.
In time of war their silence has cast a gloom around
With peace proclaimed we hear again their glad melodious sound.

These lines were written for the Women's Institute scrapbook at Wittenham Abbotts, Oxfordshire.

John Bunyan was an enthusiastic ringer at the detached tower of the parish church of Elstow, near Bedford, where he was born in 1628. He mentions bells several times in his writings, as in *The Holy War* (1682), where he talks of bells being rung in thanksgiving. In the famous *Pilgrim's Progress* (published in 1678), he writes of the two pilgrims approaching the Heavenly City and says, 'They thought they heard all the bells therein to ring to welcome them thereto.' Like Longfellow nearly 200 years later, Bunyan wrote a poem (called 'Comparison') describing the symbolism of bells. It appeared in *A Book for Boys and Girls* which he wrote in 1656, but which remained unpublished until two years after his death.

These bells are like the powers of my soul;
Their clappers to the Passions of my mind,
The ropes by which my Bells are made to tole
Are Promises (I by experience find).

My body is the steeple where they hang,
My Graces they which do ring every bell,
Nor is there anything gives such a tang,
When by these Ropes these Ringers ring them well.

If they do tole, ring out, or chime all in,
They drown the tempting, trickling voice of vice,

> Lord! when my bells have gone my Soul has bin
> As 'twere a tumbling in this paradise.
>
> Then Lord! I pray thee keep my Belfry key,
> Let none but Graces meddle with these Ropes,
> And when these naughty Boys come, say them nay,
> From such Ringers of Musick there's no hopes.
>
> O Lord if this poor child might have his will,
> And might his meaning freely to the tell;
> He never of his musick has his fill,
> There's nothing to him like thy ding, dong, Bell.

Bunyan obviously remembered his early days ringing at Elstow, and the fourth bell, which was his favourite, is still one of the six bells of the church of St Mary and St Helena.

For some reason which remains unclear, he decided quite early on to abandon ringing, which he much enjoyed, as he considered his enjoyment sinful. In his biographical book *Grace Abounding to the Chief of Sinners*, which he wrote in 1666 whilst in Bedford Prison, he explains his decision:

> Now you must know that before this, I had taken much delight in ringing, but my conscience beginning to be tender, I thought such practice was in vain, and therefore forced myself to leave it, yet my mind hankered. Wherefore I should go to the steeple house and look on though I durst not ring. But I thought this did not become religion either, yet I forced myself and would look on still. But quickly after that I began to think how if one the bells should fall? Then I chose to stand under a main beam that lay athwart the steeple, from side to side, thinking there I might stand sure. But then I should think again, should a bell fall with a swing it might first hit the wall, and then rebounding on me, might kill me for all this beam. This made me stand in the steeple door; and now, I thought, I am safe enough, for if a bell should fall then I can slip out behind these thick walls and so be preserved notwithstanding.
>
> So after this, I would yet go and see them ring, but would not go further than the steeple door, but then it came into my head, how if the steeple itself should fall? and this thought, it might fall for aught I know, when I stood and looked on did continually so shake my mind that I durst

not stand at the steeple door any longer, but was forced to flee for fear the steeple should fall on my head.

One wonders at the strength of mind of a man, a proficient and enthusiastic ringer for so many years, now deliberately giving it up as he considered his enjoyment of it to be sinful.

The other side of the coin is demonstrated by an interesting example of how keen ringers pursue their hobby into their daily lives and work. Dealing with harvest and threshing customs in Suffolk during the nineteenth century, a writer says: 'But if a company of men was threshing, the work was much easier, simply because they were together at a shared task. If the company was all bellringers they stood around the threshing floor, which was usually made of elm, and they rang the changes with the flail, in exactly the same rhythm as they did in the steeple with the bells, all coming in their proper turn, and changing and changing about at a signal from a leader. From a distance this rhythmic beating of the elm floor made an attractive simulation of the bells.'*

Mention must also be made of the various hymns suitable for special ringing services, which include:

Ring forth, ye holy bells.

Ring out! ye bells below.

Ring the bells with gladness.

Set them nobly in the steeple.

The Gospel bells are ringing.

The Sacred Bells of England.

Ye joyful bells ring out your praise.

Ye who delight to ring the bells.

There are many other ringers' hymns, of which the most popular is 'Unchanging God'.

* *Ask the Fellows Who Cut the Hay,* G E Evans. (Faber & Faber).

8
Ringers versus Clergy

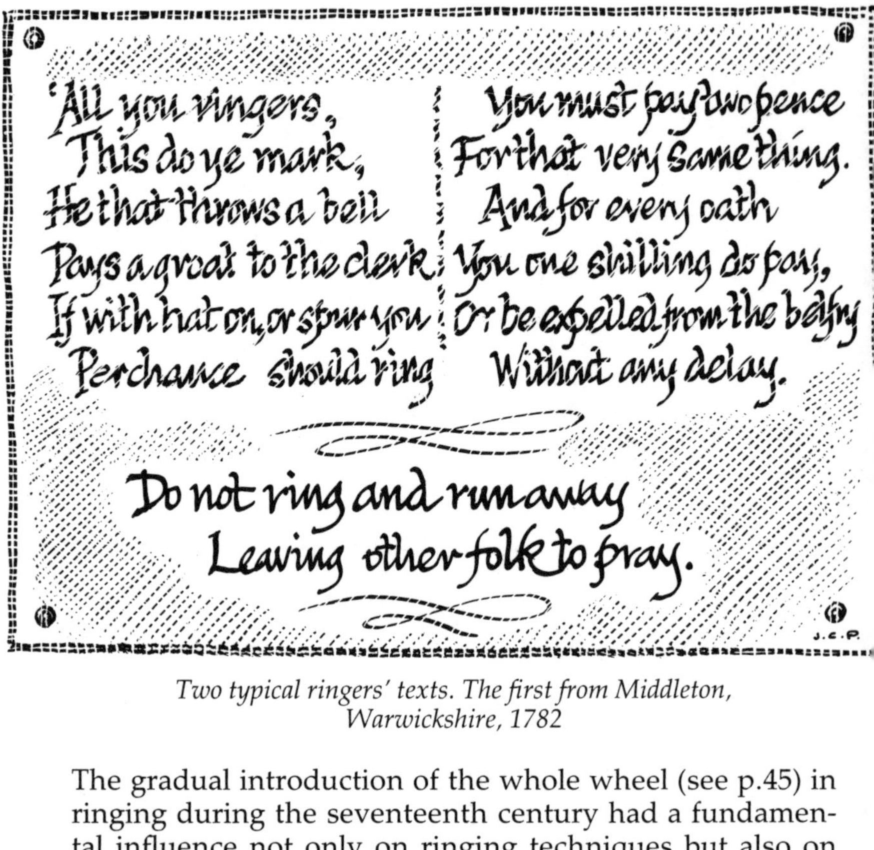

Two typical ringers' texts. The first from Middleton, Warwickshire, 1782

The gradual introduction of the whole wheel (see p.45) in ringing during the seventeenth century had a fundamental influence not only on ringing techniques but also on the relationship between ringers and clergy. The damage done to this relationship is still evident in some parishes to this day.

The trouble was that, as soon as the possibilities of whole-wheel ringing became apparent, with changes and methods ushering in an exciting new era in ringing, it was enthusiastically embraced as a hobby by many young men up and down the country who had barely been in a church before in their lives. In town and village they flocked to the nearest church with four bells or more and, often without advising the incumbent, formed themselves into bands to ring for any occasion they thought suitable. They also rang for church feasts and religious occasions, such as calling the faithful to Sunday service, for which the parson was duly grateful, but during the week they used the bells for purely secular ringing. They rang for the arrival of the London stage-coach, to signal the end of the harvest, for the squire's birthday and even for the start of the flat-racing season (the dangers of ringing to celebrate a winner are described in a previous chapter. (See p.100).

Added impetus was given to secular ringing by the publication in 1668 of Fabian Stedman's *Tintinnalogia* and his *Campanologia* of 1677 which gave explicit and detailed information on what the author described as 'the Art of Ringing'. As an example of how religious and secular ringing became intermingled, here is the programme for the purely secular ringing sessions at Westminster Abbey for the year 1692:

February 14 – Accession Day
April 11 – Coronation Day
April 30 – Queen Mary's Birthday
May 11 – Victory over French fleet (Cap de la Hogue)
May 26 – Confirmation of above
May 29 – Restoration Day
July 14 – Duke of Gloucester's Birthday
October 19 – William III returning from Netherlands
October 20 – HM King William reaching London
October 27 – Day of Thanksgiving for above
November 4 – King's Birthday
November 5 – Gunpowder Plot
November 15 – Dowager Queen's Birthday (Catherine of Braganza)
November 17 – Commemoration of accession of Queen Elizabeth I)

Early in the seventeenth century ringing societies and associations began to be formed. They were usually based on their own church or parish and rarely rang elsewhere. (Some of these early ringing societies are described in Chapter 9.)

It is understandable that, from this time onwards and well into the nineteenth century, a great deal of friction was created between ringers and the clergy. Belfry behaviour became worse and worse, and as the ringers were often paid a small amount, the proceeds went straight into the till of the local inn. Many country parsons were frightened of the ringers and their drinking, and indeed an eighteenth-century dictionary quotes the word 'ringer' as a slang definition of a drunkard.

But not all clergymen were scared of them, as the diary of the Reverend William Holland, vicar of Over Stowey, Somerset, clearly shows. His diary, which runs from 1799 to 1818,* tells of a brush with some ringers:

> 1809. Tuesday 14th November. A sad disturbance here about ringing. An Impudent Rascal of a fellow had the Impudence to come into the Garden before the house and demand the Key of the Belfry. The Clerk had told him it was with me. He replied that I had no right to keep it. I answered from the house that I could soon convince him of my right and bid him go about his business. He was very abusive. So out they went and got Farmer Landsey's Key to the Chancel and got in. I sent to them to desist at their Peril, they stopped and soon began again. I sent out a second time, sent to Farmer Landsey for the Key and they were turned out a second time. There were one or two worthless fellows beside this Joe Hill and I think of making an example of them.

Somerset clergymen seem to have been very keen on keeping diaries, and many comments on ringers and ringing are found in them during the first half of the nineteenth century and beyond. A long-running and dramatic saga concerning such topics as the propriety of ringing a celebration peal immediately after a funeral is found in the diary of the Reverend John Skinner, Rector of Camerton, kept between 1799 and 1833:

* *Paupers and Pig Killers* ed. Jack Ayres.

1821

29 July
I preached … on Death and Immortality. I was not a little hurt at the want of all propriety in the people after the service was concluded, since instead of returning quietly to their respective homes in order to reflect on the subject I had taken so much pains to impress on their minds, they banish at once all serious reflection by ringing a merry peal! This barbarous interruption to self communion, however, I soon put a stop to in person, and gave orders to the Clerk to bring in the Key of the Church in future to the Parsonage, as soon as the service was concluded.

1822

10 July
About the middle of the day the bells rang out a merry peal in consequence, I understood, of the intelligence of Miss Jarrett's marriage having been received. In the evening there was the Funeral of an Infant; and I could not help remarking how fully the tolling of the bell for the deceased had been absorbed in the more merry news.

11 July
The celebrations of Miss Jarrett's wedding continue. The poor man Dawson, who died on Tuesday, was buried this evening and a merry peal succeeded, as in the previous case. I understand that £2 are ordered to the ringers, as Dilly, the butler, asked me how I should recommend it being paid. I said, if possible, one half to be spent on beer, the other half to be divided amongst them; but I feared this could not be done. I shall be heartily glad when this scene of drunkenness and uproar is at an end.

14 July
As soon as the bells began to ring I went to the Church to request we might have no more rejoicing, as had been surfeited with it last week. Harris said it was not his intention to ring otherwise than to call people to church. I replied that it was a general order of mine that there should be no peal ringing on Sunday and that order must be abided by.
[There was trouble with the choir in the evening when they came to church drunk and walked out in a huff when they weren't allowed to sing as they wanted.]

19 July
Returning from the glebe, Stephen, the under-gardener to Mrs Jarrett, came to ask me to let the ringers give a peal, it being the King's Coronation Day, and the people at Paulton and Midsomer Norton had been ringing the whole morning.

I said I was as much attached to the King as any man in the country, yet could not see how His Majesty derived any good from people leaving their work to make a noise with the bells; with respect to the ringers they certainly did themselves much harm by frequenting the Ale Houses in the manner they had done last week, and then returning home and beating their wives to a jelly. I said as the Parish seemed so desirous of having them rung (Mr Gooch had given them a guinea and Weeks, the churchwarden, five shillings for the purpose) I would not oppose it; but recommended their not going to the Public Houses spending the money they gained in folly, which might be much better spent on their families. They accordingly commenced their ringing and I walked in the village to avoid the jingling of the bells.

23 July
After dinner Harris, the Clerk, called for the Key of the Church, saying Mrs Jarrett and her son were arrived and the people wished to ring. I replied he must have recollected what I had told him on Sunday, that I would not permit the bells to be made mere playthings of; if the ringers did not employ them for the purpose they were intended I should not consent to any extra ringing, and on these grounds should refuse the Key. He accordingly went away very sulky.

23 August
Some of the masons and carpenters working for Mrs Jarrett requested the key of the church to ring, as they said she was expected shortly to arrive home. I declined to give permission, as none of them were Camerton people, and I had made a regulation that only those who rang the bells for Church should be considered as the Parish Ringers.

They then began again on the subject of the key and told me I had no power to refuse it; that the Churchwarden ought to retain it in his possession, not me, and that he had a right to let them ring. I told him he had no right to let them ring without my consent, and I certainly should not grant it on the present occasion. They then became very insolent and I left them.

About an hour after, hearing one of the bells strike out, I went to the Church, supposing they had procured Mrs Jarrett's key from one of the servants, but all the doors being shut I called out to the man in the belfry and desired him to come down which he declining to do, I put my foot to the door and forced it open. I found three men there, whom I desired instantly to leave the Church, which at first they seemed disposed to resist, but finally they walked down the belfry stairs, and walked into the churchyard, which they absolutely refused to quit, saying they had as much right there as myself. Dilly, Mrs Jarrett's servant, then came and told them that his mistress desired them immediately to leave the premises. The men said they would do as Mrs Jarrett wished but not for me. They then went away.

1830

21 February
There was no ringing for Church: when I spoke to White (the Clerk) he was impudent, and when I told him I had given the ringers a Christmas-box on condition they would ring the bells for Church regularly, and attend themselves, he said if I minded so much about the money they would give it back to me. White told me afterwards that the reason he had not rung the bells for last two Sundays was because he had gotten drunk Saturday night and had too bad a headache in the morning to bear the sound of the bells.

15 July
[George IV had just died.] We had scarcely finished dinner when I heard a peal from the Church strike out. This rather surprised me as no one had asked for the key of the Church and I had told the ringers they should not have it without my leave, since a pack of collier lads got together to ring only for the sake of drinking afterwards. On going to the Church, they said they rang for the King, that other churches were ringing and they did not see why they should not do as the rest did. I said that if they had asked me properly for the key to toll for the King I should have let them have it … My sons came from Bath after tea and said that the shops were shut up and the bells tolling, I believe in Farmborough or Priston but I heard no such peal ringing as the worthies of Camerton chose to exhibit in honour of our deceased sovereign.

1832

> 5 December
> The ringers were very impertinent and I turned them out of the Belfry when I found they distressed my sick son.
>
> 7 December
> I visited Parfitt Bridge to speak to the parents on the misconduct of their son, a lad of 18 or 19, who was one of the ringers I turned out of the Belfry the day before yesterday. They had rung after the wedding and continued doing so until near four o'clock, which must have been a great annoyance to poor Joseph [he was dying] to hear the jingle of bells so near the whole morning – they were still ringing when Anna and myself returned from a walk at four o'clock; they seemed at first to oppose my authority but I succeeded in turning them out of the Belfry and locking the door.

The above was printed in *The Ringing World* in February 1987, and the unknown contributor comments that the Reverend John Skinner was at odds with everyone, including his family, his parishioners and the manor house. Eventually he took to drugs and at the age of sixty-seven shot himself.

There are many examples of the incumbent being on bad terms with the ringers, sometimes merely because he did not like bells or ringers, sometimes because he objected to the reason for ringing. The rector of Chesterfield refused permission for the ringers to signal the opening of the races in 1830 and was never forgiven. On several occasions the ringers were so incensed that they changed the lock on the belfry door to keep the parson out, as happened at Mortehoe, in Devon.

The reverse of this took place at Thurnby, Leicestershire, when one of the churchwardens nailed up the belfry door to bar access to the ringers, who wanted to ring in honour of a meet of the local hunt in the village. The ringers succeeded in breaking down the door and ringing but were immediately arrested. They were fined by the local magistrates but refused to pay and went to prison instead. There they languished for five weeks until the fine was eventually paid – by the parson himself!

Ringing from the tower base after the removal of the ringing-chamber floor

Even ringers who were better behaved than those in rural communities remained fiercely independent and often anti-clerical, deciding exactly what occasions they should ring on. At High Wycombe, Buckinghamshire, in 1832 the town ringers discovered that the Bishop of Lincoln (in whose diocese High Wycombe was at the time) had voted against the Reform Bill in the Lords. To mark their displeasure they refused to ring on the occasion of the bishop's visit to the town later that year.

Not only were the standards of belfry behaviour poor during the early nineteenth century but the condition of the ringing-chamber itself left much to be desired. In a prominent position stood the almost obligatory barrel of beer with the ringers' jacks by it (see p.53). The floor was often in a parlous state, while the bells and fittings were rarely inspected and often constituted a real danger to those below. Little wonder that few incumbents wished to associate themselves with bells or ringers and this produced a contentious situation.

The clergy took no interest in the ringers because of their appalling behaviour and refusal to attend divine service, the ringers, in turn, insisting that the church tower was their own particular domain and refusing to attend services or have anything to do with the church itself because the vicar was apparently not interested in them. They noted that when they rang for special services, such as Christmas or Easter or the patronal festival, the vicar, while thanking the flower-arrangers, sidesmen and others who had taken part, never thanked the ringers for their contribution. More than one curate could not stand the pace and resigned from his parish because of trouble with the ringers. By the middle of the nineteenth century the situation had become almost impossible, as witness a letter in the religious magazine *The Ecclesiologist* in 1860 on the subject of bells: 'They are abused to assist the song of the drunkard and lend a kind of revel charm to a drunken and debauched bout as is alas far too often the case. The village fair, for instance, is not a fitting occasion for the bells in the tower of our church to pour forth their scientific melody, nor any of the mad holidays or drunken festivals which occur periodically in some villages.'

But help was at hand – and from a totally unexpected source. It came from Oxford, a city with perhaps a more concentrated ringing tradition than any place in the country. In 1833 the Reverend John Keble, then Professor of Poetry at Oxford, preached his famous Assize Sermon in the university city. Together with his colleagues Newman and Pusey, he also advocated a change from the Church of England service and a return to some of the pageantry and ritual characteristic of the Roman Catholic Church. Not only were the services to be invigorated but the church itself was to undergo a physical renovation, with alterations to many interiors. The Camden Society was formed to organize these changes (later altering its name to the Ecclesiological Society), and it began work in 1839. Not that the congregation was often consulted when it came to alterations in the nave, tower and chancel, and many parishioners were alarmed at the sudden sweeping-away of much that had become familiar to them. Much attention was given to the tower and bells and even more attention to the ringers. Members of the society toured churches in each county, talking to the ringers and trying to organize them into bands, with an appointed captain to each. Swearing and drinking in the belfry were banned and it was sincerely hoped that after ringing for Sunday service each ringer would attend church. A hundred and fifty years later this is an ideal that is still far from being reached.

In those churches where the behaviour of the ringers was particularly bad, the floor of the ringing-chamber was removed and the ropes were lengthened so that ringing had to be done from the floor of the tower and visible to the congregation. This made slipping off after ringing that much more difficult. These changes were not welcomed by the ringers in many churches and there was much resistance to the work of the Ecclesiological Society. The actions of the society, in fact, brought to a head the long-standing feud between ringers and clergy. Long-standing it certainly was, for in one tower in Oxfordshire there is an early seventeenth-century noticeboard stating:

Do not ring and run away
Leaving other folk to pray.

Though the society worked hard at changing the attitude of ringers to the church, and the attitude of the clergy to the ringers, it took a very long time to accomplish.

Over thirty years after the society was first formed a letter was printed in its magazine, *The Ecclesiologist*, headed 'Successful Tactics of a Country Curate with an Ungodly Set of Ringers': 'I have never been a witness of the arcana of a belfry till I came to this parish. As you can readily conceive, Sir, I was terribly disgusted with what I witnessed; for the belfry on ringing nights was the regular resort of all the tag-rags of the village, who regarded the performance in the light of jollification, instead of "hollification".' This earnest 'country curate' solved his particular problem by inviting all the ringers to dinner at his house, giving them a talk on why they should not drink and smoke in the ringing-chamber and (perhaps most important of all) later learning to ring and ringing with them. Even then the ringers took a great deal of convincing, and one ringer insisted that the bells were available to all and proved it by insisting that the origin of the word 'belfry' was, in fact, 'bell free'!

Today the conduct of most ringers to their tower is impeccable, though discussion still continues as to whether or not ringers should attend divine service. On several occasions during the nineteenth century attempts were made to enforce church attendance by ringers, the general argument being that, if they were ringing to call the faithful to prayer, the least they could do was to attend church themselves.

Many ringers felt (as they still do to this day) that bellringing is a hobby enjoyed by many, church-goers and non-church-goers alike, and that it is unfortunate but a fact, that the only place where their hobby may be enjoyed is in a church tower. Just because they like ringing, they argue, does not mean they have to embrace a religion that is alien or even repugnant to them.

From the 1880s many incumbents formulated rules which effectively barred people from ringing if they did not attend church. At Leighton Buzzard, Bedfordshire, in 1882, for example, the vicar, the Reverend E W Langmore, issued a set of twenty rules based on a previous rule-book of 1870 which had been largely ignored. Some of the rules were:

> 1. That there shall be ten stated or regular ringers and not more than eight probationary ringers, *who must be churchmen and will be expected to attend church services.*
> 2. No drinking, smoking or bad language shall under any pretext, be allowed in any part of the church or churchyard. If a ringer is guilty of habitual neglect of public worship in church or any other improper or irreligious conduct he shall be dismissed.

Some of the band at Leighton Buzzard decided to take no notice of the new rules and continued as before. As a result five of them received a letter from Mr Langmore in which he said: ' … you are informed that your services will no longer be required, and to request you not to present yourself in the Belfry without the permission of the Vicar.' One man who received his letter was the foreman of the ringers.

Today most incumbents, even if not ringers themselves, look on ringing as an essential part of the church and its service. That the ringers do not always attend church is a continuing sorrow to many clerics, and from time to time one of them lays down the law and points out that the ringing-chamber and bells are part of the church fabric and that he has the absolute right of stating who may ring the bells.

Recently, at Chesterfield, there was an outcry against the vicar 'meddling' in ringing matters which created a considerable volume of correspondence in *The Ringing World*, the ringers' magazine. More recently, at Torrington in Devon, there was a very dramatic scene when the Reverend Jeremy Hummerstone, the vicar, sacked all his ringers because they did not attend church.

The bells remained silent for some weeks until one Saturday evening the ex-captain of the ringers, who was employed behind the bar in a local pub, suddenly heard the sound of bells from the church. Leaving his customers high and presumably dry, he sped across the road to the church only to find that the vicar had recruited a new band who were now in full swing. The ex-ringer remonstrated with the vicar and demanded the cessation of ringing. Evidently the church of St Michael and All Angels is high church, for a newspaper report stated that the vicar was 'highly incensed' at the attitude of the ringer. There was what the police like to call 'an incident', during which blood was drawn and the ringer's jumper torn. He was finally ejected from the church and returned to his bar and waiting customers. Said the vicar in a newspaper interview: 'if his jumper was indeed torn, my wife, Clarissa, will be only too pleased to mend it for him.'

Apparently the 'highness' or 'lowness' of the church service has a profound effect on some ringers, for it was the claim that incense was choking the ringers that caused them to leave immediately after ringing and not attend the service.

In 1911 the ringers of the church of St Clement in Hastings went on strike when the vicar, an art-lover, hung a replica of Raphael's *Virgin and Child* immediately above the altar of the Lady Chapel. This apparently displeased the low-church upbringing of the captain of the ringers, who ordered his band not to ring until the offending picture was removed. This created chaos in Hastings, especially amongst those who normally organized their Sunday activities by the sound of the church bells. Some (said the local paper) who were accustomed to stay in bed until the church bells began ringing remained in bed wondering why the night seemed so long. Others, again regulated by the bells, put the Sunday joint in the oven too late and had to have it in the evening. When a reporter mischievously enquired what would happen if ringers from outside were imported into St Clement's, one local ringer hinted darkly about cutting the bellropes to prevent ringing. In the event, the painting was removed to a less conspicuous position in the church, and this entertaining example of religious intolerance was ended and the ringers returned to their duties.

Occasionally one hears of a different attitude to bells. At Mevagissey, Cornwall, there were no bells installed and the parochial church council agreed to having a recorded tape of change-ringing amplified from the church tower. This was, of course, anathema to most ringers and also to many residents of the village who appreciated the former quiet of the place on Sundays. The vicar, however, was an enthusiast for bells and found that a ring of six was on sale from an adjoining parish. This discovery coincided with a decision of the Consistory Court at Truro to ban the tape recording as the result of an appeal by some villagers. The vicar pursued his objective and made enquiries about buying and transporting the bells, but found that the whole operation would cost some £27,000. This was far beyond the means of a small parish consisting almost entirely of retired people, apart from the extra cost, it was found, of strengthening the ancient tower to carry a fairly heavy ring of six.

The matter ended there, but it is an indication that some clerics *are* enthusiastic about bells and ringing. Today there are many clergymen who take an active part in ringing before divine service and on practice nights, and there is a flourishing Society of Clerical Ringers who regularly meet and ring all over the country. What was once referred to as 'the monotonous link which has bound together the Belfry and the Beerhouse'* is now largely broken. Not only has the conduct of ringers improved but, with modern ball-bearings on the timber wheels supporting the bells, it is now a less thirst-inducing pastime.

But ringers still like a drink, and many patronize the local pub after practice-nights. This custom is claimed by some to have saved lives, for at Witham-on-the-Hill, Lincolnshire in the eighteenth century, the tower collapsed only a few minutes after the ringers had downed their first pint in the local. Had they still been in the tower, the whole band would undoubtedly have been killed. There is a moral here somewhere!

* Quoted by Tom Ingram in *Bells in England*.

9
Youths and Maidens

The earliest known peal board recording Grandsire Bob Triples dated 1715, St Peter Mancroft, Norwich

Prior to the Reformation most bellringing was monastic and was performed by lay brothers specially assigned to this work and paid for it. In 1310, for example, the lay brothers of Lincoln Cathedral 'were rewarded in drink and without any other payment'.* In the small parish churches, which often had only one or two bells, the priest himself, or sometimes the sexton, undertook the ringing to announce services or other ceremonies. In various parish churches in England today one can find engravings on the stone pillars depicting figures ringing bells, sometimes using large bells and ringing with the aid of a rope, as at

* John Ketteringham, Lincoln Cathedral historian.

Belton, Lincolnshire, or using handbells, as seen at Winwick, Lancashire.

In the larger monasteries and cathedrals the ringers soon formed themselves into specialist groups. The earliest recorded 'guild' of this kind is that mentioned in a Patent Roll of Henry III in 1254 where there is mention of the Brethren of the Gild of Westminster Ringers. But even before that the right of ringing the bells of St Martin-in-the-Fields had been granted to the Saddlers Gild of the City of London, probably about 1180. Another pre-Reformation ringing guild was the Gild of St Paul's, dating from 1507. This had a lengthy set of instructions for 'the Belle Ryngeres' which not only specified their ringing duties but also gave them instructions for 'lightyng and quanching of torches and tapers' as well as instructing them on the rather odd duty of 'making clene the said crowdes'. What sort of ringing was done is not certain, for the bells were not mounted on whole wheels, so changes and methods were impossible. Fabian Stedman himself says in his *Tintinnalogia* of 1668 that, 'Within these fifty or sixty years past, changes were not known.' Nevertheless, markings scratched on some church pillars about 1600 at Moulton, Northamptonshire, indicate the changes possible on four bells, so it seems that simple changes were being rung even earlier than Stedman suggests.

The result of this growing interest in change-ringing and its possibilities caused many of the new ringers to form themselves into societies or associations, and some of these early seventeenth-century societies still exist. Others eventually vanished or were incorporated later into other societies. One early London society was called 'The Scholars of Chepesyde' and dates from February 1603. Another was the City Scholars of 1731 and the revived Union Scholars of 1736. Outside London, the Society of Lincoln Ringers was formed officially in 1612 and the Saffron Walden Society in 1623, both still in existence, as are the Painswick (Glos.) Youths, established in 1686.

Probably the most famous non-parochial society which has lasted from those days is the Society of College Youths formed in 1637 and in later years adopting the prefix

'Ancient'. It began purely as an association of 'pleasure ringers' and was modelled on the lines of a City of London trade guild. Three-hundred and fifty years later it still exists, and it is older than most of today's City Livery companies.

The several theories purporting to explain why the name 'College Youths' was adopted have been dealt with by the Society's historian, William T. Cook,* who explains that at that time most ringers were students and therefore it was natural for them to adopt the word 'scholar'or 'college' in their title. There is certainly no truth in the suggestion that the title is associated with the religious 'College of the Holy Ghost' founded in the City of London by Dick Whittington in 1424. One good reason is that the College had been disbanded in 1547, nearly a century before the College Youths were formed.

As a society of 'pleasure-ringers' it attracted the attention of many wealthy and titled young men looking for a new hobby, and its first Master was the twenty-six-year-old Lord William Brereton from an ancient Cheshire family. But in 1642 the young lord got himself caught up in the Civil War, in which he supported the Royalist cause, and he left London and presumably severed his connection with the College Youths.

There was then a gap of five years before Brereton was replaced as Master by Sir Clifford Clifton, from Nottingham, in 1647. Most members of the society in those years were wealthy, and they included Lord Dacre, the Marquess of Salisbury and various City of London aldermen. Later, in 1764, enough money was available to commission the famous Italian engraver Francesco Bartolozzi to design a handsome membership certificate, and a copy of this is still presented to new members.

The Ancient Society of College Youths, as it exists today, cannot be defined as either a 'parochial' or a non-territorial association as other societies may be. It is 'parochial' in the sense that it provides the ringing for certain London churches including St Paul's Cathedral, Westminster

* *Ringing World* March 1987.

Abbey, St Mary-le-Bow, St Michael's, Cornhill, St Sepulchre's, the Old Bailey and other City churches. Yet it is also non-territorial in that its membership of about one thousand is drawn from all over Britain and frequently ring at churches throughout the country. Any member, when in London, may join the ringing wherever the College Youths are in action in the City, or at Southwark Cathedral where they frequently practise. Monthly meetings are held in The George in Old Bailey, near St Paul's Cathedral, where administrative matters, such as the admission of new members, are dealt with in a suitably relaxed atmosphere. The annual dinner of the College Youths is an important event in ringing circles and includes a toast to the past Masters of '300, 200 and 100 years ago'.

The College Youths are proud of their history and conscious of tradition. In 1684 members rang three consecutive 'extents' of 720 changes each non-stop at Southwark Cathedral (St Saviour's), this being the longest peal ever rung at that date. Three hundred years later, in 1984, the Youths repeated the performance at Southwark with members dressed in seventeenth-century costume. The valuable regalia owned by the Society, hidden in store for many years, is now displayed and used at business meetings. Today membership is confined to men.

The second of the two most important ringing societies still flourishing is the Society of Royal Cumberland Youths. It dates from September 1747 and was based on St Leonard's, the parish church of Shoreditch, at that time in the countryside north of London. From the first it included many French Huguenot refugees from nearby Spitalfields, one of whom was a M. Dubois who later obliged by changing his name to Mr Wood and became a noted ringer. There has long been discussion as to the origin of the Cumberlands' name, though the traditional explanation seems the most obvious. In 1745 the Duke of Cumberland was a hero to many after the Battle of Culloden, and he was also a keen ringer. It is not surprising, therefore, that several ringing societies adopted his name (there was, for instance, the Oxford Cumberland Society of Ringers), and the Cumberlands of

1747 seem to have taken their name from the Duke.* He later presented to the Youths a medallion of himself which is still worn by the Master on important occasions, and a handsome oil-painting. The society then became the Royal Cumberland Youths, though other tradition, so far unproven, says that it was originally formed from the Scholars of London who were in existence in 1717.

It is a pity that not more is known about the founders and early members of the Royal Cumberlands, but one was the noted ringer William Shipway, author of the classic ringing primer entitled *Campanologia, or the Art of Ringing,* published in 1816. Of this book it has been said that, 'If all books on ringing were to be destroyed and only one retained, that one would have to be Shipway.'

As so often happens, the younger element of the Society thought the older members 'stuffy' and unadventurous, and in 1784 an important member, George Gross, formed a break-away club called the Junior Cumberland Youths. The Society of College Youths had had a similar 'revolt' against orthodoxy in their early days. Neither of these junior societies lasted long, as the young, in their turn, became old and 'stuffy' and were only too glad to rejoin the original society. But Gross remains important for at least two other reasons. He was probably the first man to ring two full peals of over 5,000 changes in one day, and in 1784, at Shoreditch parish church, he led a peal of 12,000 changes, a record at the time. So enthusiastic were the general public at this nine-hour feat of ringing that the ringers were greeted with 'great shouts of approbation and joy' by a large crowd who formed a cheering lane through which they made their way to the nearby White Hart inn.† A peal of this length would not be so remarkable today, nor would it be likely to cause much 'approbation and joy' amongst non-ringers after nine hours listening.

The history of the Society is not very exciting, though one important occurrence was in 1896 when it acquired its first woman member, and, unlike the College Youths, women are still welcomed as members.

* *Proceedings of the Society of Antiquaries,* 28 February 1891.
† *Ringing World,* 5 March 1943.

Relations between the Cumberlands and the College Youths have never been very cordial, and to this day no member of one society may belong to the other. The gulf between the two ringing associations is demonstrated in the following amusing poem on the subject, entitled; A Tragic Ballad:

It is of an old gent I'll have you to know
Who rang at St Paul's and at Cornhill also.
He lived all alone, with young William, his son,
Who was promising well, though not yet forty-one.

One evening the father admonished young Will:
'You must come down to practice tonight at Cornhill,
For afore you reach sixty, if no ill befalls,
I believe I could get you a ring at St Paul's.'

'Oh Father, dear Father,' young William replied,
'I can't tell you lies, though you know how I've tried –
I've promised tonight (and I mean to be there)
For to ring at St Martin's in Traffelgar Square.'

'My son,' quoth the sage, 'do not enter that tower,
You never shall ring with that horrible shower!
You'll change your mind quickly, avoiding disgrace,
When I tell you it's CUMBERLANDS ring in that place!'

Said William, 'A young lady ringer I've met
And on her my affections most firmly are set.
Your rooted objections to me are no barrier
For I love her, dear Father, and I'm going to marry 'er!'

'Now William,' said Father, 'Just listen to me
For if you insist it's cut off you will be,
And when I expire and am laid into dust
I'll leave all my cash to the Barron Bell Trust.'

'I've rung all my life, and I still must insist
That what you're describing can't ever exist.
I've heard people tell that there's women what ring –
But a *lady* – why, no, boy, there ain't no such thing.'

Next month they were married, that couple so bold,
And the poor father's grief was a sight to behold.
His brain is quite gone, the psychiatrist thinks,
For he even goes wrong in three courses of Cinques!

College Youths membership certificate, from the original design by Bartolozzi

But Will and his bride, also sad to relate,
Just could not escape from the vengeance of Fate.
When poverty pressed, their possessions they sold,
And now live in Devon, near Itch-in-the-Fold.

And there they are forced to go up in the tower
Ringing rounds and call changes for hour after hour.
But even that fate ain't as bad as it sounds –
For they *could* be in Cornwall – and only ring rounds!

(Anon)

From the scathing reference to women ringers it seems this poem refers to events at the turn of the century, when they were still a hotly debated novelty.

The animosity between the two societies was to continue. In 1914 the College Youths refused to ring a peal at the Cumberlands' church, St Leonard's, Shoreditch, though in 1937 there was a truce when the Cumberlands rang a peal to celebrate the 300th anniversary of the College Youths' foundation.

One member of the Cumberlands, who managed to put his ringing experience to good use and combine business with pleasure, was a certain John D. Matthews who, in the early years of the century, made a great deal of money making and selling 'The Ringers Cycle – Built to Order in only One Grade – the Best'. Bicycling had become a national craze, and one ringing society was formed called 'The Roving Ringers' who went everywhere by this means. 'The Rambling Ringers' still travel this way today.

Though the College Youths and the Cumberlands were the predominant ringing societies of their time in London, they were not by any means the only ones. There were also the Union Scholars, who are known to have rung on the new bells at St Dunstan's-in-the-East in 1713, and the London Scholars, who rang at St Bride's Church, Fleet Street, in 1717 but seem to have vanished by 1745. (It is this society that is said by some to have transformed itself into the Royal Cumberlands in 1747.) The Westminster Youths were flourishing about 1800, and the London County Association was established in 1824. It was originally called the St James Society as it met in St James's

Church just off Clerkenwell Green, before moving to St Clement Dane's in the Strand.

Probably because of Stedman's association with East Anglia, that area has long been noted as a ringing centre, and Norwich is a mecca for ringers. Strangely, the attraction is not the fine cathedral, for its bells have been hung for mechanical chiming only for well over a century. It is on that wonderful church St Peter Mancroft, with its thirteen bells (a standard twelve with a flat sixth), that Norwich ringing is centred. But though various seventeenth-century London societies were regularly visiting Norwich to become more proficient at the Art, it was not until 1716 that the ringers of the city formed themselves into the Norwich Scholars. This was a year after the first-ever recorded true peal of over 5,000 changes was rung at St Peter Mancroft, and since that time Norwich ringers have been at the forefront of the Exercise.

On the other side of the country, Bristol had its short-lived Union Youths (also known as the Society of Bristol Youths) from 1837 to 1842. Though no longer ringing as a society, the 1620 St Stephen Ringers of Bristol still meet regularly and appoint officers. Their rules still impose a fine for attending unshaven, using nicknames and 'making water in the tower'. Today Bristol, like Norwich, is a great centre for ringing and has no fewer than twenty-one churches in the city and suburbs with bells hung for ringing. These include the cathedral, with its eight ringing bells and four ancient ones in the central tower, and St Mary Redcliffe's with a fine ring of twelve and its huge tenor bell weighing fifty cwts. Nearby Bath has many good rings but no early ringing society. However, one of its claims to fame is in the strange ringing bequest of Thomas Nashe, the noted misogynist, mentioned in Chapter 5. The other is as the birthplace of the previously mentioned Thomas Shipway.

Despite the fact that both our oldest universities, Oxford and Cambridge, have a ringing tradition extending back many centuries, the formation of their respective university ringing societies was delayed until nearly the end of the nineteenth century. Though Oxford, with its many church and chapel towers and bells, presents a great opportunity for ringing enthusiasts, at one time their ringing does not seem to have been of a very high order. One Oxford ringer, Thomas Hearne, who kept a ringing diary most of his adult life, tells us that in 1733 some fifteen ringers *walked* from London to Oxford to try out the ringing there. They rang at various towers including New College, Magdalen and Christchurch, and also at Iffley. Not only were the local ringers indifferent in their Art but evidently they were also poor in belfry maintenance, for at Christchurch the tenth bell fell from its fittings and crashed to the belfry floor, while at New College a peal attempt came to nothing after two hours when a rope broke. Says Hearne, 'The Oxford men also rang and endeavoured to imitate the Londoners, but they were soon out and made a poor comparison of the others.'

Oxford has the distinction of having three separate ringing associations. First came the town ringers, the Oxford Society of Change-Ringers, founded in 1733, perhaps as a result of the criticisms of the London ringers in that year. Though many students were ringers and members of the Oxford Society, it was not until 1872 that the Oxford University Society of Change-Ringers came into being. Finally, in the 1880s, the Oxford Diocesan Guild, in common with most diocesan guilds, was formed.

As at Oxford, Cambridge was slow in establishing its own university ringing society, which came only in 1879, seven years after that of Oxford. But, like Oxford, it already had a society for students and townsfolk, called 'The Society of Cambridge Youths', which was founded in 1724 and was centred on the university church of St Mary the Great. It was not until a century and a half later that members of both universities rang a peal together, and this important event took place at Appleton, Oxfordshire, in March 1877. The official record states that, 'This is the first peal ever rung by members of the two Universities without the assistance of any other persons.' The Victorian ringing magazine *Church Bells* was even more enthusiastic when it said, 'Probably these are the first peals on record rung entirely by gentlemen of education.' This apparent gibe at the hard-drinking ringers of the early Victorian days was followed by the hope that ' …

every young clergyman should be able to ring and then be able to take his proper place in the belfry'. That is another hope that is far from being fulfilled.

Today most universities have ringing societies. Durham University is the oldest English university after Oxford and Cambridge, though not established until 1832, and its university ringing society, like theirs was slow in coming: the Durham Colleges Society of Change-Ringers was not created until 1955. At the time it included ringers from the attached college at Newcastle-upon-Tyne but in 1959, when Newcastle became established as a university in its own right, it took the title of the Durham University Society of Change-Ringers.

As we have seen, ringing societies come into various categories. First are the very few ancient monastic societies remaining, such as that at Lincoln. Next are the seventeenth- and eighteenth-century secular societies, unattached to any single church or area, such as the College Youths and the Cumberlands. Later came the diocesan guilds that exist today, formed from the parish church ringers in each diocese. (Few who ring for Sunday service in their parish church are not members of their diocesan guild, though in some areas the secular 'county' guilds replace the diocesan guilds, such as the Derby District Association and the Lancashire Association.) Last of all comes the fairly modern phenomenon of what might be termed 'trade associations' of ringers in which members of one profession or calling find additional common ground in the practice of ringing. Even so, the idea is not really new when we recall that in pre-Reformation times in London only members of a particular trade guild were allowed to ring at St Paul's.

The Guild of Medical Ringers, for example, has been in existence since 1955, though the first peal rung entirely by a band of doctors was in 1947, at Abbotts Langley, Hertfordshire. Though membership was originally confined to doctors, the rules were amended in 1957 and membership is now open to nurses, pharmacists, radiologists and in fact any member of an allied profession. The Guild meets twice a year – in London in winter and in the country in summer – and, as may be expected, rings celebratory peals for significant medical events, as it did in 1972 to mark the 250th anniversary of the founding of 'Mr Guy's' Hospital in London.

There is a Guild of Masonic Ringers, the National Police Guild of Ringers, a Guild of Post Office Ringers, a Railwaymen's Guild and a National Teachers' Guild of Ringers, to name only a few. The Guild of Clerical Ringers is flourishing, and the latest recruit to ringing is the Magistrates' Ringing Association founded in 1986. A 'drug' guild of ringers also exists formed of employees of a famous pharmaceutical company. Rumour has it that a new ringing society is soon to be formed consisting entirely of estate agents.

One ringing association founded this century is of the utmost importance. This is the Ladies' Guild dating from 1912. The first woman ever to ring a full peal on church bells was Miss Alice White of Basingstoke, a feat which she accomplished in 1896 at the age of sixteen. Other young women became interested in ringing, and by 1912 there were enough enthusiasts to form the Ladies' Guild of Change-Ringers. The first full peal rung by a ladies band was at Cubitt Town, in the East End of London, that same year. The Ladies Guild is very much alive today and boasts almost 400 members divided into six districts. Each organizes its own ringing programme, outings, suppers and social events, and the Annual General Meeting of the Guild is held every June in a different part of the country. Membership is increasing.

In the 1890s, when Alice White first rang, bellringing was considered a most unladylike pursuit, and many old ringers objected strongly to it, as has been seen. But not everyone. In the early years of the twentieth century the following lines acclaiming lady ringers were penned by an unknown author.

> Like a breath of summer laden, like a cheery ray of hope,
> Is the sight of gentle maiden, deftly handling of a rope.
> Welcome, girlhood, to our science, sunlight sweet our pathway cross,
> You can win by the alliance, all the silver from our dross.

At the same time, it must be remembered that in those

days bells were very difficult to manage and the 'deft handling' mentioned above could not have been accomplished without great physical effort. It is no longer so today.

Whilst lady ringers astonished the nineteenth-century devotees of 'The Exercise' they can still provide surprises. This they did most effectively in the summer of 1981 when they rang a peal in bikinis!

10
Handbell Happenings

Packhorses with bells crossing the bridge at Castle Combe, Wiltshire

Small bells carried by hand go back many thousands of years. They are seen in illustrations of biblical events and are prominent in the early years of the Christian religion in Britain. Similar bells have been used on animals since ancient times, sometimes on the leader to trace straying sheep (the 'bell-wether') or on goats or cows. Small bells were common on horses, partly as a form of harness decoration, while larger bells round the neck gave a more sonorous tone to dispel evil spirits when ploughing or working on the land. This was only one of the many fertility traditions associated with crops in medieval times and yet another instance of the widely held belief that the sound of bells is anathema to Satan and his works. On the ancient packhorse trains the leading horse had a bell, perhaps for the same reason, but probably more practically to announce the coming of the train near the narrow bridges and the bends of the primitive roads of the time.

Small bells and handbells were associated not only with the carriage of goods but also with the sale of goods in the market-place. A bell was used to announce the opening and closing of the market and to signal certain important events, and everyone, both buyers and sellers, was deemed to know the market regulations. An order of the town council of Oundle, Northants, dated 1475, makes this quite clear: 'It is ordayned that no person opyn ther sack or set ther corn to sale afore the hour of ten of the bell or else the undernone be rongyn.' The 'undernone' was the market bell, and to begin trading before this began to ring was a very serious offence and was known as 'forestalling'. Chipping Norton, in Oxfordshire, had a whole list of offences concerning market behaviour, and each culprit, when discovered, was publicly paraded through the streets to the sound of the market bell.

One very serious offence was to buy a product from a trader in the market at one price and then sell it at a profit elsewhere. This was known as 'regrating'. But the most serious crime of all was that of 'engrossing'. This was to buy-up the entire stock of a product and so create an artificial shortage with a consequent rise in price for the seller. This offence, though fairly rare, was dealt with most severely by every market in the country. The market bell was rung for a period of an hour or more while the culprit was hauled before the magistrates to be dealt with instantly. Normally the penalty was flogging, after which the offender was paraded round the market-place. In very bad cases a sentence of imprisonment was imposed to follow. Few traders did it a second time. Handbells are not often heard at markets today except at cattle-markets when they are used to announce the start of the next auction.

Another use for handbells was as a warning against breaching the moral codes of the time. Where a woman was known to have cuckolded her husband, a mob assembled outside her house at night and she was treated to several hours of 'rough music'. This consisted of ringing several handbells (the more cracked the better), hammering on sheets of metal accompanied by trumpets, whistles, drums and purposely tuneless singing. It was a common practice up to the sixteenth century but has fortunately lapsed today or our ears would be assailed by even more cacophany than already exists.

Street traders also used bells to advertise their wares, and each seller had a bell of a different note,* though this was banned by the 1870s.

Perhaps the most common form of handbell-ringing in the seventeenth and eighteenth centuries was that of the bellman parading the streets at night. Often he was dressed in dark robes adorned with a skull and bones and intoned: 'Awake ye that sleep and pray for the dead.' In some towns the bellman doubled for the town crier, and this form of announcing coming events may often be seen to this day in a revived form in towns favoured by tourists. In the islands of the Hebrides the handbell is still used to summon the ferry.

Whether town criers or night-watchmen, eighteenth-century bellmen were a primitive form of police, and there were many cases of bribery. Prostitutes interrupted at night while entertaining customers were expected to 'pay off' the bellman and no doubt considered it part of what might be described as their 'overheads', just as prostitutes today do. Possibly because they spent a good deal of time on their own, bellmen were in the habit of composing doggerel as they walked their various beats. Most of them were unprintable, not because of the terms used but from the appalling standard of versification. Here is an example 'composed' in 1743 by George Gutheridge, a bellman working in the Shoreditch area, and complaining of his difficulty in seeing the correct time by the church clock, which had been installed in the tower at great expense in 1742 and which was the work of a certain John Sluice of Bethnal Green. Evidently Mr Gutheridge did not approve.

* Mayhew *The Street-Traders' Lot* (London, 1862).

To look upon the church askew by some is deem'd a crime
But all must do it at Shoreditch church, all who would
 know the time.

The figures on the dial plate 4 5 6 7 8,
Being hid behind the pediment, if you look at it straight,
The brains sure of the architect must in confusion been
When he five figures of the twelve prevented being seen.

The matter was corrected in 1881 when a new clock, with chiming bells, was installed, though the bells for ringing were not affected.

In some instances, notably at Hardrow in Yorkshire, handbells were used as a substitute for tower bells. Here it is said that when the bells of the church had been removed, in the mid seventeenth century during the Civil War, one of the sextons would climb the tower and, putting his hand and a small bell through the louvres, would signal the start of the service or the beginning of the sermon. Another Yorkshire church in Wensleydale has an even more curious story on the same lines. This church had no bells at all, not even handbells, and the sexton would go to the top of the tower and shout 'Boom! Boom!' to signal the start of the service.

In the more fortunate churches, where handbells were available, they were often used to keep young choristers interested in church affairs after their voices had broken. Today handbell concerts are frequently given to raise money for the re-hanging or maintenance of the church bells. But here we move into another aspect of handbell ringing which needs explanation.

With the coming of change-ringing on church bells there grew an interest in ringing methods on handbells. Apart from that, the method could be practised on handbells before actually ringing it in the tower, making the situation better for ringers and listeners alike. Up to this time it had been customary to 'tap' handbells rather than ring them 'in hand'. Tapped handbells were mounted on a rack and struck, while bells rung 'in hand' meant that one or two bells were held in the hand and rung separately. Yet another means of ringing was to stand the bells on a table, each being picked up in turn and rung by a ringer for the appropriate note.

Handbells light enough to be rung 'in hand' and tuned to scale were probably first made in Wiltshire by the Corr family foundry about 1700. The alloy used is eighty per cent copper and twenty per cent tin. A double leather strap forms the handle, and the clapper is usually tipped with leather or wood pegs so that metal never comes into contact with metal during ringing. This is the reason for the characteristic mellow tones of handbells and also allows the overtones to be heard to advantage.

One immediate result of the interest in using handbells for ringing methods was the realization that handbells were not limited to this. Sets of bells could be made amounting to almost any number, and semi-tones could be introduced so that with them, unlike tower bells, recognizable tunes could be played. Again, handbells being portable by definition, experiments could be made ringing them out of sight of other members of the team. There is an account of 1758 where four handbell ringers, each holding a bell in each hand, rang a peal of over a thousand changes in the house of one of the ringers at Shifnal, Notts. The host, John Nock, rang bells 1 and 2 in the parlour, John Debney rang 3 and 4 in the brewhouse, Samuel Lawrence 5 and 6 standing in the bedroom and Thomas Clempson made a sepulchral contribution by ringing 7 and 8 in the cellar! Obviously, each ringer was out of sight of the others, and if the peal was rung in this manner for a bet, as seems likely, it denotes a very high standard of ringing.

In more recent times a few 'trick' handbell peals have been rung, as happened in 1923 when a band of Cumberland Youths started ringing a peal of 5,056 changes of Bob Major in a train leaving Paddington at 6 p.m. and completed it two hours and twenty minutes later as the train drew into Stroud Station in Gloucestershire. The peal had the dubious distinction of being rung in six counties. Since then a similar feat has been performed in a train leaving London for Edinburgh, thus establishing a record for a peal rung in two different countries.

Another apparently pointless peal on handbells took place on the night of the full moon of 24 August 1972. According to *Ringing World* two weeks later a band of

Medieval actors with handbells at Chislet, Kent

ringers from Wirral, Cheshire, consisting of two girls and three men, walked the 1,820 feet up to the top of Moel Fammau, a North Wales mountain. Here, at the base of what was once intended to be a monument to George III, they rang 5,200 changes in two hours and forty minutes for the North Wales Association. It seems that the old county boundary ran straight through the base of the monument, and we are told that the ringers of bells 1 and 2 and those of 9 and 10 were ringing in Flintshire, the others in Denbighshire. 'Surely', says the report in *Ringing World,* 'it must be a record.'

Handbell ringers addicted to change-ringing never need to look far to find a reason for ringing. Muffled handbells are often rung at the graveside of a departed ringer, and accounts of handbell peals are a feature of the *Ringing World* every week. But in 1920 there was consternation amongst handbell ringers when a certain Arthur Morris, from Harwich, Essex, submitted a peal to the magazine not 'rung in hand' but 'tapped' as they hung on a rack in his living-room. *Ringing World* refused to accept this as a genuine peal, on instructions from the Central Council of Church Bell Ringers, and to make matters worse the local Essex association of ringers also refused to recognize its validity. The result was some of the most heated arguments ever seen in the pages of *Ringing World* (where the letters occasionally cast doubts on the mental stability of some ringers). The correspondence became hysterical and also personal to the extent that by the end of 1921 the editor was forced to intervene and close the matter on the grounds that, 'The consequences of infringement of the law of libel may well fall upon the publisher as well as the writer.' Arthur Morris resigned from the Essex Association, though he continued to submit 'tapped' peals, and died a few years later a broken and embittered man. It is a sad story and indicates the intensity of feeling and emotion that can be aroused amongst those who live only for their hobby. Today many church bell ringers also ring changes on handbells. There also exist some handbell societies, mainly secular, devoted to the Art and meeting in each other's houses. Probably the best known is the Dronoldore Society of North Derbyshire whose name is a compound of three Derbyshire towns – Dronfield, Old Whittington and Dore, where its first members originated.

The discovery that with a suitably enlarged set of handbells, properly tuned, recognizable airs could be played took a long time to seize the popular imagination. From the latter half of the eighteenth century it became customary for handbell ringers to perform at village fêtes, and by the accession of Queen Victoria in 1837 it had become a recognized village pastime.

In the North of England it had taken root with much enthusiasm and from 1826 regular competitions were mounted in the famous Belle Vue Gardens in Manchester. This enormous building was the equivalent of London's Crystal Palace in later years and was the cultural and entertainment centre of the North of England for a century and more.

Cheshire, Yorkshire and Lancashire produced some of the finest handbell bands in the country and enormous crowds flocked to Belle Vue to hear them during most of the nineteenth century. The Lancashire ringers who competed became so famous that in 1845 the noted American showman P.T. Barnum engaged them for a tour of the United States. For reasons best known to himself, he refused to bill them as coming from England but dressed them in an extraordinary pseudo-Alpine costume and advertised them as 'the famous Swiss Bell Ringers'.

After World War I handbell ringing began to die out in Britain, despite the publicity engendered by the exploits of Arthur Morris in Harwich. A few village schools kept small sets of tuned bells for the purpose of ringing Christmas carols or for other occasions, but by 1926 the great ringing festivals at Belle Vue were things of the past.

Not for the first time the United States of America were responsible for the revival of a British tradition. A ringer from Boston, Mrs Margaret Shurcliff, visited Britain in 1923 and rang with the College Youths. As a parting gift the Youths presented her with a fine set of handbells. Once home again, Mrs Shurcliff promptly formed the Beacon Hill Ringers of Boston, an organization of handbell enthusiasts still very much alive today, and who occasionally visit Britain.

Though church bells were silenced during most of World War II, this did not apply to handbells. An interesting tradition was maintained at Liverpool, near Pier Head, where the motor vessel belonging to the Mission to Seamen was moored. On the pier was a small chapel dedicated to those who went to sea, and during the war every Sunday morning without fail, the ringers of the nearby St Nicholas Church assembled in the entrance to ring handbells.

Handbells are still very much associated with the northern counties. In churches in Yorkshire and Lancashire old bells are being discovered and there are impressive sets of handbells in some Yorkshire schools. Ecclesfield School, for example, has no fewer than 165 tuned handbells, the same number as Clifton, and in 1986 an important find of over 200 handbells was unearthed at Crossland Moor near Huddersfield. Ecclesfield School has another claim to fame in that its pupils hold the world record for marathon handbell ringing, which stands at fifty-six hours three minutes.

This may well be a record in terms of endurance, but what must surely be unique in reasons for ringing handbells, and perhaps a new tradition, took place in the City of London on 1 October 1986. On that day, near St Paul's Cathedral, three members of the College Youths and one Cumberland rang a short touch on handbells to celebrate the official opening of the first convenience for disabled people in the City of London.

The very small enclosed bells, called crotals, have long been a form of embellishment on dress. They may still be seen on the costumes worn by morris-dancers and help to establish the rhythm. At Congleton, in Cheshire, there was once a pre-Reformation tradition concerning nineteen small bells attached to three leather belts. The bells were surprisingly loud and deep-toned for small bells, five being attached to one belt and seven each on the other two. The belts were said to represent the chains which bound St Peter (the dedication of the parish church), and on the patronal feast-day three altar-boys would each don a belt and run round the town calling the faithful to prayer. The Reformation put a stop to this but in 1559 the bells, and the tradition, were handed over to the important Stubbs family, of which the mayor was a member. By the end of the seventeenth century the tradition of 'belting' round the town had deteriorated into a custom carried out on every occasion possible and was becoming a public nuisance. The Stubbs family by that time had suffered ill-fortune and were by now chimney-sweeps. They were only too glad to sell the bells to the corporation for 10 shillings. The corporation still retains the right to ring these belted bells in this way but so far has refused to revive the custom.

Bells on clothing could also indicate the mental state of the wearer, as evidenced by Shakespeare in *Henry VI,* Part 3, Act I, Scene i, where Warwick says about himself:

> Neither the King, nor him that loves him best,
> Dare stir a wing when Warwick shakes his bells.

Here the Earl is equating himself with a hawk adorned with bells in the pursuit of sport.

Small bells were once hung on birds in cock-fighting contests, and in the equally cruel sport of 'hen-hunting', whereby players were blindfold and then required to kill a hen by chasing it with a stout pole, the location of the bird being denoted by a bell round its neck. Both these games were popular in early nineteenth-century boarding schools, where the masters frequently bet with the boys on the outcome of the competitions and also extracted money from them to buy fresh birds. The so-called 'sport' of cock-fighting, unfortunately being secretly revived, is very old, and the earliest cock-bell known is dated 1514 and is a dainty silver model just two inches in height. It was found at Pocklington, Yorkshire, and because of its quality is thought more likely to have been a prize rather than part of the bird's adornment. Similar bells of silver, though usually rather larger, were often given to successful jockeys in important races, the earliest known example being at York in 1590. In Scotland prize bells for racing were presented at Paisley in 1688.

Brewer mentions the story of 'belling the cat', which goes back as far as William Langland in 1370, who describes how a colony of mice, constantly harassed by a cat, decided that warning of the animal's approach could be given if a bell were to be hung round its neck whilst asleep. This was generally considered a brilliant idea – but unfortunately no mouse could be found willing to 'bell the cat'.* So the phrase is generally used to mean that whilst a certain course of action may be of benefit to the community, nobody is likely to be found to sacrifice himself for it.

Modern bells occur everywhere in our lives and have few traditions. It is therefore pleasant to record that the old interest in handbell ringing is now very much revived and that the Handbell Ringers of Great Britain were formed in 1967 at Norbury near Manchester. Some 700 handbell teams are now part of this association, and the size of a set of bells may be anything from one to six diatonic octaves, often with duplicate and triplicate bells to achieve a high standard of performance.

As was common a hundred years and more ago, handbell teams are once again found in many villages and are not confined to the North of England. Indeed, one of the best-known handbell teams since the 1950s has been that created by the late Frederick Sharpe of Launton in Oxfordshire. Handbell concerts are in great demand as fund-raising devices for hospitals, hospices, drug-addiction centres and the like.

Although the Handbell Ringers of Great Britain now exist officially, the members are mainly ringers who provide recognizable tunes. Other handbell ringers still continue ringing methods and changes, as rung on tower bells, but sometimes appear a little superior in their attitude to the 'tuneful' ringers because of their lack of knowledge of the intricacies of the Exercise.

One type of small bell is neither a handbell nor a crotal but an open bell mounted on a metal spring. Rows of these may still be found in some Victorian kitchens and are a relic of the days when servants in plenty were employed to minister to the needs of the more affluent families. But

* *Dictionary of Phrase and Fable* (Cassells, 1968).

the use of bells to summon servants is much older than that, and Dean Swift, in his satirical *Directions to Servants* of 1755, says that, 'No servant should answer a bell unless it has been rung three or four times, for none but dogs come at the first whistle.'

Yet servants in the seventeenth century and later had every reason to complain of their treatment and the incessant ringing of bells. Beau Brummell, being asked by a friend which of the lakes in Cumbria he liked best, merely rang for his valet. 'Which of the lakes do I admire most, Robinson?' he enquired. 'Windermere, sir,' said the valet. To which the Beau replied, 'Ah, yes, Windermere it is. Thank you Robinson'.*

One manservant in the early years of the nineteenth century was so upset at being called by bells to his master upstairs that finally he picked up a carving-knife, stormed into the room and practically decapitated his victim. At that time it must have been particularly upsetting to be summoned by bells, especially when the sound of the bell and the sight of it going up and down on its spring went on for some time after the bell had ceased to be agitated from above. Later, though the bells continued, a system was devised that indicated which room had rung, and later still the rows of bells were replaced by an electric gong and a similar visual system.

Intolerance to domestic servants was a marked feature of upper-crust Victorian life. Walter Bagehot, in his *Literary Studies* of 1879, makes a remark which is on a par with Marie Antoinette's celebrated comment about 'letting them eat cake'. Bagehot says: 'Poverty is an anomaly to rich people. It is very difficult to make out why people who want dinner do not ring the bell.'

* Quoted by E.S. Turner, *What the Butler Saw* (Michael Joseph, 1962).

11
Big Ben & Co.

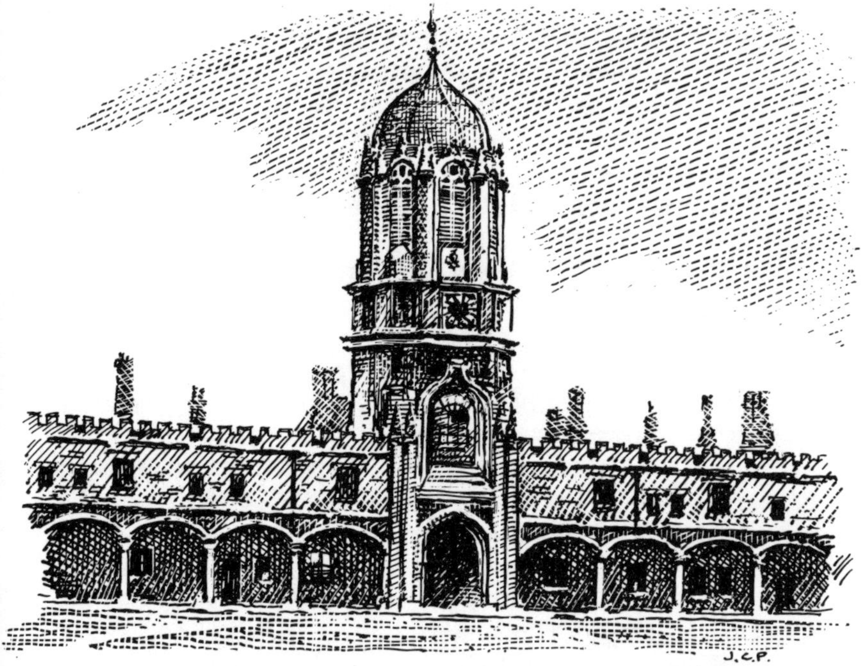

Tom Tower, home of Great Tom, Christchurch, Oxford

Though bells form part of our everyday lives and are largely taken for granted, there are some bells which, perhaps because of their size, history or purpose, have an interesting story to tell.

In Britain, for example, bells are not normally associated with steam locomotives, though they are compulsory on them in the United States. It was for this reason that when the GWR locomotive *King George V* went on a tour of America and Canada in 1937 it had to have a large bell fitted. The bell, provided by the Baltimore & Ohio Railway, is on the locomotive to this day. The *King George V* is now owned by the Bulmer Cider Company of Hereford and may be seen in steam during the summer at various rallies and steam outings. Also, though bells are not a part of the British Rail scene officially, they are occasionally seen mounted on works locomotives and shunters to warn wandering staff of the engine's approach.

Electric bells still play a big part in signalling the imminent arrival of a train, both on station platforms and in the signal-box. One conventionally shaped bell, once used for this purpose on a station in Scotland, seems to have had a curious history. It is inscribed 'Lady Gordon 1785' and was on the station at Lossiemouth for many years though the railway did not reach this part of Scotland until 1852. According to Ernest Morris*, it originally belonged to Lady Gordon of Gordonstoun who in 1772 was officially separated from her husband but continued to live alone in her large mansion. Her two sons lived in smaller houses in the grounds, and in 1785 Lady Gordon had the idea of having a bell cast so that she could summon them or ring for help should an emergency arise.

When Lady Gordon died, the house was bought by a retired sea-captain who transferred the bell to the harbour to serve as a signal to mariners in foggy weather. Unfortunately the arrival of the railway in Lossiemouth dealt a severe blow to passenger traffic by sea, and the harbour became of minimal importance. The captain, evidently determined that his bell should continue to perform a useful function, this time had it hung in the station to signal the arrival of trains. There it remained for over a hundred years until access to Lossiemouth by rail was ended by Dr Beeching in the 1960s. It is now on view in the Fisheries Museum, Lossiemouth.

Museums in port areas of Britain can usually provide examples of bells from ships lost at sea, and the north of Scotland has a plentiful supply. In 1890 the freighter *Nar* was lost in Spey Bay while carrying a cargo of coal and with all hands drowned. The *Nar*'s bell now hangs in Whitehills harbour, and for many years sea-coal could still be gathered in the area after a severe storm. Another area notorious for the loss of ships at sea is the Scilly Isles, and

* *Tintinnabula* (Robert Hale, 1959).

on the main island, St Mary's, four of the five chapel bells in use were salvaged from the sea.

Probably the most famous of all ship's bells is the Lutine Bell which hangs in the Underwriting Room at Lloyd's of London. This bell originally belonged to the French frigate *La Lutine* (*The Sprite*) which surrendered to the British fleet at Toulon in 1793 during the Napoleonic Wars. She was then inducted into the Royal Navy and re-named HMS *Lutine*. In October 1799, while carrying a cargo of gold and silver bullion from the Port of London to Hamburg, she was lost with all hands in a storm off the Dutch coast. During the years that followed, many attempts were made to salvage the cargo, said to be worth nearly £2 million in today's money, but it was not until 1859 that the ship's bell was recovered together with bullion worth £100,000. HMS *Lutine* was insured at Lloyd's, who paid out in full, and since that time the Lutine Bell has hung in the palatial premises of Lloyd's in the City of London. It is rung once to announce that a ship is overdue, and twice to indicate that all is well. Contrary to popular belief, it is NOT rung to announce a wreck or loss at sea. Because of the efficiency of modern communications, it rarely has to be rung today and is used mainly on ceremonial occasions.

At sea there still exists the long tradition of ringing a bell to mark the various watches, though today the bell is most likely to be an electric one. Conventional bells are still found on Royal Navy vessels and are cast and made at the Ministry of Defence depot at Portsmouth. Another important bell is that of Nelson's *Victory* still preserved under a handsome carved canopy.

The Great Fire of London in 1666 put an end to some of the most famous bells in folklore. These were the bells of St Mary-le-Bow in Cheapside, for ever associated with the legend of Dick Whittington and his cat. The story was first told in broadsheet and in pantomime in 1605, some 200 years after the events described.

According to this the young Dick Whittington was employed as a scullion in the house of the wealthy alderman Fitzwarren in the City of London. Dick fell in love with Alice, the alderman's daughter, but considering himself too lowly ever to be considered as a suitor, he determined to run away, with his sole possession, his cat, and seek his fortune elsewhere. He travelled as far as he bottom of Highgate Hill, where he rested, only to hear the sound of the distant Bow Bells which seemed to be saying to him:

> Turn again, Whittington,
> Thrice Lord Mayor of London

Having been accustomed to doing what he was told at the house of Fitzwarren, Dick returned there just in time to hear that a projected sea expedition to North Africa was in trouble because of the infestation of the ship by rats. Dick promptly offered to lend his cat to the captain, and the experiment was highly successful both on board and at the North African port. As a result Dick became famous, made a great deal of money and later married Alice Fitzwarren.

The sound of Bow Bells is an integral part of the story, but how much the rest of it is true remains debatable. Richard Whittington certainly existed, though never a poor man. In about 1380, at the age of twenty, he decided to leave London to seek his fortune, only to return quickly and unexpectedly. He became an influential Londoner and member of the Mercers' Company and was elected Lord Mayor of London four times (not three) – in 1397, 1398, 1406 and 1419. He died in 1423. His decision to return to London as a result of the sound of Bow Bells is marked by a stone tablet in a metal grille at the bottom of Highgate Hill.

There is no doubt that Whittington's return to London, whether or not as a result of hearing the bells, proved of great benefit to the capital. He was a very generous man. During his lifetime he paid for the extension of the nave at Westminster Abbey, restored St Bartholomew's Hospital and built several almshouses and schools. Other less well-known acts of this remarkable man were his fining the powerful Brewers Company a considerable sum for supplying bad beer to the London taverns, and lending Henry V a sum which, at today's valuation, would represent £1 million, to enable the King to invade France.

The pantomime version of Dick Whittington includes more bells than the facts allow, which is no bad thing. First we hear Bow Bells while Dick is resting on Highgate Hill, then there is often a 'transformation scene' depicting a fairy bell-foundry and finally the wedding bells ringing out for Dick and his Alice. It is a charming story, loved by children for nearly 400 years, and we would not want to change a word of it.

After Bow Bells had been destroyed in the Blitz, a new ring of twelve was installed in 1961 and dedicated in the presence of the Duke of Edinburgh. Some pieces of the old bells were incorporated in the new ring.

There is another legend concerning Bow Bells claiming that only a person born within their sound can be considered a true Londoner. There is some opposition to this claim. The Cheapside Bow Bells are so named because of the arcades of the original tower. The real Bow Bells (say the pundits) are those hanging in St Mary's, the parish church of Bow, three miles east. This is more logical (it is said) because the bells of Bow church would have been more likely to have been heard by Cockneys living in London's East End than the bells of the church in Cheapside. The East Enders consider themselves the only true Cockneys – and they are. There still exists confusion on the point when folk from outside the capital insist on referring to all Londoners as Cockneys. This irritates both the ordinary Londoner and the true Cockney, the latter easily distinguished by the marked accent.

Another casualty of the Great Fire of London was the cathedral of St Paul's together with its bells. The original building had been started in 1087, and by 1222 the central tower was completed and fitted with five bells. In 1561 the central tower was struck by lightning and demolished, so losing its bells. But according to Stow in his *Survey of London* (1603) there were four more bells in a detached tower to the north-west of the main building. Stow tells of '... a great high clochier, or bellhouse, four square and built of stone, and in the same a most strong frame of timber with four bells, the greatest I have ever heard. These were called Jesus bells and belonged to Jesus chapel, but I know not by whose gift; the same had a great spire of timber covered with lead with the image of St Paul on the top.'

There is a legend that after the dissolution of the monasteries Henry VIII (who now owned the tower and bells) lost them to Sir Miles Partridge against a bet of £100 while playing dice. Sir Miles had the bells removed and broken up for scrap, bell-metal being the most valuable form of this commodity. Later Sir Miles was lodged in the Tower of London and eventually beheaded in 1552. Dr Thomas Fuller DD made the somewhat cryptic remark that, 'He bought the bells to ring in his pocket, but the ropes afterwards catched about his neck.'

Little remained of Old St Paul's after the fire of 1666, and a new cathedral, to the design of Sir Christopher Wren, began rising on the site in 1675. Building began at the east end, and the twin towers at the western end were not completed until 1700. Even then a shortage of funds prevented bells being hung in them, though one bell had to be provided to indicate the start of a service, in accordance with the instructions of the 1662 Book of Common Prayer. By great good fortune a large bell became available when the stone campanile of the Palace of Westminster was demolished. This was the four-ton Great Tom of Westminster and is the chief character in a curious tale.

About 1690 John Hatfield, a guardsman at Windsor Castle, was court-martialled and sentenced to death for being asleep at his post at midnight. His defence was that he had not been asleep at that time, and to prove it he swore in evidence that he had heard Great Tom of Westminster strike thirteen. He was not believed, but between his conviction and his sentence several affidavits were obtained from people living in the area that Great Tom had indeed struck thirteen on the night in question. Guardsman Hatfield was reprieved and lived on to enjoy a successful career in the Guards.

Great Tom was transferred to St Paul's some years after this incident but fell off its trolley *en route* at Temple Bar. The present Bell Yard is said to mark the spot. But the accident cracked Great Tom, and in 1708 it was recast by the founder Wightman who inscribed it with the words:

'BROUGHT FROM THE RUINES OF WESTMINSTER.' The new bell was not a success, being poor in tone, and in less than a year was replaced by another bell cast by Richard Phelps, at the time in charge of the Whitechapel Foundry. Only eight years later it was decided to recast this bell, and the result was today's five-ton monster with its deep and sonorous note. It may be tolled by swinging its clapper and is used in this manner on the death of a royal or important non-royal person. (Only two non-royals have so far been honoured in this way, the Duke of Wellington and Sir Winston Churchill.) On these occasions the bell is tolled for an hour on the day of the death and an hour on the day of the funeral – an interesting survival of the medieval use of a bell to impart grave news.

It is odd that it was not until nearly 200 years after the completion of Wren's masterpiece that St Paul's was provided with bells hung for ringing. After discussions lasting several years, a ring of twelve bells was cast and installed by Taylor's of Loughborough in 1878. Eleven of the bells were the gift of various City Livery companies, and the tenor bell was presented by the Corporation of the City of London. After a trial ring by the College Youths in October of that year, the bells were officially dedicated at a service on 1 November.

One of the prime movers in the matter of the bells had been that infuriating polymath Sir Edmund Denison, later Lord Grimthorpe. He was a Queen's Counsel and an expert on almost everything, but particularly concerned with bells, clocks and watches. He had already managed to annoy the Whitechapel Bell Foundry twenty years before in dealing with Big Ben (of which more later) and this time chose Taylor's to provide the ring of twelve. When asked why he had not chosen the Whitechapel Foundry, only a mile away, he gave the reasons for his decision but made some unfortunate remarks about the London foundry. The result was a famous libel action brought by Whitechapel against the know-all lawyer, which the foundry won. They were awarded £2,000 damages against Grimthorpe – a vast sum in the 1870s.

Despite an apparent lack of interest in bells at St Paul's going back 200 years, once the ring of twelve was installed, the dean and chapter, urged on by Denison, began thinking about having a really big bell in what was, after all, the most famous cathedral in Britain. They envisaged a bell of about fourteen tons and once again began raising the necessary funds. This time, though the City Livery Companies obliged as before, the Corporation of the City of London refused to co-operate, considering it a needless expense. In the event enough money was raised to enable an even larger bell to be cast by Taylor's. This bell weighed 16¾ tons and was successfully cast on 23 November 1881.

The bell, named 'Great Paul', then had to be transported to London. Its weight and size (nine feet six inches wide at the mouth) presented problems, not the least being the capacity of the bridges it would have to go over and under. It eventually left Loughborough on 11 May 1882 on a specially strengthened low-loader hauled by a steam traction-engine. Its departure from the town of its birth was greeted with the ringing of church bells from all over the area, a feature which continued throughout its ten-day journey to London. Hundreds of people turned out to accompany the bell on its route, and there was great excitement all the way. So great was the enthusiasm that the bell had to be guarded by the police during the nightly stop, especially after it was discovered that a man had been caught during the hours of darkness just about to inscribe his name on the bell with a punch and hammer.

Through Leicester, Kettering, Northampton, Dunstable and St Albans, Great Paul travelled until it reached the steep Highgate Hill on 20 May. Here it had to stay a day whilst a second traction engine was attached to act as a brake going down the hill, but finally, on Monday 22 May, it arrived safely outside St Paul's. No bell of that size had ever been hoisted aloft before in Britain. The Royal Engineers were called in from Woolwich Arsenal and brought equipment with them normally used for moving 35-ton cannons. All went according to plan and in the surprisingly short time of fifteen hours Great Paul had been lifted into its tower. After more work by the bell-hangers, the bell was ready to be tolled and the dedication service took place on 3rd June 1882.

Though the largest bell in the country,* Great Paul's note was considered a disappointment by many. Mellow as the note was, it did not seem to carry very far, and one correspondent of *The Times* was of the opinion that it had made more noise on the road from Loughborough to London than it had since being installed. So concerned were the general public after the excitement of seeing the bell that a broadsheet was printed and sold on the streets with the headline: 'Great Paul Tongue-Tied: Why Don't He Speak Out?' The fault was not in the bell but more likely in the way it had been hung, a fact noted by Denison. After much discussion involving the location of the bell and the nearby clock mechanism, the bell was raised another sixteen feet and provided with a full wheel. This enabled it to be swung through an arc of nearly 90 degrees though it required four men to do it.

In later years Great Paul was rung daily at 1 p.m., thus reviving the medieval apprentice bell. By 1963 this custom had to stop through lack of volunteers, but in 1971 it began again when an electrical timing and striking device was installed by the Friends of St Paul's. The note remains rich and mellow, though strangely subdued for such an enormous bell.

If Great Paul is the biggest bell in Britain, there is little doubt that Big Ben is the best loved. Probably the most famous bell in the world, it hangs in the clock-tower of the Houses of Parliament at Westminster. For many people Big Ben *is* the clock-tower, but, in fact, it is only the hour bell of the Westminster chimes. It weighs 13½ tons and was not installed at Westminster without incident.

The first attempt at producing a suitable bell for the Houses of Parliament was made in 1856 when a sixteen-ton bell was cast by the Warner foundry at Stockton-on-Tees. Taken to West Hartlepool by rail, it then travelled to London by sea and was hauled by road from the London docks to Westminster. Here, in Palace Yard, it was mounted on a frame a few feet off the ground

* It is sometimes stated that Great Paul is the largest bell ever cast in Britain. This is no longer so. An 18¼-ton bell was cast in 1928 by Gillett & Johnson of Croydon and is now the deepest bell of the carillon of Riverside Church, New York.

Great Paul on its way to St Paul's, May 1882

and became one of the sights of London. It was not, however, intended only as a spectacle but was hung in this manner so that the optimum weight of the hammer which was to be used to strike it could be calculated. Needless to say, the experiment was supervised by Denison (not yet Baron Grimthorpe) who at the time was president of the Horological Society. The idea was to drop lead balls of increasing size onto the bell to see how much weight it could stand. The optimum safe weight was discovered when the next heaviest ball was dropped on the bell and cracked it! There was consternation amongst the experts, and Denison, who was extremely unpopular with the press, was lampooned in the *Illustrated London News* and other periodicals.

The Warner foundry was asked to take back the bell and recast it but seemed unwilling to do this, quoting a completely unrealistic price for the work. In the event the Whitechapel Foundry was given the contract, broke up the original sixteen-ton bell and recast into a smaller bell weighing 13½ tons. This time the calculations regarding the hammer were made first, before experiments began, and the foundry stipulated that a hammer weighing not more than 4 cwt should be used. In July 1859 the bell was hauled to the top of the tower and sounded for the first time.

Londoners took it to their hearts and named it Big Ben. This may well have been a compliment to Sir Benjamin Hall, Chief Commissioner of Works, an enormously fat man who had had a great deal to do with the design and eventual installation of the bell. Though this theory is often propounded, it seems much more likely that Big Ben was named after Ben Caunt, a seventeen-stone prize-fighter famous in his day whom the public had known as Big Ben since 1856. Like the bell named after him, he was described as being 'the heaviest in his class'.

Though Big Ben's sound became familiar to Londoners, it did not last long, for in less than three months it was reported that the bell was cracked. This sparked off an immediate quarrel between Denison, the bell-hangers and the Whitechapel foundry. The foundry said that, despite their recommendations a hammer of more than 4 cwt had been used. There was some justification in this as when the hammer was weighed it proved to be 7 cwt. The bell-hangers, on the other hand, insisted that the hammer had nothing to do with it and that the bell had cracked in the foundry, but this fact had not been divulged at the time and the crack hidden before delivery. In the meantime Big Ben was silent for the next three years while controversy raged and litigation was threatened. In 1862 the bell began to ring again after a lighter hammer had been installed and the bell turned slightly so that the hammer hit the sound-bow at a different spot. Big Ben remains cracked to this day, a fact apparent to a sensitive ear, and its imperfect note is known all over the world since it made its radio debut ushering in the year 1924 via the BBC studios in Savoy Hill, just off the Strand.

Though in Great Paul and Big Ben London has the heaviest and third heaviest bells in Britain, in between them comes the 14¾-ton bell of Liverpool Cathedral. Other big bells include York Minster's 'Great Peter' of 10¾ tons and the hour bell of Nottingham Exchange known as 'Little John', weighing 10½ tons.

It must be appreciated that none of these very heavy bells is mounted on a wheel for full-circle ringing but is normally tolled, by swinging the bell in a short arc until the clapper strikes the bell, or chimed by hitting the bell externally with a hammer. Most of these big bells are fairly modern or have been recast from ancient bells, as has happened with Oxford's 'Great Tom' (6¼ tons), originally cast in the fourteenth century at Osney Abbey and brought to Oxford and recast in 1612 and at various times later. Exeter has its four-ton Great Peter recast in 1676 from the original bell of 1484 dedicated to Bishop Peter Courtenay.

Canterbury Cathedral is justifiably proud of its bell called Great Dunstan (3¼ tons) which was cast in a pit in the cathedral precincts in 1762. The cathedral has a smaller and older bell called Bell Harry cast in 1635. Through the generosity of the Anglia Building Society in 1981 Great Dunstan, together with a clock and chimes, was installed in Arundel Tower, which was built in the first half of the nineteenth century but contained no bells.

Not until we get down to a weight of about four tons do we meet bells that can be rung full-circle and in peal. The heaviest of these is the tenor of Liverpool Cathedral known as Emmanuel, with a weight of 4 tons 2 cwt. Other heavy cathedral bells hung for change-ringing include Exeter's Grandison, the tenor of St Paul's Cathedral and the tenor bells of York Minster and Wells Cathedral, all weighing between 2¾ and four tons.

Surprisingly, the ten bells of Westminster Abbey are not all that noteworthy. The old ring of just four bells was increased to eight in 1919, when the first true peal was rung, and all the bells were recast and augmented to a ring of ten in 1971. There is no full ringing for services, though a bell is chimed. The Westminster Company of Ringers ring peals or touches for special occasions throughout the year such as royal weddings or births. A peal of 5,040 changes was rung on 26 June 1982 to mark the birth of Prince William a few days earlier, and a similar peal on 22 September 1984 after the birth of Prince Harry. The bells are also rung at a service marking the start of the legal year in the autumn at which the Lord Chancellor, judges and members of the Bar are present.

One of the best-known London churches is St Clement Danes in the Strand, rebuilt by Sir Christopher Wren in 1682. Eleven years later 'eight noble bells' were hung in the tower but it was not for another forty years that a full peal was rung on them, a feat accomplished by the College Youths in February 1733. When the bells were increased to ten in 1843, St Clement Danes became one of the most popular venues for ringing in London. At the beginning of World War II the bells were taken down for safety and housed in the base of the tower. One night in May 1941, when all London seemed ablaze and even St Paul's was diminished in its inferno of flame and fire, St Clement Danes was gutted by incendiary bombs, only the tower and walls remaining. The bells, red-hot from the flames and then swamped by water from the hoses, were cracked beyond repair. In 1955 the Royal Air Force restored this famous church as a memorial to the Commonwealth airmen who lost their lives in the war. The bells were recast and rehung by the Whitechapel Foundry and have been rung regularly since 1958. There is also a carillon provided playing the famous nursery tune 'Oranges and Lemons'.

A more fortunate City church was St Michael's, Cornhill, which, though losing most of its peal-boards in a small fire, remained largely undamaged throughout the war. The present building dates from 1728 and was one of the first churches to have a ring of twelve installed, thus attracting the 'scientific' ringers of the day. Another record is held by St Bartholomew the Great in Smithfield, a church founded by Rahere in 1123. A victim to the Reformation, when it was a priory, the present buildings date from 1630. Despite this it has the oldest ring of five bells in existence, and the cost of installing them is noted in the churchwardens' accounts of 1510.

Outside London some interesting church bells are found at Windsor, in the Curfew Tower of the Chapel of St George. A tower was built at Windsor in 1230, and there is a document recording the hanging of four bells there as early as 1249. The present chapel was built in 1475 by Edward IV, and three years later the old bells moved to the new tower. The eight bells hanging there today date from the seventeenth century and are hung anticlockwise. They are rung in peal for royal and ceremonial occasions. A 300-year-old tradition persists in connection with the three services held daily in the chapel, Holy Communion, Matins and Evensong: one bell is chimed to summon the sacristan to the chapel, the second to send for the lay clerks and the third bell for the choir to be ready, after which the remaining five bells are tolled for a short time until the sacristan intones the words 'Toll down.' At this point the procession of choir and clergy move into the chapel. The Round Tower of Windsor Castle is famous but has only one bell. Cast in 1755 and called 'The Raven', it was captured at Sebastopol and brought back to Windsor as a trophy of the Crimean War. Its harsh and anguished note is rarely heard, for it is tolled only at the death of a monarch.

Windsor and its castle may have a tradition going back a thousand years but in a remote corner of the British Isles a single bell recalls the simple faith of the first Christian missionaries to Britain. This bell hangs in the Abbey of Iona, on that island off the west coast of Scotland where St Columba landed 1,400 years ago and established a community. Over the centuries the site became neglected and desolate, the buildings in ruins, but still able to cast a magical spell over those who visited the island. Said the great Samuel Johnson: 'The man is little to be envied whose piety would not grow warmer amongst the ruins of Iona.'

At the beginning of this century the Iona Community began to re-establish religious life on the island and by 1931 the abbey had been rebuilt by members. Taylor's of Loughborough were asked to cast a 22-cwt bell which was hung on a full wheel for ringing. But in the absence of any experienced ringer it was chimed for the next forty years, until 1971, when two ringers travelled from the mainland and gave the community the required instruction. A few days later the full sound of this superb bell was heard calling the faithful to Evensong, and it is said that its voice could be heard that Sunday evening in Oban, thirty miles away across the sea. Truly the prophecy of St Columba has been fulfilled when he said: 'Iona of my heart, Iona of my love, instead of monks' voices shall be heard the lowing of cattle. But before the world's end Iona shall be once more as it was.'

Odd materials have been used for making bells in the past, one of the oddest being the ring of 'ceramic' bells hung in a garage at Liss, Hampshire. The first strange bells in this 'tower' were a set of metal buckets made by Messrs Spear & Jackson, the well-known makers of agricultural implements. These were replaced by the present 'flower-pot' ring cast (if that is the right word) by a pottery at Farnham, Surrey. The tenor weighs 7¾ lb and there are fourteen bells in all. Though peals on these bells were not officially recognized at first, they now appear in *Ringing World*. The ringers of Liss have formed themselves into a ringing society and are active ringers on conventional bells. Twelve churches in England have rings of steel bells including Thornborough, Buckinghamshire, restored in 1986 after being unringable since 1952.

For various reasons carillons of bells have never found

much favour in Britain. In Belgium and Holland, where the full-circle method of ringing was never adopted, the system was taken up with enthusiasm.

A carillon is a method of playing a large number of tuned bells by hand or by automatic striking. They are tuned to the normal scale, as in a piano, and to be classified as a true carillon there must be a minimum of twenty-three bells. Today there are only seventeen true carillons in the British Isles, one of the largest being that of St Nicholas Church, Aberdeen, which has forty-eight bells including the deepest bass bell at 4½ tons. Bournville Schools in Birmingham also has forty-eight bells but there the bass bell is much lighter. Manchester Town Hall has a carillon of twenty-three bells plus an eight-ton hour bell called Great Abel.

Carillons are played by hand at a kind of keyboard, where the 'keys' are banged with the fist, though today most modern carillons are played by an automatic or even computerized device.

Curiously, London only has one true carillon, of twenty-three bells, and this is on commercial premises in New Bond Street, formerly the headquarters of Atkinson's, the perfume company. At the premises of the Houndsditch Warehouse Company in the City is found a set of ten bells hung 'dead' for chiming and a very small set of bells rung automatically at two o'clock.

To hang bells 'dead' but capable of being chimed (i.e. struck externally in turn) is a device midway between bells hung as a true 'ring' for method-ringing, and the vast range of the average carillon. It is also used, as we have seen, when it is inadvisable to use church bells for full ringing because of the state of the tower. In Newcastle-upon-Tyne we find examples of both in the same city, for the church of St Andrew has six bells hung for automatic chiming only, whilst the Civic Centre has a superb twenty-five-bell carillon.

In London one famous church has an automatic chiming mechanism that should be noted. This is All Hallows on Tower Hill, where a church has existed since the first little chapel was dedicated by St Ethelburga, Abbess of Barking, in 675. Over the years the chapel was enlarged and managed to survive the Reformation. In 1649, however, it suffered great damage in an explosion which was thought to be a political act, as Charles I was being tried in London that same day. After World War I All Hallows became closely associated with the Reverend 'Tubby' Clayton, the founder of Toc H, but in World War II was again severely damaged by enemy bombing. The tower survived and in 1948 the remainder of the church was rebuilt and bells were installed, due largely to the generosity of Mr John McConnell of Montreal. Later examination of the tower indicated it to be too frail for full-circle ringing, and today the church has eighteen bells, of which the heaviest weighs a ton, hung for chiming. These bells were cast and hung by Taylor's of Loughborough, and a device has been installed enabling them to be used also as a carillon.

It has occasionally happened that full-circle ringing is not performed in a church tower, not because of any danger but because no ringers can be found. This happened at the unusually dedicated church of St Cyr at Stinchcombe, Gloucestershire, where, because no ringers were available, a chiming device was installed. But this device was rather more sophisticated than most and was geared to 'play' changes and methods with perfect 'striking' which sounded very like a good team of ringers in action. Local ringers soon got to hear of this and were so incensed, or perhaps so ashamed, that within weeks a band of ringers had been formed, and conventional ringing goes on at Stinchcombe once more. The chiming machine is now on view in the church and is a source of great interest to both ringers and those who are mechanically inclined.

As carillons in the British Isles are not very common, we list below the seventeen which are true twenty-three-bell machines and the number of bells in each carillon:

Aberdeen: St Nicholas Church	48
Birmingham: Bournville	48
St Helens, Merseyside: St Mary's	47
Loughborough War Memorial	47
Cobh, Ireland: St Colman's Cathedral	47

Armagh: St Patrick's Cathedral	39
Parkgate, Cheshire: Mostyn House School	37
Perth: St John's Church	35
Kilmarnock: St Mark's Church	30
Eaton Hall, Cheshire	28
Newcastle-upon-Tyne: Civic Centre	25
Manchester Town Hall	23
St Andrews: Holy Trinity Church	23
Saltley, Birmingham: RC School	23
Dumbarton: RC church	23
London, New Bond Street: J. Fox & Co	23
Spalding: South Holland Centre	23

No reference to chiming bells could be complete without mentioning the various devices for signalling the time found on many buildings and known as clock 'jacks'. Some merely tell the time by striking, others are part of a complicated mechanism involving moving figures, knights in armour and the like. Probably the most famous of these is at Wells Cathedral, where two knights in armour strike the bells with their battleaxes. Another figure, a short distance away, is known as Jack Blandiver and strikes the quarters on two bells with his heels. In London two famous clock jacks, known as Gog and Magog, were enormous painted wooden figures carved by Captain Richard Saunders in 1708 to be carried in the Lord Mayor's Show complete with clock. They were formerly outside St Dunstan's Church in Fleet Street but are now in London's Guildhall. Figures ringing bells are found in various churches and cathedrals, though few are as magnificent as Wells, and some are not working at all. Examples may be found at Oxford (Carfax Tower), Minehead, Launceston, Rye and York Minster.

12
The Bell Tower

The church bellcage at East Bergholt, Suffolk

Whilst this book has been concerned mainly with the history, legends and traditions of bells, there is much of interest to be discovered in the many types of towers and buildings in which the bells are housed. For many years the standard view has been that a church should look like a church – and a medieval church at that. Only recently has this view changed, and even in the United States, where change is often confused with progress, the Episcopal Cathedral at Washington DC, which received its bells as recently as 1963, still bears a remarkable resemblance to Worcester Cathedral.

Nevertheless, even amongst churches that have been built mainly to the same pattern from the fourteenth and fifteenth centuries, an amazing variety of architectural features may be found. One thing that had an effect on church architecture, as it had an effect on so many things, was the introduction of the whole wheel in belfries and the development of full-circle ringing. In some churches the tower, particularly if centrally placed, could not bear the weight of the additional bells that needed to be hung and the tower was demolished and rebuilt at the west end. This sometimes happened for purely architectural reasons unconnected with ringing, as at the parish church of High Wycombe, Buckinghamshire, about 1540.

Wordsworth says of a spire that, 'Its silent finger points to Heaven' but both towers and spires vary enormously. It may be slender and tall as at Salisbury Cathedral, or squat and on the ground like the strange bell-cage at East Bergholt, Suffolk. A tower may be a physical part of a church or detached and standing apart. A tower may be square, which is usual, round, or even oval. The church of St Augustine at Brooklands, Kent, is one of the strangest of all. It is of timber, is detached and is in the form of a six-sided pyramid in three sections, one above the other.

Round towers are a particular feature of East Anglia, and of 174 such towers in Britain, 160 are in Suffolk and Norfolk. Other isolated examples may be found in Cambridgeshire, Essex, Sussex and Dorset. Various theories exist as to their origin but the most widely accepted is that were built as a form of defence by the Saxons against the marauding Norsemen. They are round because the dressed stone and corner-stones, so essential for the construction of square buildings, were not readily available and the local flint and rubble were therefore used. More evidence of their use in defence is provided by the siting of the east door of the tower which is always at least ten feet from the ground. A local historian* is of the opinion that this suggests that the tower could be reached only by ladder and that, once the terrified Saxons were inside, the ladder was drawn up after them.

The original Saxon towers prior to the ninth century

* A.C.C. Hedges, *The Gunton Story* (Weathercock Press, 1985).

were probably built free-standing, with a church added during the following centuries and bells provided later. At the village of Bramfield, in Suffolk, one free-standing tower still exists to which a church has never been attached. Round towers remain a fascinating feature of the Eastern Counties and a memento of the fierce and cruel invaders from overseas. The theory that they were originally deep wells, dug into the ground with the surrounding soil later washed away, simply does not hold water.

At Hexton, Northumberland, two sides of the square tower collapsed but the remaining sides have been strengthened and retained, giving a very odd effect.

Other church towers have developed a list away from the true, as has happened with the church of St Laurence at Surfleet, Lincolnshire, a county that seems to specialize in 'leaning' towers, as witness the old rhyme:

Gosberton church is very high,
Surfleet church is all awry.
Pinchbeck church is in a hole,
And Spalding church is big with foal.

At Surfleet the tower and spire reach a height of 120 feet, and the top is six feet four inches out of true. A plate set in the floor near the west door indicates that one is immediately under the apex of the spire. Oddly enough, the tower began to lean before the spire was added. Had there already been a spire when the tower began leaning, it would by now be thirteen feet out of true.

Surfleet is certainly an architectural oddity but by far the most famous of all 'leaning' towers is the crooked spire of St Mary and All Saints, the parish church of Chesterfield, Derbyshire. Many are the legends surrounding this spire which the Victorian novelist, Harrison Ainsworth, likened to the tail of the dragon of Wantley. It leans six feet out of line to the south and over four feet to the west, thus producing the 'corkscrew' effect for which it is famous. The most popular legend concerning it is that Satan, on a flight from Nottingham to Sheffield, stopped for a rest on the spire. A service was in progress at the time and he suddenly caught a whiff of incense from the church below. This caused him to sneeze violently and thrash about, so twisting the spire on which he sat.

The scientific reason for the twisting of Chesterfield's spire is said to be the action of the sun on the southern side of the spire, causing the lead-covered timbers to warp. From time to time the tower has been scheduled as unsafe but each time it is reprieved, and its fine ring of ten bells is regularly heard.

Chesterfield is reported as having had bells in medieval times, though the present ones date from 1820. A peal was rung on them by the Sherwood Youths of Nottingham that same year, and the peal-book states that a Mr Peat, who conducted the peal, had his coach fare paid for him but the remainder of the band 'started on foot from Nottingham to Chesterfield'.

Another famous crooked spire is found at the church of SS Peter and Paul at Ermington, Devon. A pleasant legend purporting to account for it says that the very first bride to be married in the church was so beautiful that the spire twisted round to have a good look at her! Many other towers exist which lean slightly, such as the spire of Salisbury Cathedral, Britain's highest at 404 feet, which is just over two feet out of true. A more serious deflection was found at Yapton, Sussex, where the tower had to be supported by a buttress.

Though the external appearance of the tower is of great importance to the viewer, internal access to the bells is of even greater interest to the would-be ringer, and it varies enormously. In most churches the route to the ringing-chamber is by way of a narrow spiral staircase built into, or sometimes onto, the wall of the tower. It is usually a clockwise spiral constructed purposely in this manner so that a person defending the tower from above would have his right arm free to deal with the interlopers trying to get to the top. But some stairways are anticlockwise, and not all of them are narrow. The ancient Saxon church at Brixworth, Northamptonshire, has a very wide semi-circular stone staircase, and in some churches one finds a wide wooden staircase. In the village of Cumnor, Oxfordshire, for ever associated with the mysterious death of Amy Robsart in 1560, the parish church of St Michael has a very odd free-standing wide wooden staircase.

Access to the bells is not always as simple as this and not always comfortable for the ringer when he arrives. Charles Dickens, in his unfinished novel *Edwin Drood,* has his hero murdered in what is considered to be Rochester Cathedral, by being pushed off a beam in the tortuous passage leading to the ringing-chamber. This is, of course, fiction and few towers are so dangerous.

Cottingham, near Hull, has a dark and narrow stairway which, surprisingly, ends amongst the bells themselves in the belfry. To gain access to the dungeon-like ringing-chamber below, ringers must descend to it through a trapdoor. At Merton College, Oxford, there is an odd situation in that there is no ringing-chamber in the accepted sense, ringing being performed from a three-foot-wide gallery round the wall of the tower. Sixty feet below is the floor of the chapel, with nothing between. Because of this strange arrangement the ropes from the bells are diverted to the ringers at an angle which makes ringing extremely difficult.

Another bizarre ringing-chamber is that in the great lantern tower of the Abbey Church of Pershore, Worcs. This tower, begun in 1330, is 125 feet to the top of its pinnacles and is one of the finest examples of fourteenth-century architecture. Inside the tower massive beams spring from the thick walls and meet in the centre, seventy-two feet above the floor of the church. On this structure is a twelve-foot square 'cage' with its corners facing the walls, so giving it a diamond appearance when seen from below. This extraordinary 'cage' (designed by Gilbert Scott) is reached by a narrow spiral staircase and then by a bridge across one of the beams, carefully railed on each side. The bells themselves are only sixteen feet above the heads of the ringers but, despite the eccentricities of the ringing-chamber, are a pleasant and easy ring of eight. Scott's unique design was intended to avoid obscuring the view of the internal architecture of the tower.

Damage has been done to church fabric, and towers

have fallen down for a variety of reasons. Sometimes, as at Darfield and Hatfield, in Yorkshire, mining has created dangerous subsidence which has put an end to ringing. Sometimes it is just through old age, as happened at Hempstead in Essex (the birthplace of Dick Turpin) in 1882. The new tower and its six bells date from 1962.

An interesting attempt to avoid such misfortune has been made at Horley, Surrey. Here, in 1970, a completely new *iron* tower was built inside the timber one and a new frame for the bells installed. It was originally intended to demolish the church but it was finally decided that, if the tower could be saved, a brand-new church would be built alongside, and this was done. A similar 'face-lift' was carried out at Acle in Norfolk. In Suffolk, at the wonderful church at Long Melford, repairs to the church fabric were required due to the bell-frames being mounted diagonally in the tower – a very rare feature.

A disaster of a different kind took place at Spitalfields Church in London's Commercial Street in 1836. Though the tower was not destroyed, much damage was caused by a fire in the ringing-chamber. So fierce were the flames that the massive timber bell-frame was burnt through, and the twelve bells were completely destroyed. Whilst many people in the past have fulminated against strong drink in the ringing-chamber, nobody seems to have thought of banning food, for this calamity was caused by a visiting band of Cumberlands having a 'fry-up' which got out of hand.

As one writer has pointed out,* fears that a tower may collapse because of the swinging tonnage of the bells may not always be justified. He cites the situation at Peterborough Cathedral where for many years it was thought that, if the ten heavy bells were rung together, the west front would collapse. Five of the bells were therefore removed but a more recent survey has revealed that such fears were overstated. In 1986 a new ring of ten bells was installed and dedicated, though appreciably lighter. In 1987 three of the heavy old bells were bought by an American for use in Pittsburgh, Pennsylvania.

* *Bellringing* Ron Johnston.

A vitally important factor in the stability of the tower is the manner in which the bells are hung. Traditionally they are hung in such a way that the movement of each bell cancels out the strain of each other bell when swinging, for the horizontal force exerted is enormous. If the position of the bell frame is dangerous and makes it unstable, it may have to be dismantled and rebuilt. This is a job for a professional bell-hanging team and even then may cause complications.

On a fine Sunday afternoon in 1972, a lady living over a shoe-shop in Marske, Yorkshire, thought she heard suspicious noises coming from the Midland Bank next door. Soon police cars with flashing lights had surrounded the premises, but the loud thumping noises continued, though there seemed no sign of entry into the bank nor anyone within. It was at last realized that the noise of hammering and banging was coming from the church tower next door, where it was found that six stalwarts were engaged in dismantling the iron bell-frame, blissfully unaware of the chaos they were causing below. The sound was directed downwards through the louvres of the tower. (Louvres, incidentally, though having little tradition or folklore associated with them, are of infinite variety and a source of unfailing interest to church architects and historians.)

Another complication in a tower affecting the ringing is the way the bell-ropes come down from the bells into the ringing-chamber. If the bells are mounted in the standard manner on the frame, the ropes usually fall into the ringing-chamber in a circle, clockwise, starting with the treble and ending with the tenor. But this does not always happen. At the Suffolk church of Beccles, for example, the ten bells are hung in such a way that the ropes fall in a circle 1-9-7-8-10-2-6-5-4-3. Another odd feature of this fascinating church is that it has four staircases, one in each corner of the tower. One leads to the ringing-chamber, one to the bells, one to the clock mechanism and one to the roof. Beccles also has one of the finest examples of a leather ringers' beer jack or jug dated 1827, and according to the late George Symonds of Ipswich, it was one of the last church towers in England where smoking and drinking beer were permitted. Perhaps it was due to the fact that Beccles is also a detached tower that induced a more relaxed atmosphere.

Detached towers are found in many parts of Britain, and at one time were a feature of most English cathedrals, including Norwich, Salisbury, Ely, Rochester, Worcester and Chichester. Over the years most have been replaced with a conventional tower, though in some instances, as at Norwich, the tower is unsuitable for ringing. Chichester retains a separate campanile of eight bells plus a clock with a 73-cwt bourdon bell. Another example is at St David's Cathedral, Dyfed, which has a ring of eight hung in the gateway of the monastery. At Oxford both the cathedral of Christchurch and the chapel of New College have separate towers, while the Carfax Tower, in the city centre, is the detached tower of the long-vanished church of St Martin of Tours and is a fine vantage point from which to view the ancient university city.

In Worcestershire the church of All Saints at Evesham has a handsome detached 'bell tower' with a roadway running through its base. King's College, Cambridge, once had a low, timber bell-cage on the north side which was demolished in 1754. But the most famous surviving example of this genre is the belfry in the churchyard at East Bergholt, Suffolk. Here the five bells are housed in a shallow pit with a timber frame round the top, the whole surmounted by a tiled roof. They have no ropes and are rung by their headstocks, though mounted on whole wheels. Needless to say, there are various legends accounting for this phenomenon, one being that the Devil tried to run off with the bells but, pursued by the parson and his flock, dropped them in the churchyard, where they remain to this day. Another story is that the lord of the manor in medieval times was not a lover of bells. When he offered to rebuild the church, he did not want to have bells but was persuaded by the parson to instal them. He compromised by having the bells mounted in a cage in the churchyard at ground level, so that the sound would not carry, and also on the opposite side of the church to his house, again to reduce the noise. A more modern legend, only 450 years old, tells how Cardinal Wolsey, who hailed

Quex Tower at Birchington in Kent was erected privately by a local ringer in 1819

from nearby Ipswich, generously offered to pay for a new ring of bells for East Bergholt church. They were delivered to the churchyard in 1530 but in that year Wolsey was summoned to trial for displeasing the King and died on his way to London. No money was available to hang the bells properly, so there in the churchyard they remain.

Another famous detached tower is at Elstow, Bedfordshire, where John Bunyan rang, as described in a previous chapter.

A strange situation exists at Berwick-on-Tweed where the parish church was built without a tower or bells, the latter being provided by the ring of eight in the town hall. This building looks so much like a church that on one occasion the local militia were marched in for a service, and hunted-looking visiting preachers have been found sobbing to be admitted in time for them to preach to the converted.

Berwick is a curious example of a secular tower and bells being used for religious ringing, but there are many towers in Britain whose origins are secular and whose bells exist purely for the enjoyment of *aficionados* of the Exercise.

Some of these towers were provided by the community, often as a watch-tower with bells to signal an alarm, others, like Berwick Town Hall and Manchester Town Hall, by the civic authorities. Another example of the latter is the somewhat unfortunate case of the Queen Anne Tower of Imperial College at South Kensington in London. This 300-foot tower was built in 1887 to commemorate the Jubilee of Queen Victoria. Today it could also be classified as a detached tower, for the original buildings of what was then called the Imperial Institute have gone and a new Imperial College has been built nearby. Opened by the Queen in 1893, the institute was first conceived partly as a smaller but more permanent exhibition hall intended to replace the highly successful Crystal Palace, home of the 1851 Exhibition in Hyde Park which owed so much to the activities of that astonishing man the Prince Consort. Although it was not designed to carry bells, immediately after the publicity attending the opening, an American lady, Mrs Elizabeth Millar, living at Kew, offered to pay for a ring of ten bells. They were cast by Taylor's of Loughborough, and Mrs Millar, by then eighty-three, was offered honorary membership of the Ancient Society of College Youths, which she gracefully declined. The ten bells, each named after one of the Queen's nine children and one after Her Majesty, all bear the inscription:

> Elizabeth Millar gave me –
> The Loughborough Taylors made me.

Unfortunately this heavy ring of bells is hung at the very top of the tall tower, with the ringing-chamber immediately below. This causes a sway and makes good striking difficult. These problems were apparent from the first, and at the official opening the ringing was in the hands of John Taylor himself, who had a certain amount of difficulty in obtaining first-rate ringers from every ringing association in the country, which had been his brief. That he did so is greatly to his credit, and the Queen is reported to have stopped her carriage on the opening day so that she could better hear the bells. The bells of the Queen Anne Tower of the Imperial College are still rung for royal occasions, and the first full peal was rung in 1902 to mark the coronation of Edward VII. Short lengths are rung on them every few weeks by both Cumberlands and College Youths but full peals are rare.

Some secular towers have been built by private individuals, and by far the best known of these is the result of the activities of a bellringing country squire. He was John Powell Powell, squire of Quex Park near Birchington, Kent, who in 1819 built himself an extraordinary edifice of brick with a curly cast-iron spire, which he called the Waterloo Tower and in which he had hung twelve bells. It is a very fine example of the Gothic style then in vogue and was built as a result of Powell's frustration at being able to ring on only six bells, which was at the time the complement of his own parish church. The whole edifice is about 100 feet high, so making it (as the publicity leaflet of the day said) ' … a noble sea-mark, being only one mile from that briny fluid'.

Both Cumberlands and College Youths were invited to

the official opening on 4 August 1819, and ringing went on all that day and for most of the next day. Not only 'Youths' took part but virtually anyone who could ring at all, and those sailing peacefully on 'the briny fluid', whilst appreciating the new sea-mark, must have been somewhat puzzled at the sounds from shore which did not stop for two days.

Today Quex Park is very popular with ringers from all over the country and its twelve bells are in constant demand. The tower is noted for the large number of peal-boards which adorn the walls, the first of which was a somewhat ornate stained-glass specimen in a wooden frame. It reflected John Powell Powell's interest in the sea, and the design incorporates two sailors as well as the traditional (for Quex) all-seeing eye and an upturned bell. The board commemorates the first full peal rung in the tower by Powell's original 'Quex Institution' at which Powell himself rang the tenor. In later years the tower was vandalized and the peal-board damaged. Latterly, due to the activities of the re-named Quex Park Society of Change-Ringers, this most interesting peal-board has been restored with the help of local craftsmen. Another curiosity at Quex is the four air-ducts built into the tower walls to convey the sound of the bells to the ringers below. A concealed compass has been discovered in the roof of the tower.

For over 130 years the Waterloo Tower at Quex Park was the only privately owned ringing tower in Britain. In 1951, however, Mr Charlie Jarvis, a farmer and keen ringer at Balscott, near Banbury, built a tower on his land and installed a ring of small bells. Initially they were six in number, with a 1¾-cwt tenor, and were cast by the former foundry of Gillett & Johnson at Croydon. Because of the smallness of the bells and the construction of the tower, conventional wooden whole-wheels were not possible, and the ingenious Mr Jarvis first adapted bicycle wheels for his purpose. In 1961 the ring was increased to ten and later augmented yet again to twelve. The bells are now hung on a solid metal frame and with aluminium wheels. The treble bell weighs a mere 14 lb.

The tower is twenty feet in height, and the chamber is a

useful eleven feet by ten. The bells are rung exactly as in a conventional church tower, complete with slider and stay, and the whole thing is an incredible achievement by a man who claims to have no technical knowledge but has 'just listened to people talking'. The village church at Balscott has only two bells, so the Jarvis bells are in great demand for weddings when they are usually rung by members of the Banbury branch of the Oxford Diocesan Guild.

One other place in Britain with a comparable private ring is Stoulton, Warwickshire. Here Arthur Jopp has made a collection of old school bells, had them properly tuned and hung them in the first floor of a cottage adjoining his house. Once again all the correct equipment is there and the ten bells are hung properly for full-circle change-ringing.

Conclusion: Outings and Oddities

Nobody knows the precise number of ringers in Britain today but an estimated figure is 40,000. Many of these ring only occasionally or confine themselves to rounds and call-changes. Method ringers (sometimes known as 'scientific' ringers) are estimated at about 25,000 and represent the hard core of the Exercise.

Most regular ringers are members of their own diocesan guild or county equivalent, and their activities are supervised by the Central Council of Church Bellringers. This body includes ringers who are architects, historians, bellfounders and clerics and so covers every aspect of ringing as well as establishing certain rules and regulations. It also publishes a large number of books for ringers from the *Beginner's Handbook* to technical treatises for architects and other ecclesiastical experts.

There is also a weekly newspaper for ringers called *The Ringing World* which first appeared in 1911, not long before the Victorian *Bell News* ceased publication. It was founded by John Goldsmith, a newspaperman, who remained editor for thirty years and who, in true journalistic tradition, ensured that the content of the journal should be hard news and not history. Today, published in Guildford under the editorship of David Thorne, it prints details of peals and quarter-peals as they are submitted by bands from all over Britain and also records handbell achievements. There is plenty of up-to-date news but there are also many entertaining snippets from the past.

Back numbers are a valuable source of information on the social history of ringing and may be relied upon to furnish many strange stories and curious facts. From the pages of the March 1987 issue, for example, we learn that if one rings Westminster Abbey, the telephone 'holding tune' (that fearsome invention of British Telecom) is, perhaps predictably, the Westminster chimes. This tune was composed in 1793 by the noted musician William Crotch for a church in Cambridge and was adopted by London's Royal Exchange in 1845 and by Westminster in 1860. In 1890 the first commercial electric recording of the famous chimes was marketed, and since then this tune has been adopted by many carillons and chiming devices throughout Europe.

Rather more spectacular was an account in *The Ringing World* of July 1980 of two ringers from Birch-with-Fallowfield (Manchester) who performed a sponsored parachute jump to raise money for the bell-fund of their parish church. The paper reported that at a special service the following Sunday to commemorate the event the hymn chosen was 'O Thou who camest from above'.

An odd and potentially dangerous incident was reported in November 1986 when an old lady was accidentally locked in the base of a church tower in Liverpool for three days. On the previous Sunday, during Evensong, a violent storm had erupted. The old lady, being of a nervous disposition, had not wanted to leave the shelter of the church and had slipped inside the door of the tower leading to the belfry. The captain of the ringers, who had attended Evensong, came from the church and locked the tower door without first checking that nobody was inside. The old lady remained there in the cold and dark, and without food, until ringers arrived for practice on the Wednesday evening, when she was discovered. Said *The Ringing World* 'She was revived by the clergy with a cup of hot tea and seemed none the worse for her ordeal.'

It was just as well for this lady that she had not got herself locked in the tower in 1914, for in November that year *The Ringing World* reported that some churches had suspended practice-night ringing so that, 'It may not be of possible assistance to the enemy's aircraft in locating our cathedrals and churches.'

Unlikely as this belief may be, others even less likely are commented upon in the 'Letters' page of the journal from time to time. One reader revives the superstition that, if the church clock strikes during the hymn before the sermon or during the announcement of the text, a death will occur in the parish during the coming week. Another correspondent reminded readers of the ancient belief that a child born while the church clock was striking 3, 6, 9 or 12 (the 'chime hours') would have the gift of 'second sight' and the ability to cast out devils.

As the pages of *The Ringing World* demonstrate, the activities of ringers are not limited to service ringing in their own tower. Most ringers visit other towers from time to time, such as when they are on holiday, and on these occasions are usually welcomed warmly and invited to 'take a rope'. During the summer months visiting other towers is more organized and usually takes the form of the traditional 'ringers' outing'. Each year a day is decided, a coach booked and the ringers, accompanied by relatives and friends, sally forth to ring at towers in the adjoining county or counties. At each of these they ring for about half an hour while the non-ringers in the party take the opportunity of looking round the church or exploring the village. Some six to eight churches are normally visited in the course of a day's outing.

In 1987 one Dorset band organized an outing by canal, ringing at canalside churches. Homeward bound a stop is made for food and drink, and on a fine day a ringers' outing can be one of the most enjoyable episodes in the ringing year, even for those who do not know the difference between a hammer and a headstock. For the organizer it means a great deal of preliminary work, for the coach must be hired and the route planned, and the incumbent of each church it is proposed to visit must be asked for his permission to ring. This is not only polite but avoids the visit clashing with some other function, such as a wedding. Many vicars pass on requests to ring to their tower captain, but unfortunately it sometimes happens that an absent-minded cleric forgets to do this. The party arrives ready to ring, only to find the tower locked and the captain away for the day. This situation may be overcome if the vicar can be found, but little is possible when another visiting band is in possession of the tower.

These days ringers' outings seem to be becoming much

more widespread, and in 1981 one band from Hertfordshire travelled to Inverness to try the ten bells of St Andrew's Cathedral and those of other churches in the area.

Individual ringers have travelled even further afield, a popular venue being the United States, and in 1987 a party of ringers visited Moscow. As ringing the British way is not possible in the USSR, the journey was presumably to see the heaviest bell in the world, the enormous Tsar Kolokol bell weighing an estimated 170 tons. It stands on the ground today but in the past is said to have been hung a few feet off the ground and actually swung, though it required the efforts of some fifty men to do it.

Competitive efforts between ringers have up to now been mainly confined to striking competitions. Now there seems to be a move towards competitions of a different kind, and we read of evenings involving inter-tower darts matches. As these normally take place in the local inn, the bond between the belfry and the beerhouse, so deplored by Victorian clerics, does not seem to be breaking. Indeed, it appears to be strengthening. Inter-tower bowls seem to be the latest development.

As new recruits join the ringing fraternity, tuition is sometimes needed rather more expert than can be obtained in a small rural band. The diocesan guilds run seminars for learners and also for those who are reasonably expert but who want to improve their knowledge and technique.

Something that is new, but which may well be the beginning of a tradition, is the first-ever commercial 'ringing break' organized by an hotel. Arranged by the Eastern Branch of the Norwich Diocesan Association, the venue was Gunton Hall, near Lowestoft, Suffolk, and lasted four days in October 1987. The idea was that ringers from far afield could join together and ring in various churches in Norfolk and Suffolk while excursions and entertainments were available for the non-ringing members of the party. The scheme was evidently a great success and may well be copied by other hotels.

Today people are much more 'bell-conscious' than they were, and this includes those who fulminate against them after buying a house next to a church. The Central Council has a fund especially for redundant bells so that bells not being rung in one church may be transferred to another church needing them. This is being done more and more frequently with new churches, and as a ring of new bells may cost anything from £40,000 to £100,000 it is a worthwhile development.

Even our city planners are becoming more aware of bells and their attraction. In Cambridge the ancient church of St Andrew the Great, opposite Christ's College, was converted into shops in 1987. The outward appearance remains little altered and the tower, with its ring of eight bells, has been preserved and the bells ring regularly.

Perhaps the final accolade of acceptance is that the very word 'bell' has now become an accepted part of English slang. No longer does one person say to another 'I'll give you a ring tomorrow.' Today the modern expression is 'I'll give you a bell.' This may not represent a vital new awareness of campanology, as suggested by a writer in the *Daily Mail,* but it certainly indicates a new context for the word describing this ancient and evocative instrument.

Bibliography

Bells in England, J.J. Raven, (Methuen, 1906)
Bells thro' the Ages, J.R. Nichols, (Chapman & Hall, 1928)
History of Change-Ringing, E. Morris, (Chapman & Hall, 1931)
Legends o' the Bells, E. Morris, (Sampson Low, 1935)
English Custom and Usage, Christina Hole, (Batsford, 1941)
English Town Crafts, Norman Wymer, (Batsford, 1949)
Bells of all Nations, E. Morris, (Robert Hale, 1951)
Bells in England, Tom Ingram, (Frederick Muller, 1954)
Towers and Bells of Britain, E. Morris, (Robert Hale, 1955)
Tintinnabula, E. Morris, (Robert Hale, 1959)
The Science of Folklore, A.H. Knapp, (Methuen, 1961)
Encyclopedia of Superstition, Hole/Radford, (Hutchinson, 1961)
Discovering Bellringing, John Camp, (Shire Publications, 1968)
Bells in Our Lives, Mary Cockett, (David & Charles, 1973)
Folklore of Rural England, Margaret Baker, (David & Charles, 1974)
Folklore of East Anglia, Enid Porter, (Batsford, 1974)
Folklore of the Cotswolds, K. Briggs, (Batsford, 1974)
English Traditional Customs, C. Hole, (Batsford, 1974)
Bellringing, John Camp, (David & Charles, 1974)
Folklore of Hertfordshire, D. Jones-Baker, (Batsford, 1977)
Bells of Hereford Cathedral, John Eisel, (Friends of Hereford Cathedral, 1977)
Bells, Felicia Law, (Collins, 1977)
Ring Out – a Book of Bells, Jane Yolen, (Evans, 1978)
Church Bells in Britain, R.H. Dove, (Viggers, 1981)
Bells and Man, Percival Price (OUP, 1983)
Westminster Abbey Bells, W.T. Cook (Central Council, 1984)
The Story of Great Paul, Trevor Jennings (Taylors Foundry, 1986)

The Royal Way of Death, Olivia Bland (Constable, 1986)
Bellringing, Ron Johnston, (Viking, 1986)

The above is a list of the main works consulted in the writing of this book. Other sources are noted in the text.

Index